"Nason and Nesbit have brought together a daring group of thinkers to reimagine the techniques and tools available to urban citizens, and map makers alike, in capturing the urban construct— one that unfolds in front of us as this ubiquitous field of seemingly infinite manipulations and possibilities. Within this context, *Chasing the City* gives us the unique opportunity to seriously explore the emergent urban landscape in its full capacity."

– Petra Kempf, author of *You Are the City, Observation, Organization, and Transformation of Urban Settings*

"*Chasing the City* presents a counter perspective on city making. Rather than setting out to impose a mental and physical control on the constantly shifting urban terrains and processes, this edited volume asks the audience to begin by first seeing and investigating the city with the level of rigor and intensity demanded by the rich, complex, layered, incomplete, incongruent, and even contradictory realities of the lived environment. More than looking at the city as-is, *Chasing the City* offers a critical lens for repositioning ourselves relative to the city as a dynamic field."

– Jeffrey Hou, Professor of Landscape Architecture, University of Washington, Seattle

CHASING THE CITY

Historically, many architects, planners, and urban designers solicit idealistic depictions of a controllable urban environment made from highly regulated geometrical organizations and systematically defined processes. Rather than working as urban "designers" who set out to control and implant external processes, we shift our approach to that of urban "detectives," who set out to chase the city.

Charged with approaching the city more responsively, we investigate what we do not know, allowing the city to direct our work. As urban detectives, we have the ability to interrogate and respond to the elaborate patterns emerging from self-generated, internalized urban interactions. *Chasing the City* asks what are the current design trends shaping how we, first, understand the cities of today to, then, produce informed decisions on the continuously undefined evolving city of tomorrow. Intentionally, the work here does not adhere to rudimentary notions of supposed singularities or rely upon past generations of idealistic utopian models. Rather, *Chasing the City* delineates current models of urban investigation that seek to respond to the nature of cities and develop heretofore-urban strategies as concurrently negotiated future urbanism.

This edited volume provides a collection of innovative design research projects based on shared notions of Chasing the City through three bodies of strategic frameworks: (1) Mapping, (2) Resource, and (3) Typology. This structure ultimately allows readers, as fellow urban detectives, access to exploratory tools and methods of detection that accumulate from our environs, both practical and projective in our chase of the city.

Joshua M. Nason, educated at Cornell and Texas Tech, is an Associate Professor of Architecture at the University of Texas at Arlington as well as the director of the experimental design research firm Iterative Studio. His teaching, research, and design work explore dynamic and dependent contextual relationships and issues of city identity through analytic mapping processes.

Jeffrey S. Nesbit, a doctoral candidate at Harvard University's Graduate School of Design, studies sporadic development, dismantled landscapes, and the evolution of military infrastructure in the 20th century. He is founding director of Haecceitas Studio, a design-research group, director of Seoul Studio, a research program in South Korea, and has taught architecture and urban design at the University of North Carolina Charlotte and Texas Tech University.

CHASING THE CITY

Models for Extra-Urban Investigations

Edited by Joshua M. Nason and Jeffrey S. Nesbit

NEW YORK AND LONDON

First published 2019
by Routledge
711 Third Avenue, New York, NY 10017

and by Routledge
2 Park Square, Milton Park, Abingdon, Oxon, OX14 4RN

Routledge is an imprint of the Taylor & Francis Group, an informa business

© 2019 Taylor & Francis

The right of Joshua M. Nason and Jeffrey S. Nesbit to be identified as the authors of the editorial material, and of the authors for their individual chapters, has been asserted in accordance with sections 77 and 78 of the Copyright, Designs and Patents Act 1988.

All rights reserved. No part of this book may be reprinted or reproduced or utilized in any form or by any electronic, mechanical, or other means, now known or hereafter invented, including photocopying and recording, or in any information storage or retrieval system, without permission in writing from the publishers.

Trademark notice: Product or corporate names may be trademarks or registered trademarks, and are used only for identification and explanation without intent to infringe.

Library of Congress Cataloging-in-Publication Data
Names: Nason, Joshua M., editor. | Nesbit, Jeffrey S., editor.
Title: Chasing the city : models for extra-urban investigations / edited by Joshua M. Nason and Jeffrey S. Nesbit.
Description: New York : Routledge, 2018.
Identifiers: LCCN 2018022350| ISBN 9780815384885 (hardback) | ISBN 9780815384892 (pbk.) | ISBN 9781351202992 (ebk)
Subjects: LCSH: Cities and towns—Forecasting. | City planning—Forecasting.
Classification: LCC HT151 .C524 2018 | DDC 307.76—dc23
LC record available at https://lccn.loc.gov/2018022350

ISBN: 978-0-8153-8488-5 (hbk)
ISBN: 978-0-8153-8489-2 (pbk)
ISBN: 978-1-351-20299-2 (ebk)

Typeset in Sabon
by Swales & Willis Ltd, Exeter, Devon, UK

CONTENTS

Acknowledgments	*ix*
Notes on Contributors	*x*
Foreword: Chasing the City in the Age of *New Geography*	*xiv*
DAVID GRAHAME SHANE	

1 Introduction: Chasing the Neo-utopian Paradox   1
  Joshua M. Nason and Jeffrey S. Nesbit

PART I
Mapping   **9**

2 Chasing the Awkward City   11
  Joshua M. Nason

3 Chasing #Antidrone   37
  Derek Hoeferlin

4 Chasing the Logistical City and Its Spatial Formations   61
  Clare Lyster

viii Contents

PART II
Resource   **83**

5 Chasing and Rewiring Resource Territories   85
  Neeraj Bhatia

6 Chasing Military Logistics in the Urban Void   106
  Jeffrey S. Nesbit

7 Chasing Lines of Engagement   127
  Edward Becker

PART III
Typology   **153**

8 Chasing Strategies for the Post-crisis   155
  Emmanuelle Chiappone-Piriou

9 Chasing Ambiguous Conditions of Coexistence   179
  Peter Winston Ferretto

10 Chasing a Genealogy of X   201
  Choon Choi

Afterword: Chasing Composition   *215*
DAVID SALOMON
Index   *221*

ACKNOWLEDGMENTS

We would like to acknowledge, with sincere gratitude, all of the individuals who have contributed to this project. Without a doubt, this body of work would not have manifested into a collection of inspiring and speculative works on our chase for the city without so many talented people.

In 2014, we co-organized a session at the Association of Collegiate Schools of Architecture annual conference in Miami. The response to this call was immense, creating a second subsequent session. Although many of the presenters of the conference papers are not formally included in this edited volume, we would also like to thank each of them for their interest in our early stages of this topic. Following the conference session, we continued the conversation, which ultimately has led to the framework for this volume.

Special thanks to our families, who have supported the numerous hours of work required to manage this project. It is their understanding and sincerity that have allowed us to work well beyond our regularly scheduled tasks to make this project possible. This is dedicated to them: Yoon, Celine, and Teah, Dallin, Carter, and Miley.

CONTRIBUTORS

Edward Becker is an Assistant Professor of Architecture at Virginia Tech and co-founder of the Finnish architectural investment firm Vör (Vör Architecture + Vör Capital Investments AB). As a registered, practicing architect in Helsinki, Finland and a member of the Finnish Association of Architects, he is currently engaged in ongoing housing projects in both Finland and the United States with particular focus on timber construction/innovation. Previously, Edward taught housing and urbanism in Aalto University's master's degree program in Espoo, Finland and was Visiting Guest Researcher in Aalto University's Department of Architecture. He holds a Master of Architecture, with Distinction, from Harvard University.

Neeraj Bhatia is a licensed architect and urban designer from Toronto, Canada. His work resides at the intersection of politics, infrastructure, and urbanism. He is an Associate Professor at the California College of the Arts, where he also co-directs the urbanism research lab, The Urban Works Agency. Neeraj is also founder of The Open Workshop, a transcalar design-research office examining the negotiation between architecture and its territorial environment. He is co-editor of the books *Bracket [Takes Action]*, *The Petropolis of Tomorrow*, *Bracket [Goes Soft]*, *Arium: Weather + Architecture*, and co-author of *Pamphlet Architecture 30: Coupling—Strategies for Infrastructural Opportunism*. Bhatia received his Master's degree in Architecture and Urban Design from MIT and received his Bachelor of Environmental Studies and his Bachelor of Architecture from the University of Waterloo.

Emmanuelle Chiappone-Piriou, an architect and architecture historian, works as a curator and writer. Her research addresses the architectural field as one that stands "at the edge of everything else" (Choi, Trotter) and proceeds by building genealogies from the 1960s' radical practices to contemporary ones. From 2011 to 2016, she has been the Program curator at the Frac Centre (Orléans, France), where she has curated exhibitions and events, including *Relief(s)* (2015) and *The City as a Vision* (2014), and was Assistant Curator of the ninth edition of ArchiLab's *Naturalizing Architecture*. Previously, Emmanuelle has collaborated in numerous exhibitions, first in the institutional context of the Centre Pompidou and Centre Pompidou-Metz, then at OMA/AMO (*OMA/Progress*, Barbican Art Gallery, 2011).

Choon Choi is an architect based in Seoul. He has collaborated with curators to design exhibition spaces for *Gwangju Biennale* and *Seoul Media Art Biennale*, and collaborated with artists for the *Sangha Farm Project* and *Asteroid G*. He has independently participated in group exhibitions at Platform in Kimusa, Seoul Station, and Ilmin Museum. Various built projects include Jeomchon Middle School, Kkummaru at the Children's Grand Park, Sangha Farm Village, and unbuilt projects, including the National Museum of Contemporary Art and Forest Church, have been introduced in various international publications.

Peter Winston Ferretto graduated from Cambridge and Liverpool Universities and worked as a registered architect for several international architectural practices, including Herzog & de Meuron in Basle, before establishing his own firm, PWFERRETTO, in 2009. Peter teaches as an Associate Professor of Architecture at the Chinese University of Hong Kong, and previously held an Assistant Professor position at Seoul National University in Korea. His main research focus is the relationship between architectural design and the city. He has written many essays on architecture and the city, is also the author of several books such as *Place/Seoul* (2015) and *Architectural Notes* (2014), and in 2016 was awarded the General Research Fund by the Research Grants Council of Hong Kong for *Urban Pauses: Reclaiming Hong Kong's Residual Urban Spaces*.

Derek Hoeferlin is a registered architect, and teaches in the Sam Fox School at Washington University in St. Louis. Derek directs "Deltas + Watersheds (D+W)," conducting collaborative research on global comparative deltas and watersheds—primarily focused on the Mekong, Mississippi and the Rhine—to inform adaptive design strategies. Currently Derek is design lead for STUDIO MISI-ZIIBI, one of eight multidisciplinary finalist teams in the *Changing Course* competition for Louisiana delta coastal restoration strategies. He was valedictorian and was awarded multiple commencement honors at Tulane University, and received the Charles O. Matchum scholarship at Yale University.

Clare Lyster is an architect, educator, writer, and an Associate Professor at the University of Illinois at Chicago School of Architecture. Her work

xii Notes on Contributors

explores architecture and urbanism from the perspective of contemporary theories in landscape, infrastructure, and globalization. She is the author of *Learning from Logistics: How Networks Change Cities* (2016), and editor of *Envisioning the Bloomingdale: 5 Concepts* (2009) and *306090*, vol. 9, *Regarding Public Space*, with Cecilia Benites (2005). Clare is a registered architect in New York and Illinois, and holds a BArch from University College Dublin (Ireland) and an MArch from Yale University. She has also taught at Syracuse University, University of Toronto, and Harvard University, and was the Gillmor Lecturer at the University of Calgary in Fall 2017.

Joshua M. Nason, educated at Cornell and Texas Tech, joined the University of Texas at Arlington as an Associate Professor of Architecture in the Fall semester of 2012. His work explores dynamic and vacillating collisions, synchronicity, and reciprocities via stratified analytic processes as director of the experimental design research firm Iterative Studio. Some of his recent lectures include "Design: A Work in Process," "Draw In/Draw Out: Participatory Maps as Event Urbanism," "Awkward Mapping," "Mapping + Change," "Drawing [on] Urban Complexity," "Anomalic Urbanism," and "Place Pavilions: Inhabiting the Map." His drawn and built work has been featured in exhibitions such as *Divergent Convergent: Speculations on China* in Beijing, *Common Ground* in New York City, and *The Place Pavilions* in both Lubbock and Dallas.

Jeffrey S. Nesbit is a doctoral candidate at Harvard University's Graduate School of Design, and a researcher in the Office for Urbanization. His research focuses on the evolution of post-industrial landscapes through the lens of historical technology, political uncertainty, and environmental unpredictability. He is also the founding director of Haecceitas Studio, and Director of Seoul Studio, a design research program in South Korea. He has taught at the University of North Carolina at Charlotte and Texas Tech University, along with leading a number of design studios in the contemporary megalopolis, including China, Korea, and Spain. Jeffrey holds a Master of Architecture from University of Pennsylvania and a Bachelor of Science in Architecture from Texas Tech University.

David Salomon is an Assistant Professor of Art History at Ithaca College, where he is also the coordinator of the Architectural Studies program. He is the co-author, with Paul Andersen, of *The Architecture of Patterns* (2010). His wide-ranging research has been published in *Grey Room*, *Log*, *Harvard Design Magazine*, *Places*, the *Journal of Landscape Architecture* and the *Journal of Architectural Education*. Forthcoming publications include a book on the history of symmetry in architecture, math, and science (Buenos Aires: Di Tella), and articles on the history of the driveway (*Buildings & Landscapes*) and the relationship between Michael Heizer's land art, bulldozers, and suburban tract developments (*Journal of American Culture*).

David Grahame Shane is Adjunct Professor in the Urban Design program at Columbia Graduate School of Architecture, Planning and Preservation. He studied architecture at the Architectural Association, London, and continued with an MArch in Urban Design (1971) and an Architectural and Urban History PhD (1978) with Colin Rowe at Cornell University. During the 1990s David wrote about New York's urban fragmentation, enclaves, and heterotopias for many professional and international publications. He published *Recombinant Urbanism: Conceptual Modeling in Architecture, Urban Design and City Theory* (2005) and co-edited with Brian McGrath the *Architectural Design* title *Sensing the 21st Century City: Close-Up and Remote* (2005) and *Urban Design Since 1945: A Global Perspective* (2011). His recent work includes *Block, Superblock and Megablock: A Short History* (2014) and *A Short History of Hong Kong Malls and Towers* in Stefan Als' edited volume *Mall City* (2016).

FOREWORD

Chasing the City in the Age of New Geography

David Grahame Shane

Geography has traditionally involved mapping, categorizing resources for extraction or exploitation, as well as indexing urban developments in a hierarchical series of typologies, such as hamlet, village, town, city, and metropolis. *Chasing the City* attempts to side-step this imperial and colonial approach through an emphasis on heterotopic systems of analysis that do not require a central master planner or planning agency, and allow for emergent systems, creating a wider context of a New Geography, as explored by Charles Waldheim (2009). Citizens have a role to play in this new open-source, emergent mapping approach that exploits the potential of the Internet, handheld devices as well geographic information systems and the Global Positioning System. At the same time, *Chasing the City* is realistic about the total transformation in our urban experience brought about by these systems, especially as embedded in modern, global systems of logistics. City services can be summoned via handheld devices anywhere—city, suburb, peri-urban belt of countryside are all potentially urban under this dispersed, petro-chemical- and electronics-fueled logistical regime.

Chasing the City deepens this line of research, especially in its treatment of logistics and modern informational systems based on handheld devices as fundamental to a New Geography. In *Chasing the City*, Mapping, Resources and Typology are intended as new urban apparatuses for viewing the new city territory, following the example of Michel Foucault. There is no history provided for such devices, but Foucault provided the basic outline in a famous, often-quoted statement in an interview in 1977 at the head of this Preface: "firstly, a thoroughly heterogeneous ensemble consisting of discourses, institutions, architectural forms, regulatory decisions, laws, administrative measures, scientific statements, philosophical, moral and philanthropic propositions . . . the apparatus itself is the system of relations that can be established between these elements." He continues: "secondly, what I am trying to identify in this apparatus is precisely the nature of the connection that can exist between these heterogeneous elements" (Foucault 1977). Many philosophers have since asked, "What is a dispositif?" including Deleuze (1992), Agamben (2009), and most recently Matteo Pasquinelli (2015), who links the term to Foucault's educational background and training with Canguilhem, the French historian of modern science and computation. Pasquinelli highlights how Canguilhem used the same term in his teaching, being especially critical of German and Nazi organic, racial, and *Lebensraum* (organic-racial-space-to-live) theories, using the term in 1952.

Such an apparatus was an instrument intended to reveal a hidden reality, an "other" system for seeing the city, partially through its rejects and blind spots. For Foucault such a dispositif or apparatus, including his heterotopia (the place of the "other" that contained the exceptions that made consistency possible), formed an essential, logical, organizational, often spatial device symbolizing the system being studied (Shane 2005). In a powerful spatial turn in an interview with architects, Foucault (1967) provided Jeremy Bentham's unbuilt scheme for a Panopticon Prison (1791) as an example of a state apparatus designed as part of a larger system of laws and intellectual disciplines to improve society and the lives of those imprisoned, creating a new citizen-worker able to operate efficiently in the emerging bourgeois, industrial society.

Later, in *Discipline and Punish* (1975/1977), Foucault emphasized how the Panopticon device was a utopic response to a dystopic contemporary situation of medieval prisons filled with unemployed peasants and debtors taking refuge in expanding industrial cities. Bentham intended that the omnipotent, all-seeing jailer housed in the central tower would become internalized by the prisoners, creating new, modern self-regulating citizens. Almer (2012) commented: "The Panopticon is an ideal architectural figure of modern disciplinary power. The Panopticon creates a consciousness of permanent visibility as a form of power, where no bars, chains, and heavy locks are necessary for domination any more." In the 1970s Foucault was very critical of the authoritarian French state and its expanding welfare state apparatus with its rigid, fixed norms of administration that impinged on individual rights and freedom.

The New Geography in *Chasing the City* opens up links to older urban geographic studies that drew attention to Foucault's concept of the heterotopia as a real built space, an urban fragment, that contained a utopic element, part of a wider network of legislation, communications, and logistics. Edward Soja, for instance, in *Postmodern Geographies:*

xvi David Grahame Shane

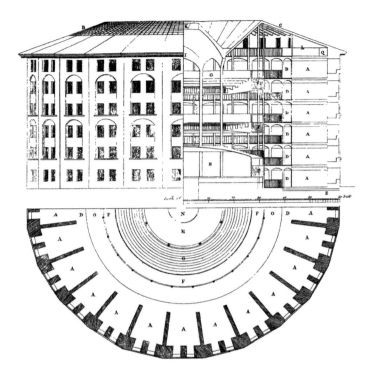

FIGURE 0.1 Reveley's plan and section of Jeremy Bentham's Panopticon.

The Reassertion of Space in Critical Social Theory (1989), contrasted Foucault's real heterotopias with the vast abstraction of the previous, number-crunching, mathematical models of the traffic engineers and housing specialists of the 1970s and 1980s. Similarly, David Harvey's *The Condition of Postmodernity: An Enquiry into the Origins of Cultural Change* (1989) outlined the abstract global financial structures that sought to invest their profits in real estate, driving the transformation of global cities as investors sought rent from a "spatial fix" without any concern for issues of social justice in the city. Harvey's case study of the reconstruction of downtown Baltimore around the harbor provided the perfect link between the "fictional" global capital that would end in the 2008 financial debacle and the precise spatial locations chosen by developers on the abandoned waterfront of the industrial city.

Soja and Harvey's geographical emphasis on Foucault's "spatial turn" made concrete and real the forces driving the fragmentation of society in the global financial system emerging in the 1990s and 2000s. Soja showed how the fragments linked together into systems using the highway structure of Los Angeles, as well as the new information systems and global communications. Later researchers, like Corner and Maclean (1996), Berger (2006), and Easterling (2016), would document the global reach of this fragmentary system of enclosed patches, including vast man-made agricultural and environmental structures best seen from the air, resource extraction sites that provided commodities for global manufacturing systems or Special Economic Zones for manufacturing. In *The Birth of Territory* (2013) the geographer and Foucault scholar Stewart Eldon linked Foucault's late lectures with their concepts of subjectivity, self-creation, individual freedom, and minimal state governance (based on his concept of bio-power) to the expanded urban territory made possible by new communications and logistics, creating a New Geography of sublime proportions.

The Mapping apparatus in Part I of *Chasing the City* clearly builds on earlier models of the metropolis and megalopolis (Shane 2011), now expanded by the new information systems of the cloud and Internet into the metacity, allowing for a huge extension of urban reach across a wider territory. In Part II, "Resource," *Chasing the City* demonstrates this enormous scale jump in supra-regional, utopian projects for resource management in Latin America in the face of climate change. A similar scale jump in North America examines the fate of the Fordist mass-production shipyards constructed by the US Navy across the country as the manufacturing paradigm shifts to Post-Fordism and a neoliberal recreational model. An even larger jump in scale examines the New Geography of the Arctic Circle as the long-sought North West Passage between Europe and Asia opens to modern logistical systems, creating a new corridor of potential urban development.

In his 1967 interview Foucault outlined a system of "sites," fast-changing places, "heterotopias of illusion" as dynamic sites, in contrast to the "heterotopia of deviance" like Bentham's Panopticon, a fixed and rigid system to normalize the deviant in the new industrial city. As an example of the heterotopia of illusion, Foucault offers the glass-covered Parisian shopping arcade, beloved by the Parisian Surrealists in the 1930s (Geist 1985). Walter Benjamin (1935) also chose the arcade as the symbol of the destructive-creative power of capitalism based on consumption and fashion that made Paris the "Capital of the 19th Century." Benjamin linked this urban apparatus to a system of display, including advertising, department stores, world fairs, and exhibitions that provided an index of the constantly shifting capitalist phantasmagorias or utopic fetish structures (Somani 2016). Foucault in his 1967 interview included all these structures, extending the argument to art galleries, museums, brothels, and the stock market itself, as fast-changing sites of illusory, shifting tastes. Like his teacher Canguilhem, he included a reference to computers and the digital world as an example of this new geographic and spatial system, speaking of mobile, shifting "sites" held in complex relationships (Pasquinelli 2015).

xviii David Grahame Shane

The final part of *Chasing the City* follows this heterotopic logic of the New Geography in trying to keep open the multiple registers of activity toward the larger systems of display and consumption, erasing the old micro/macro dichotomy in a new emergent complexity. While the editors gave Part III the title "Typology," performative "platforms," dispositifs, or apparatus would perhaps have been more appropriate, as traditional morphology plays a very small role in the analysis. Again the analysis focuses on the new information systems of the cloud and Internet, allowing for a huge extension of urban reach across a far wider territory, but this time turning toward the spatial implications for cities and traditional buildings. Here *Chasing the City* examines the earlier, simpler, and ultimately self-contradictory, closed utopian models that in the 1960s and 1970s tried to imagine a new society based on leisure and pleasure (with automated manufacturing, allowing for a new personal freedom). A huge jump in scale projected utopian megastructures attached to elevator towers that sprawled above historic Paris (Friedman) or on pilotis across the Dutch countryside (Constant). Studies of three-dimensional projects in East Asian cities, Taipei and Hong Kong, contrast with this European megastructural scale jump with real Asian counter-spaces, also complex and three-dimensional, that accommodate community needs with far more modesty and sensitivity.

Foucault in 1967 never imagined the future commercial or corporate mega-dimensions of his nascent heterotopia of illusion, with its emphasis on pleasure and leisure. He did study and contest the Chicago School of neoliberal economics, with its similar emphasis on the individual and care of the self. From 1976 Foucault in his last lectures wrestled with what might be the form and organization of the geography of a non-authoritarian, less state-based city and society, examining many other systems of thought and social organization from ancient Greece to contemporary revolutionary Iran. Many scholars, like Reinhold Martin (2016), have extended the commercial apparatus of the arcade to the shopping mall and then linked it to global supply chains, Walmart, big box retail (LeCavalier 2012), and the emergence of the Internet as a huge system of communication, coordination, and information, a vast metacity of information available now for analysis, including tracking the mining of commodities in remote locations (Brenner and Schmidt 2012).

The central spatial problem for the New Geography is both the displacement of the city and at the same time its precise localization as a set of services intimately linked to contemporary life, as Clare Lyster's Chapter 4 on the logics of global logistics in *Chasing the City* clearly demonstrates. Lyster (2013) argued that with a handheld device, city services and information are theoretically available anywhere there is cell service or Wi-Fi. Pasquinelli (2009) detailed how Google's free search engine using page ranking based on Internet searches has created a fortune for its inventors through targeted advertising based on individual searches. Now the accuracy of the information available is not guaranteed, as hackers using bots and websites can reverse engineer the search engines to privilege false information. Still contemporary philosophers like Agamben (2009) and Serres (2014), both Foucault scholars, have identified the smart phone as a "dispositive," a contemporary apparatus of great power, heralding a New Geography.

Any new research such as *Chasing the City* inevitably raises further questions. In this case, the question must be whether these three first lenses are enough for an emerging New Geography. What other lenses (as pursued by Harvard Graduate School of Design's *New Geographies*) might be useful, and how does the new dispositif of the handheld device, with its attendant metacity dimension, fit into this New Geography? The New Geography as a device for seeing the world raises important questions, especially how this new vision as an intellectual device intermeshes with previous dispositif constructions and how all such devices intersect with life/bios in Foucault's theories. It often seems that life is the "other" beyond the various conceptual devices created by agents of the state or commercial-corporate interests in the city territory. Foucault raised the question of this self-regulating system of life as biopower, a messy amorphous system outside the state, but which the state, and now commerce, seeks to control and exploit, perhaps through handheld devices. This new contested territory represents the ground from which the figure of the New Geography is emerging.

Bibliography

Agamben, G. *What Is an Apparatus? And Other Essays*, trans. by D. Kishik and S. Pedatella (Stanford, CA: Stanford University Press, 2009), p. 5.

Almer, T. *Towards a Critical Theory of Surveillance in Informational Capitalism* (Frankfurt am Main: Peter Lang, 2012), p. 22.

Benjamin, W. "Paris, Capital of the 19th Century" (1935), in *Illuminations: Essays and Reflections*, ed. H. Arendt (New York: Schocken, 1969).

Berger, A. *Drosscape: Wasting Land in Urban America* (New York: Princeton Architectural Press, 2006).

Brenner, N., and Schmidt, C. "Planetary Urbanization," in *Urban Constellations*, ed. M. Gandy (Berlin: Jovis, 2012), pp. 10–13.

Corner, J., and MacLean, A.S. *Taking Measures across American Landscape* (New Haven, CT: Yale University Press, 1996).

Deleuze, G. "What Is a Dispositif?" in *Michel Foucault Philosopher*, ed. T. Armstrong (New York: Routledge, 1992).

Easterling, K. *Extrastatecraft: The Power of Infrastructure* (New York: Verso, 2016).

Eldon, S. *The Birth of Territory* (Chicago, IL: University of Chicago Press, 2013).

Eldon, S. *Foucault's Last Decade* (Cambridge: Polity Press, 2016).

Evans, R. *The Fabrication of Virtue: English Prison Architecture, 1750–1840* (Cambridge: Cambridge University Press, 1982), pp. 193–235.

Foucault, M. "Of Other Spaces (1967), Heterotopias," https://foucault.info/doc/documents/heterotopia/foucault-heterotopia-en-html (accessed June 29, 2018).

Foucault, M. *Discipline and Punish: The Birth of the Prison* (New York: Pantheon Books, 1975/1977).

Foucault, M. "The Confessions of the Flesh" (1977), in *Power/Knowledge: Selected Interviews and Other Writings 1972–77*, ed. C. Gordon (New York: Pantheon, 1985), p. 194.

Geist, J.L. *Arcades* (Cambridge, MA: MIT Press, 1985).

Harvey, D. *The Condition of Postmodernity: An Enquiry into the Origins of Cultural Change* (Oxford: Blackwell, 1989).

LeCavalier, J. "Patrons and Prototypes: Walmart's Catalytic Urbanism," *Architectural Design* 82(5) (2012): 26–35.

LeCavalier, J. *The Rule of Logistics: Walmart and the Architecture of Fulfillment* (Minneapolis, MN: University of Minnesota Press, 2016).

LeCavalier, J. "All Those Numbers: Logistics, Territory and Walmart" (May 2010), https://placesjournal.org/article/all-those-numbers-logistics-territory-and-walmart/ (accessed June 29, 2018).

Lyster, C. "On Demand Urbanism: Learning from Amazon," in *The Petropolis of Tomorrow*, ed. N. Bhatia and M. Casper (Barcelona: Actar, 2013), pp. 406–423.

Martin, R. *The Urban Apparatus: Mediapolitics and the City* (Minneapolis, MN: University of Minnesota Press, 2016).

New Geographies, www.hup.harvard.edu/collection.php?cpk=1332 (accessed June 29, 2018).

Pasquinelli, M. "Google's PageRank Algorithm: A Diagram of Cognitive Capitalism and the Rentier of the Common Intellect," in *Deep Search*, ed. K. Becker and F. Stalder (London: Transaction Publishers, 2009), http://matteopasquinelli.com/google-pagerank-algorithm/ (accessed June 29, 2018).

Pasquinelli, M. "What an Apparatus Is Not: On the Archeology of the Norm in Foucault, Canguilhem, and Goldstein," *Parrhesia* 22 (2015): 79–89, http://matteopasquinelli.com/what-an-apparatus-is-not/ (accessed June 29, 2018).

Serres, M. *Thumbelina: The Culture and Technology of Millennials* (Lanham, MD: Rowman and Littlefield, 2014).

Shane, D.G. *Recombinant Urbanism: Conceptual Modeling in Architecture, Urban Design and City Theory* (Chichester: Wiley, 2005).

Shane, D.G. *Urban Design Since 1945: A Global Perspective* (Chichester: Wiley, 2011).

Soja, E. *Postmodern Geographies: The Reassertion of Space in Critical Social Theory* (New York: Verso, 1989).

Somani, A. "Walter Benjamin's Media Theory: The Media and the Apparat," in *Grey Room* 62 (Cambridge, MA: MIT Press, 2016), pp. 7–41.

Waldheim, C. "An Interview with Charles Waldheim" by Meg Studer, *Scenario 01: Landscape Urbanism* (Fall 2011), https://scenariojournal.com/article/an-interview-with-charles-waldheim/ (accessed June 29, 2018).

1

INTRODUCTION

Chasing the Neo-utopian Paradox

Joshua M. Nason and Jeffrey S. Nesbit

FIGURE 1.1 Plan of Miletus (Hippodamus, ca. 460 BCE).

Chasing the City is inquiry. It is the act of searching for inherency, for potential, for improvement—all through rigorous reflective processes bounded among urban and extra-urban territories. The investigations for understanding our contemporary city must be expanded, both physically and geo-politically. It is not based on the reliance upon unattainable ideals or the adherence to antiquated formal models. In fact, *Chasing the City* looks at the city through a critical lens of existing components, techniques of analysis, tools for actuation, and speculative propositions for the distant future supported from within. The city is an integrated field from which the future may be exhumed. By looking at the city as a complex cross-roads of influences, contingencies, reciprocities, and interactions, designers can draw from the existing to determine what tomorrow may hold without segregating the city from its inherent and attainable potentials.

The city of tomorrow has long fascinated humanity. For generations projective urban thinkers have pondered on the future city as an idyllic utopia. Continued today, such depictions of a controllable urban environment made from highly regulated geometric organizations and systematic idealism fail to identify both cultural and social legacies, lacking sensitivity and responsiveness to contextual qualities and needs. The contemporary city is complex, full of irregularities, and composed of continuous oscillations of local and global intersections that require constant attention, adjustment, and reinforcement.

Urban models popularized in the first half of the 20th century, based on control, efficiency, and systematization, failed to adequately deal with the changing diversity of cities. One-size-fits-all master planning models tended to ignore context, history, environment, and many other vital urban influences. Focusing on growth and delaminating layers of the city into distinct structures failed to meet the realities of the emerging city. Post-World War II cities began to decentralize, extending into territories beyond the proper municipal boundaries. Postmodernist planning attempted to return individual qualities of cities and respect some divergence from standardization. Lasting utopian tendencies still pushed city plans toward idyllic proposals—this time overloaded with references amalgamating "other" places and times. Both looked to outside models in order to develop the future city. However, each failed to recognize the vitality of cities as specific, encompassing organisms.

The city is beholden to a host of mutually dependent forces that reside outside the designer's purview, but are integral to the behavior of cities. Seemingly, such varied design authorship contradicts singular and idealized urban visions. Instead, urban design that incorporates various professions and vantage points can lead to adaptive and responsive proposals helping the city to evolve over time, rather than stagnate it in the now (or, more likely, past). This fosters an understanding of the city as an interconnected series of forces and relationships layered over conflicting isolated moments and processes. This, at times, culminates in unpredictable outcomes. While unpredictability can be unsettling, it can also be productive for its transformative potential. In fact, it is that very unpredictability which forms alternative futures for the city that are impossible to be arrived upon through singular processes and externalized visions. Cities are undergoing rapid change in population, cultural proliferation, and technological interconnectedness. Such changes in the city require us to rethink our interpretations of what they are, and what we can understand.

Therefore, "city" in this book is not merely describing either singular or specific municipalities, but rather conditions of human civilization and ideas of processes impacting the globe. These can be geographically based or less localized. They can be physical, digital, or systematized. They can be synonymous with specific cities, but can also be regional and encompass a larger integration of several cities. Such cities can also be manifested at smaller scales, such as neighborhoods, specific sites, or as bits of data and mobility. The reality of the contemporary city is akin to many of the transformations we have seen in society: boundaries are continuously being reinterpreted, realigned, and even erased in the face of the complex, connected, and connective nature of urbanism today. Therefore, the city must be read and lived in at multiple scales. And as such, those scales include elements and influences previously nonexistent (or that may have been unrecognized).

Consequently, a shift in thinking and a subsequent reassessment of the role of the designer must occur. Approaching design as a fruitful exchange begins when designers accept the futility in attempting to fully dictate the future city. One must work in dialogue with existing and emergent urban components, trends, and behaviors. But designers must be willing to do so, even if it means compromising personal claims, politics, and philosophies to provide authorship embedded within the city and the consequences of the city. The utopian, and even authoritarian, tendencies of individual designers must be deferred in order to pursue access necessary to find what the city already is, and in turn its needs. Through this, designers can develop a more responsive working process rich within each urban instance discovered and potentially folded back into its own fabric, perpetuating an internal process of self-improvement.

Herein lies the neo-utopian paradox. The ideal city does not exist as a prototype to be laid across the globe as a singularity. However, the ideal—or at least broken fragment of the ideal—for each city lies inherently within the conditions that make up the city. For ideal models to be interpreted through a design process, designers, acting as detectives, must resist the tendencies to implant foreign, idealized masterworks upon the cities in which they work. The neo-utopian paradox is an anti-utopian model responding to the reality of contextual elasticity within site-specific conditions shaping the urban domain. Such conditions include ecological impact, cultural context, and continuously changing outputs of data and communication. The grid of Hippodamus expresses our earliest example of the ideal city.[1] As history shows, the impacts of ignoring topographical and environmental considerations, and even in some cases processes leading to such transitions from extraction of raw resources to social consumption, unfortunately thrive for control. The ideal city cannot be built through the superficial implantation of foreign idealized masterworks, as seen with Roman Colonization planning, modernism's universal anti-historicism, urban design principles, and contemporary derivatives of New Urbanism (among other -isms). In fact, the implantation within or superimposition of ideals upon a fabric can actually tear it apart—killing its identity in the process of trying to perfect it. Instead, it is through the active extraction and re-presentation of inherent qualities within the city that it becomes its ideal self.

Capitalizing upon these inherent qualities of the city is the process by which you chase it. As such, it is the primary role of the designer, as the chaser, to detect, expose, and respond to the latent and emergent essences already established in the stratification of city. This chasing is the central strategy within the neo-utopian paradox—a fruitful paradox defined by the inputs of extracted resources combined with conditional urban outcomes and excesses expressed through the physical form and informational output of the city. It is through engaging the challenges of this paradoxical neo-utopian model that designers chase the contemporary city rather than sacrificing its immediate potential for an unattainable future ideal.

Instead of outlining a new paradigm, *Chasing the City* intends to reframe and cross-reference some critical positions in urban discourse. This situates the book in an established intellectual context, aspiring to contribute to an urban design that is dependent upon examinations of and within places shaped outside normative master planning practices. The role of designers and planners in the building of a vibrant and connected urban future requires acceptance of and participation in the evolutionary historical context. As a continuation of ideas aimed at challenging utopian idealism, *Chasing the City* seeks to uncover an anti-utopian accumulation of contradictions and contingencies shaping our current design disciplines. Similar to Camillo Sitte's 1889 principles based upon the irregularity of the medieval organization, the neo-utopian future considers contemporary urbanism to be folded and unfolded—acknowledging the unbalanced and unpredictable as crucial urban design criteria.[2] Yona Friedman's ten principles of spatial urbanism from 1959 provide further pioneering examples of urban divergence, offering flexible programs of spatial agglomeration, unpredictable at its core while simultaneously offering a structural and relational matrix as means of undertaking the whole.[3] Reyner Banham's 1971 seminal book *Los Angeles: The Architecture of Four Ecologies* lays out an integrated model of understanding a city's individuality through examining its integrated built, topological, and cultural forces rather than denigrating its inability to fit pre-supposed, foreign urban models or best practices.[4] The Situationists' skepticism of the commodification of the city and its coinciding conformity to linear development practices fostering streamlined, anti-experiential norms of sameness provides a vital model for the inquisition of acceptance of city design as business as usual. Although each of the models mentioned above frames an intellectual context shaping irregularity, flexibility, and integration, *Chasing the City* moves beyond their fixed manifestos of principle-based regulation and suggests a more ongoing interaction with the city itself.

A closer look at such examples reveals tremendous possibilities held within a paradox intentionally confronting the realities of a city framed by its own imperfect utopian potential. Inherent in the neo-utopian paradox lies the duality both of an active human endeavor for civilization and community as well as the city as indeterminable consequences of colliding forces, cultures and ages—each superseding simplistic attempts to tame them. On one hand, the city continuously attempts to become efficient, reaching toward an idealized state. On the other, due to the complexity of interactions, the city is organized through conflicts of varied ideals, thereby producing behaviors beyond the prescribed and predictable. Therefore, a true chasing of the city requires layered, integrated, and evolutionary processes that involve and capitalize upon such a paradox—not merely ignore it. Designs that fail to embrace this two-edged nature of the contemporary city are rendered inadequate, at best, and possibly dangerous in more extreme cases. The authors in this book capitalize upon this tenuous relationship to deploy design strategies as detecting and revealing, beyond any over-idealized, superficial reading of pre-supposed truisms.

Utilizing responsive approaches to urban design, this book postulates a series of essays and design projects curated in accordance with these dualities. Categorized thematically, the chapters explicate the investigation of cities through three main partitions: "Mapping," "Resource," and "Typology." Each part categorically establishes modes of inquiry for chasing identity and potentiality within the city, therein deploying existing contextual processes that explicate the city's inherent qualities: namely reading, production, and identification processes, respectively. Such modes are not intended as mere descriptors of the city nor tools with which it can be measured. Rather, these processes are frameworks embedded within the city—they are part of it. Further, each chapter signifies a chase that identifies the nature of the city through integral processes. They are not urban-ism, but are urban. The city is in part the fragmentation of ideas that comprise it—a nesting of influential forces inherently shaping its present and future. And since the city is varied, complex, and evolutionary, so should be the ideas in and about it. Thus, the following chapters intentionally span a wide collection of topics and locations. The aim is twofold: to tie together the varied methodological ideas of chasing the contemporary city, and to redefine how we conceptualize the city in order to more successfully detect its possible, speculative futures.

"Mapping," the first part, collects chapters that propose processes to contextually read the city as a whole through its integral component parts. Chapter 2, "Chasing the Awkward City" by Joshua M. Nason, investigates and offers an overview of mapping processes particularly intended to uncover emerging city identities, otherwise unknown. By drawing (and drawing from) places commonly misunderstood and/or conflicted within the city, one understands underlying, vital, and identifying urban conditions. Chapter 3, "Chasing #Antidrone" by Derek Hoeferlin, examines the impact of water-based systems on the urban realm. Low-technology recording/mapping processes are deployed in order to educate the public about their own urban contexts, teaching them how to read these highly varied ecological circumstances and understand their relationships to larger contexts. "Mapping" ends with Chapter 4, "Chasing the Logistical City and Its Spatial Formations" by Clare Lyster. Here, Lyster describes reading the city through logistical processes that produce highly robust networks of urban infrastructure, transportation, and technological storage. This inquiry looks at processes of transfer expanding the city beyond the boundaries of singular municipalities. Such an expansion communicates the city as simultaneously being handheld and global.

Part II, "Resource," gathers evidences of extraction and production processes from the inherent and established contextual situations within cities. Naturally occurring and long-standing, these processes, which are ultimately informed by ecological influences, embed into landscapes, the synthetic integral components of a city. Chapter 5, "Chasing and Rewiring Resource Territories," introduces the conversation of industrial resource and extraction processes. Here, Neeraj Bhatia, examines the impacts of pipeline production processes on territorial and cultural factors, even after their original use expires, reconsidering such infrastructures as potential urban tools to redefine the cities they identify with and connect. Chapter 6, "Chasing Military Logistics in the Urban Void" by Jeffrey S. Nesbit, examines historically rich industrial productivity in manufactured shipyard landscapes as urban contemporary design process. Utilizing the consequential voids of shipyards in support of ecological speculations, the fluctuations of economic uncertainty become productive testing grounds in their cities. Chapter 7, "Chasing Lines of Engagement" by Edward Becker, tracks the processes and procession of urban resources from their extraction to their consumption. Doing so deepens one's understanding of the highly networked nature of contemporary site-specificity and the ramifications of our production processes, thus linking people to place to exchange as a definition of community.

Part III, "Typology," identifies processes, patterns, conditions, and narratives within urban environments and discourse that potentially redefine how cities are identified, designed, and perceived—all of which reveal the inconsistencies of standardized urban types while trending toward more authentic methodological readings of the city. In Chapter 8, "Chasing Strategies for the Post-crisis," Emmanuelle Chiappone-Piriou posits the powerful roles of architectural and urban speculation in the face of a permanent crisis state. Chiappone-Piriou proposes, as a divergence from reliance upon utopian problem-solving typologies, contextually specific, ground-up design as a tool through which crises can be reframed as opportunity for cultural and built advancement. In Chapter 9, "Chasing Ambiguous Conditions of Coexistence," Peter Winston Ferretto challenges generic typological definitions of the dense contemporary city. Through a process of identifying Hong Kong's ability to adapt specifically to its own evolving conditions, he describes how it has subsequently become a city defined by its strain of reactive conditions. Chapter 10, "Chasing a Genealogy of X" by Choon Choi, innovatively recites the city through social, political, and symbolic voids that transcend physical place, marking new strategies for architectural form. Through an inquisition of the typology of voids found in Seoul, Choi identifies process through which flat voids are transforming the city's use of space.

Charged with approaching the city more sensitively and responsively, this book investigates what designers do not presently know, attempting to learn from the city's inputs and outputs simultaneously. This allows the city to participate in its own evolution by directing the work of its designers. Designers, as city chasers, will then have the ability to interrogate and respond to the elaborate urban patterns of form as manifestations of the internal processes and self-generative interactions of the city itself. Approaches outlined in the subsequent chapters allow for the identity and diversity of global cities to remain intact—to continue supporting their own individual structure, culture, and behavior. This calls for evolution, not transplantation or blatant historicism. *Chasing the City* demands that design processes deviate from the formulaic, generic, and/or detached proposals of our utopian ancestors. Sensitive, progressive city design must evolve from the very city fabrics that foster the heterogeneity and duality of the neo-utopian paradox.

Notes

1 Francis Haverfield, *Ancient Town Planning* (London: Oxford University Press, 1913). Hippodamus provided clear strategies for designing the proper urban plan through wide streets, and especially described programmatic organization as the primary role for keeping activities segregated.

2 Camillo Sitte, "City Planning According to Artistic Principles" [1889], trans. by George Collins and Christiane Collins, in *Camillo Sitte: The Birth of Modern City* (New York: Rizzoli, 1986), p. 130. As a formative framework for this book, Sitte utilized conditions found in the evolved medieval city in order to produce an extended set of guidelines for the future city. It is in this spirit that *Chasing*

the City attempts to uncover lessons learned, to then re-embed those formal and logistical processes back into that very condition.

3 Yona Friedman, *Pro Domo* (Barcelona: Actar, 2006). Although Friedman describes a flexibility built out of a megastructure soaring above Paris, limits of evolutionary domains remain (see Chapter 8 for more information regarding models defined by Friedman).

4 Reyner Banham, *Los Angeles: The Architecture of Four Ecologies* (New York: Harper & Row, 1971).

PART I
Mapping

2
CHASING THE AWKWARD CITY

Joshua M. Nason

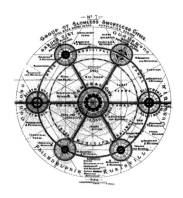

FIGURE 2.1 Ebenezer Howard's Garden City of To-Morrow, in all its sectioned splendor.

On Urban Identity

Utopia has long fascinated humanity, especially those who work in cities. To imagine the perfect city, and more so, to be a part of its making, is an exercise speaking to the core desires of many designers and planners. Generations hunting for utopia remain grasping for the ideals upon which a collective perfection could be based. Unfortunately, there is no collective perfection, and the superimposition of individual perfections has proven to be misguided in some instances and disastrous in others. As the world globalizes, intensified, continuously layered human differences engender complexity within global cities that collectively thwart any supposed efficacy founded within singular ideals.

As the world's growing population dramatically urbanizes, coupled with the globalization of influences and connections, urban communities are mutating at unprecedented rates where global and local identities melt into one another, leaving policy makers, planners, and designers grasping for means to keep up. What does this all mean for today's and tomorrow's cities? Is it futile to even attempt to read and understand them? Certainly not. Rather, it is more crucial than ever for those who work in and on the built environment to understand cities (or at least attempt to), even if the cities are in the midst of complex evolution. In *Far from Equilibrium*, Sanford Kwinter and Cynthia Davidson call for urbanists that integrate the complexity of the city into their work, rather than subdue or trivialize it:

> No longer content with the milquetoast urbanism of merely remedial design propositions, nor the camp urbanism that transforms the advancing, often savage deprivals of the modernization process into cult objects (i.e., suburbs, nets, edges, and spectacle), what we need is a genealogical urbanism that both invents and unearths embedded histories-in-the-making, and through such invention transfigures and transvalues the very landscape on which it operates.[1]

However, such an undertaking must be done sensitively, with the full understanding that modes and mediums of analysis and design are integral

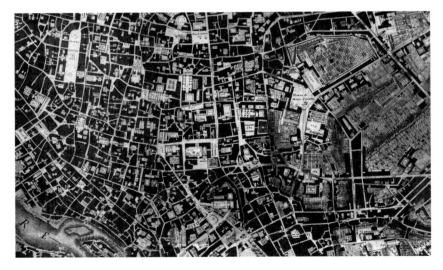

FIGURE 2.2 Giambattista Nolli's map of Rome subtly superimposes public space over a seemingly straightforward figure-ground, showing the city beyond solid and void, but rather as a dichotomy of inhabitabilities.

to and impactful on their outcomes. Projective mapping is one way to tangibly investigate and affect urban contexts—not in search for utopian ideals or moments to transplant pre-set prototypes into local fabrics, but rather, through mapping, which, when used to extract from cities the moments that define them and give them authenticity, can be a powerful tool for investigation and change within and for cities. Such drawings do not merely represent the stereotypical, but advocate for and give direction to cities.

On Mapping

Although innumerable definitions of mapping vary greatly depending on what is being mapped and the specific execution of the map, most concur in explaining maps as simplified diagrams of complex systems.[2] These flattened illustrations are vital in their ability to assist in gaining an understanding of orientation within the more complex system. This orientation, although usually geographic in nature, need not be limited to helping a person get directions from one physical place to another. Maps can be orienting on many fronts: ideological, social, economic, political, and more. An underlying thread through this list of mapping's orienting capabilities is the common need for someone or something to be found or identified within a context. This need, rooted in the desire for some semblance of orientation, can be that which compels one to refer to such figures in the first place. Therefore, the purpose of a map is to clearly and succinctly communicate information necessary to facilitate orientation of the individual within that system, whether it is a building, a city, a landscape, a concept, or a social or cultural context. However, such a definition of mapping ostensibly makes some assumptions.

An orientation-based definition of mapping assumes that the system is presently understood by the cartographer, and therefore navigable by others via graphic direction. This is not always the case. In fact, it is, at times, impossible to completely understand the system being mapped. Such an assumption leaves one with a cursory scan rather than delving into notions of exploration of what place can potentially mean. Places are complex, multivalent systems that require volumes to be adequately communicated. No cartographer can understand all of these complexities, much less convey them in a single map. In fact, not all systems are inherently understandable or communicable, further complicating the cartographer's task. Another assumption embedded in the statement above is that map users indeed desire to be oriented, guided, and/or found within the system. This, too, is not always the case. In instances such as these, maps can become misinformed, misinterpreted, inadequate, or in a word, *awkward*. Such *awkward maps* should not be discounted as useless or insufficient. They can be used to generate new understandings of places and systems. An awkward map can get the visitor sufficiently lost, guide one to new, uncharted territories, and expose unique or unplanned juxtapositions, and therefore lead to unpredictable discoveries not transmissible via traditional methods. Awkward maps can explain places as they are while not worrying about what others think they should be. They ignore the idyllic while focusing on the endemic, no matter how awkward it may be. It is the awkwardness that delineates the identity of place. Normative mapping is ill-equipped to navigate beautifully flawed contexts, untapped or misunderstood resources, experiential or spatial systems, or to communicate spatial complexities not lending themselves to merely directional graphics. Such qualities and events must be mapped through inventive means not intending to explain understood systems. Rather, such maps attempt to simultaneously extricate and communicate the potentiality held within the inexplicable and at times irreproducible moments within a system. Awkward maps ask questions, explore possibilities, take risks, and leave room for their own expansion.

Such projective maps, those leading to the discovery of new systems, are the focus of this chapter. Concurrently, maps that do nothing more than reproduce a small, closed-system par value will be ignored. In accordance with claims made by the likes of Gilles Deleuze, Felix Guattari, and James Corner, it is accepted here that such illustrations are more akin to "tracings" than viable maps. Deleuze and Guattari explain:

> What distinguishes the map from the tracing is that it is entirely oriented toward an experimentation in contact with the real. The map does not reproduce an unconscious closed in upon itself; it constructs the unconscious . . . . The map has to do with performance, whereas the tracing always involves an "alleged competence."[3]

Corner describes the ability of the map to construct new knowledge as its agency to unfold. This is linked to the map's inherent revelatory potential as both analog to physical place and abstraction of information related thereto. Corner argues:

> The analogous-abstract character of the map surface means that it is doubly projective: it both captures the projected elements off the ground and projects back a variety of effects through use. The strategic use of this double function has, of course, a long alliance with the history of mapping.[4]

Such maps, those that are involved in the shaping of the world rather than just representing its pre-supposed stasis, hold tremendous potential considering the changing nature of the world's cities.

On Vital Awkwardness

"Awkward" is not the most flattering of terms in the English lexicon. When one speaks of "awkward," it is usually in reference to another, or rather an "other" individual—not one that is a recipient of the narrator's verbal affection, but rather a social outlier, a nuisance. Dictionaries use such terms and synonyms as "clumsy," "lacking dexterity," "embarrassing," "unruly," "socially uncomfortable," "adverse," and "antagonistic" to define what is awkward.[5] Some go as far as to define awkwardness as "backwards," "perverse," "inconvenient," "unfavorable," "without grace," "hazardous," "uncivilized," and even "barbaric" (although this seems a stretch on all accounts).[6] Aside from semantics and etymology, if we look closely at all of the claims against awkwardness, they seem to hold to one truism: awkward is different—not different in an appreciatory unique or exotic manner, but different in a way akin to something to be avoided, ridiculed, and feared.

Definitions of "awkward" that gravitate toward solely negative connotations are merely reflecting the limited bias in favor of the norm. They are prejudicial, and certainly incomplete. Aspects of awkwardness are (or can be) incredibly positive. There are several types of awkwardness. Two such types exemplify the poles of its range of meaning: the awkward as outcast, and the awkward as vital. Consider forms of vital awkwardness—for example, the awkwardly tall tower which offers way-finding and acts as an emblem of progress, or the awkward diner that acts as a special tradition, an oasis from the sameness of its fast-food neighbors. Vital awkwardness is mediating. It offers intimate connection between person and place in personally relevant ways. Vital awkwardness stems from complex interrelationships principally linked to the identity of the whole that yet hold their own distinct authenticity.

While such vital awkwardness is essential and identifying to a city, it is not always easily recognizable nor understood at first glance. In order to understand what within a city is vitally awkward and how it relates to the rest of the city, one can employ *awkward maps*, which reveal analytic mapping processes aimed at exposing and interrogating such moments in the city.

Awkward maps are particularly well suited to draw out characteristics within a city that evade the limitations of normative mapping. Namely, in drawing characteristics such as complexity, change, and relational contingencies (all of which are defining to contemporary cities), a cartographer is well served to focus on the city's awkward moments which exhibit tension and evolution within its fabrics. Focusing on these three as the initial characteristics used to identify vitally awkward urban components, one can better understand the contemporary city. Complexity, the result of layered global and local as well as past and

16 Joshua M. Nason

present influences, offers opportunities for multicultural authorship and participation, thus fostering evolution within the identity of contemporary cities. Akin to such complexity is the inevitability of change—not change in a linear or causal manner, but integrated and contingent change, change that requires thinking about cities as ecological systems and processes of evolution as integrated, algorithmic entities that are hard to predict and must be treated responsibly and responsively. Stating that cities are ecosystems is not enough, we must think ecologically. Such integrated thought focuses on relationships in an attempt to understand contingencies, connections, and reciprocities within part-to-part and part-to-whole correlational structures.

On Awkward Characteristics

Complexity: Sameness and the City's Identity Crisis

The world's unprecedented rapid urbanization, while economically beneficial, puts tremendous strain on cities as urban contexts radically transform. It also seems to engender a strange contextual dumbing-down in the face of cultural multiplicity. Replicative urban development patterns replace local fabric with homogenized, internationally recognizable typologies that many consider to be "best practices." Such trends are apparent across the United States, particularly in areas of rapid growth. However, many cities change negatively, digressing to the standard corporate norm of chain stores and suburban sprawl. These changes are subsequently producing new and significant transformations in the urban context such as fatigued and failing infrastructure, volatile economic networks, and compromised political systems. Finding viable and architecturally sustainable solutions to address the influx of people is a significant challenge. While cities are attempting to deal with (not prepare for) this rapid growth in various ways, many are trending toward the faceless norm—a new ideal in which ubiquitous comfort and familiarity take precedent over uncomfortable city realities. Perhaps this is actually a facet of the "McDonaldization" of society.[7] This phenomenon surely counters Kevin Lynch's focus on a city's "imageability" as a character-defining quality. When cities begin to assume the same image, they normalize themselves through commercialization, losing identity in the process.[8]

Cities are simultaneously existential, inexplicable, experiential, and most certainly variable due to intimate connections and vacillating contingencies. Cities, due to their enigmatic scale, have always attracted the attention of those seeking to tame and define the city. However, cities, due to their enigmatic scale, tend to undermine that desire they perpetuate. And while experts throughout history have labeled, sorted,

FIGURE 2.3 Dallas' sprawl, while a powerful reality of suburban growth, is also a growing stereotype that neither adequately describes the city nor gives insight into its qualities and potentials for new and authentic urban form outside pre-configured models. Photo by Exploredinary.

and catalogued cities into compartmentalized, segregated pieces, cities (the world over, throughout history) continue to evade absolute definition and classification. Considering the plethora of utopian proposals that created more problems than they solved, one would assume that designers and builders would recognize the futility of superimposing "there" onto "here." Yet the beat goes on. Countless books, drawings, speeches, and curricula have purported the new ideal: the city so good it will replace all other, inferior, models. And yet each of these plans gives way to the next in a chain of broken idealized promises. Such plans are not only shortsighted, but dangerous in their attack on local and specific fabrics that give cities their identity. Better urbanism will never come from a can.

It is in their multiplicity and mutations that future cities will find their benefit. Designers simply need to operate among the multiplicities rather than peddling the standard. It is crucial to seek urban models that are multiple, mutating, and contextually specific in nature. But in order to do so, one must operate in medium-conducive exploration.

Change: Shift and Eco-logics

For recent generations of urban researchers, a shift in focus has occurred—a shift that is more focused on thought processes than design styles. This shift focuses more on the integration of multiple models that embrace the complexity of the city, and avoids notions of singular design solutions as silver bullets aimed at solving all of the problems of the city. In reality, no single solution could fix the issues of a neighborhood, much less explain what transpires in the world's megacities. But this shift is not just in design and planning. It is a cultural shift reflected across disciplines. This shift, however, is directly linked to the built world, as it usually represents the largest scale at which humanity operates on a daily basis. Cities are the manifestations of daily life and culture in palpable ways. They therefore reflect the growing cultural awareness of the morphing of those very cultures. The generations where life was understood as linear, simple and isolated are long gone. The shift toward thinking ecologically, meaning that thinking and working processes are integrated, focused on multiple inputs and outputs, does not necessarily mean that all thought is focused on natural systems, or formal "ecologies." Rather, if we can think about design relationally, determined to incorporate the integrated and interconnected aspects of as many influences as possible, we can derive more robust and inclusive projects for and by the city. Such eco-logic thinking is similar to algorithmic processes, in that they require the inclusion of complex, varied, and even changing information in order to develop more nuanced and specific solutions. Change is an urban quality that can be better understood through such thinking, and studied through awkward mapping.

Mario Carpo, in *The Alphabet and the Algorithm*, describes this change and advancement in our collective language of thought, not just a modification of symbols and representations.[9] Our world and cultures now operate more akin to flows of interactions and exchanges than to processions of cause and effect. This new algorithmic thinking, while not universally accepted and deployed, allows for cognizant, multifaceted ideological collisions more advanced than standard linear deduction. It is a fittingly complex analytical model well suited to understanding increasingly complex ecological conditions. And while algorithms are being developed to better understand ecologies, the more poignant development is deeper than the analysis of ecologies of things, it is the fundamental understanding that those ecologies of things operate algorithmically. The actual revelation is that more robust and layered analytical systems better grasp ecological systems because they operate on similar structural terms. Similarly, this is the intent of awkward mapping.

In accordance with such thoughts is David Grahame Shane's elaboration on urban systematic layering and mutations similar to those employed in DNA recombination.[10] Also influenced are authors and designers such as Fumihiko Maki[11] and Thom Mayne,[12] as evidenced by their investigations into collective form. All of these authors employ integrated thinking and design methodologies within their work. Certainly, they are not alone, but this exemplary work explicitly discusses urban design and criticism in what could be termed eco-logic or algorithmic ways.

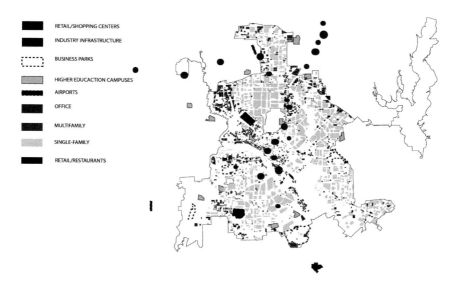

FIGURE 2.4 Identifying specific programmatic types within a city can be the beginning of mapping archetypal displacement as evidence of cultural change. Map drawn by Joel Martinez.

We may be, out of pure necessity, on the precipice of another paradigmatic shift in the way in which we comprehend and inhabit our cities. However, there is no real way to speak to that possibility until it has unfolded to an undeniable degree. One thing that is certain is our need to, at the very least, adapt how we deal with our environments on a daily basis. Rather than adhering to rudimentary notions of supposed singularities, more inclusive and projective urban strategies should now investigate cities as concurrent topographies. This provides for new opportunities in identifying multivalent urban organizational systems as communities of interacting urban agents. We can no longer afford to underestimate our ecological environments, both natural and synthetic, as archipelagic collections of isolated, or even tangentially related, pieces circumstantially gravitating to one another. More inclusive and encompassing urban alternatives would lend themselves to a better understanding of complexity, eliciting new methods of understanding the interconnectivity and integration of formal, social, infrastructural, cultural, and political forces. Analytical methods can foster such understanding if they extend beyond mere representation and, through the revealing and proposing of new relationships, present new defining connections within our cities. Despite this potential, many of our current analytical models are unable to adapt to our need for contemporary urban spaces, making us guilty of what Reyner Banham terms an inability to "find new bottles for new wine."[13] In this regard, mapping is a well-equipped vessel.

For designers of the built environment, contextual relationships are undeniably crucial to how a project or piece of the city relates to the whole. But one could expand that contextual understanding to the critique of typological transplantation in general. Beyond deploying Banham's work as an illustration of urban identity and as a mode for differentiating one city from another, the brilliance of his ecologic view of urban environments holds true over four decades later. His insight into the interconnected nature of components within the city at varying scales (both internal to each ecology and across the collection) sets a precedent for understanding the complex relationships within the even more volatile cities of today. Specifically vital is his ability to surpass seeing these ecologies and their parts as wholes and pieces Their relationships are nuanced and crucial to their function as well as their impact on the rest of the city.[14]

Relational Contingencies: Defining Correlations

To begin: a description of very specific relationships and/or instances within the city could potentially redefine how one understands the design assessment of the urban component. To do so requires a few key definitions (or possible re-definitions). Here, we will examine three adjectives as describing relational types within the city: the *aleatoric*, the *meronymic* and the *anomalic*.

First, *aleatoric* refers to something that is dependent on uncertain contingencies. It is left to or resulting from a chance process. Many describe it as a roll of the dice.[15] To be clear, it is not that something is truly left to

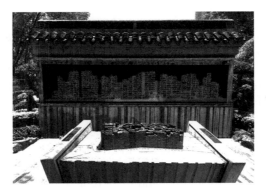

FIGURE 2.5 The Kowloon Walled City Model and Cross-section, as displayed in Kowloon Walled City Park, Hong Kong. The drawing appears to be an inverted replication of Kazumi Terasawa's 1993 section of the housing block as published in 1997 in *Kozuru Castle* by Kowloon Castle Expedition. Photo by Joshua Nason.

FIGURE 2.6 The Eiffel Tower is more than a mere landmark. While certainly not representative of the entirety of Paris, for many this unmistakable icon is synonymous with the city. Photo by Cheryl Donaldson.

chance or entirely unpredictable; it is merely that its contingencies are not fully understood at present. In this lies the possibility of learning those contingencies through an examination of that which seems *aleatoric*. It is not entirely without reason; it is simply part of a context which has not yet been properly excavated. It is not the relationships that are lacking, it is the understanding of those relationships. This speaks of emergent or multi-influenced authorships. In urban design, "aleatoric" refers to something so linked to its context that it exceeds the designer's expectations or preconceptions. It has developed a life of its own, or works at levels deeper than intended. While almost always the case to some degree, this is specifically referring to the significant outcomes emerging from the newly altered context. The impact must be noticeable and significant for the relationship to be *aleatoric*.

Second, *meronymic* refers to a relationship in which a part expresses the nature of the whole.[16] It is a reference, or inference, where the constituent part is so indelibly linked to the whole that it can either reference or even reflect it. This can be exampled by a spokesperson so connected to the body they represent that they are indeed a voice of the people, or a strand of DNA giving identity to the organism. In cities, it could be a place within that city that gives it identity. Kevin Lynch would argue that it is a part of the city that represents its image[17]—for example, the Eiffel tower in Paris.

Lastly, there is the *anomalic*. Commonly used dictionaries do not recognize the word "anomalic."[18] In fact, they usually re-route the searcher to "anomaly" or "anomalous." However, there is an important difference between "anomalic" and "anomalous," both of which describe conditions surrounding anomalies. Anomalies are irregularities, deviations from the common (or natural) order, exceptional conditions or circumstances.[19] While both "anomalous" and "anomalic" describe the existence of such

FIGURE 2.7 Relationships such as Singapore's integration of jungle and city or Shanghai's superimposition of past and present hold the potential to generate anomalic moments within the city. Photos by Joshua Nason.

irregularities, it is in the specific relationship of those irregularities to the norm where their difference comes to be.

"Anomalic," most frequently used in specializations such as astronomy, chemistry, computer science, and music, describes elements, traits, or phenomena that actively evade description and yet convey highly specific characteristics. Anomalic conditions do not lack purpose or organization—quite the contrary. It's simply that those purposes or organizations are not yet fully understood. Where anomalous conditions are those that are "unconformable to the common order; deviating from rule, irregular; abnormal,"[20] anomalic behavior deviates with the purpose of redefining the system entirely. The anomalous condition is a misfit. That which is anomalic is evolutionary. It can evidence curious juxtapositions between elements within a city, or even draw attention to a tension between a moment and the whole. Either way, anomalic traits within a city begin to explain subtly iconic aspects, character-building fissures in the fabric, or even identify frictions that speak to the construction and potential for a city to evolve.

In describing these three urban relational types, it is key to note that their mere existence is not what is most important in identifying awkward moments within the city. It is in fact the potential coexistence of such conditions that brings lasting identity to a city. Such moments occur in a city when a place therein is singular and identifiable yet so indelibly linked to its fabric that its quality exceeds its planning effectively enough to catalyze new typologies within that city. This, potentially a form of urban catharsis, clarifies or even redefines the city's identity, becoming truly crucial to the city and its future. However, this redefinition does not require, nor even benefit from, a spreading into other parts of the city. It

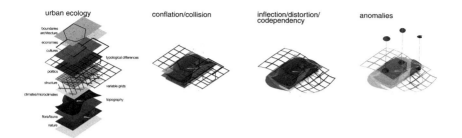

FIGURE 2.8 Joshua Nason's "Anomalic Emergence Diagram" depicts the interaction, conflation, and distortion of seemingly simple city components as morphological layerings that can drive authentic moments within a city.

is through the moment's autonomy that it affects the whole in a productive manner. It should not be copied. It should be cherished. Indeed, it is the moment's awkwardness that offers its hierarchy. It is not a misfit within the city—not an urban stranger. It is the city itself, the underlying reality of its best self-emerging from the sea of superimposed *elsewheres* and norms composing a masquerade-tapestry covering its true fabric. It is in this presence that the city's identity exists. It is in the communication of such presence that awkward mapping becomes most effective: in drawing the unadulterated and unedited here and now that comprise the city's most vital awkwardness.

On Awkward Process

As previously stated, vital awkwardness mediates between people and place. Further, while not easily understood, vitally awkward moments can make our cities home, making them strangely intimate and familiar by embodying specific combinations of the *aleatoric*, *meronymic* and *anomalic* moments that unite people with their context and build a sense of place. Vitally awkward places are linked to the identity of the city while deftly maintaining their own distinct authenticity. It is through this that such places can be both contextual and iconic. Designers must then work in processes that embrace the efficacy of such moments while avoiding the lack of fidelity in urban identity that comes through formulaic or replicative processes.

The Situationist International (SI) understood the efficacy of the awkward. SI members Guy Debord and Asger Jorn, among others, concocted a multitude of psychogeographic maps not only as drawings of *dérive*, or wandering, but also as registrations most important within Paris.[21]

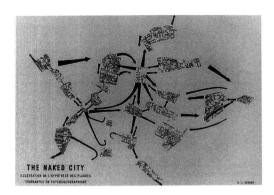

FIGURE 2.9 Guy Debord's psychogeographic map known as "The Naked City" explores the experiential city laid bare, beyond the landmarks or traditional pathways.

To them, Paris was not merely the iconographic landmark the tourist visits. Paris was a series of experiences and connections of place, cultures, and opportunities to engage. It was not just spectacle, but an integrated superimposition of past, present, and future. It was the essential "here" that interested them. It was the sincere, reciprocal, and selective immersion in the city that made it real at a time when they felt simulations were beginning to compromise the efficacy of life, specifically life in the city. Fast-forward roughly six decades and examine where our cities stand in terms of sincere, reciprocal, and selectively immersive experience. Guy Debord would be horrified at how deeply into the simulation we have regressed. Beyond a social critique on technology or modern comforts, the very nature of urban spectacle and the eradication of "here" in favor of the implantation of "there" is alarming.[22] It is emblematic of the erosion of the awkward within our cities.

As city growth continues to outpace projection and preparation, frenetic complexity results. Designers and planners with limited capacity erroneously extinguish the vitally awkward in favor of the accepted stereotypes. This reaction-based operation ultimately fosters the distillation of place and the perpetuation of urban homogenization. When such rapid growth is coupled with the globalized streamlining of influences and products, the immediacy of preconfigured capital, and the inactivity of those who challenge unfettered system models, the attainability of socio-architectural and urban stereotypes becomes prevalent. Therein lies the problem. Essentially, each city gets what it wants: a different city. Through the grafting of stereotypical urban typologies over existing fabrics, world cities regress to the norm, where no cliché is left behind. And cities are left staring at mere traces of themselves absorbed in the banal sameness of everywhere else.

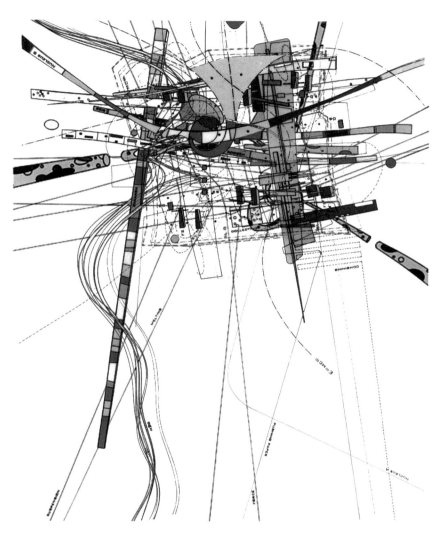

FIGURE 2.10 Petra Kempf's "You Are the City" gives readers the opportunity to alter layer combinations of city systems in order to reframe how the city is understood and engaged. Kempf describes each layer as its own diagram—a diagram that may stand alone without meaning, but possesses the ability to describe a "circuit or an action." When one begins to layer them, they become the map.

Designers must not only labor keenly to adequately add to the identifying gems of a city, but must also be vocal in their retention, participatory in their evolution, and insightful in their impact upon the future city. Focusing on retaining the vitally awkward moments within the city and sensitively adding new life to them will allow the city to continue to grow in appropriate, specific, and contextual ways. The city can morph and mature without losing what it is: rare idiosyncratic collections of hundreds of years of various types of people working together to build an authentic place to claim as home.

As designers and planners, when talking about city life, we are many times discussing experiential microcosms, contextually rooted in both the obvious and invisible, the planned and the circumstantial. The conspiring of such forces differs for each local place in time, and thus must be observed firsthand—bite by bite. This form of tacit and tactical research contextually informs design, hopefully catalyzing hypotheses and designs into appropriately adaptable spaces that host dynamic patterns of urban life. The role of such observation and research in design processes is crucial in the development of public spaces as places of exchange at the edge of change and tradition. Such a delicate balance is only exacerbated when rooted in the freneticness of the contemporary megacity. Entrenched observational urban research tactics akin to the processes of investigators help one to make informed, contextually responsive, and adaptable design decisions able to be beneficially folded back into the urban fabric. However, one must precede such decisions with in-depth investigative work. This is where mapping becomes ever-fruitful through its ability to help identify vitally awkward moments within cites and subsequently place and connect them to the future thereof.

On Drawing Conclusions

Intelligent, precisely crafted, and applicable studies augment understanding and intensify the communication of the effects of urban growth and adaptation. Through garnered sapience, one is able to recognize, embrace, and wield one's skills and talents in the cultivation and implementation of numerous shifts in projective ways. Studying cities as integrated urban ecologies, defined by their awkward characteristics, through intense mapping exercises exposes the components within the examined systems, their relationships to other constituent parts, and the overall relational adaptations.

If one can create and analyze such structured maps with applicable identity, complexity, and adaptability, one can better apply these skills and characteristics within cities. Through this, one not only orients individuals within their contexts, but also informs urban actors how to affect their contexts, empowering them with tools to employ change as a progressive

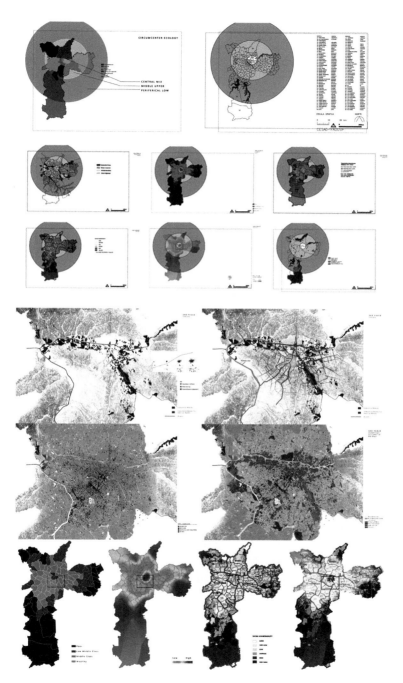

FIGURE 2.11 "Scalar Sao Paolo," a student's maps exploring city components, traits, and activities at varying scales. Maps by Ricardo Simoes Bandeira.

power. Maps as frozen images of contained conditions are only representational tools. Alternatively, maps focusing on the multifaceted, multivalent evolutions of the environments prove to be more indicative of cities, as they are more accurately complex. This is particularly productive when such maps focus on the vitally awkward moments within a given city.

The key to understanding why awkward mapping is a good fit for such explorations is that it is a proven tool for testing relationships, the building blocks of an urban ecology. Mapping exercises produced in the office, studio, or laboratory need to do several things well to truly test these relationships. They must operate at varying scales, oscillate between general and specific conditions, focus on contextual meaning and influence, and expose forces within each city and its vitally awkward places. If one aims to test the *anomalic*, *meronymic* and *aleatoric* nature of places within a city, several actions prove to be productive tools as analytical mapping exercises.

Varying

Operating at varying scales benefits most design ventures, specifically those covering large entities and collections, such as cities and ecologies. The Eames' film *The Powers of Ten*[23] exemplifies the usefulness of such scale variation: by zooming in to the molecular scale and out to the cosmic scale, the movie shows organizational, formal, and relational similarities

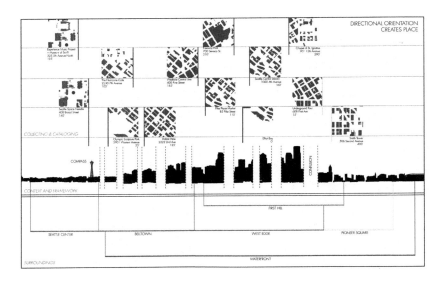

FIGURE 2.12   "Seattle Gems" extract for closer inspection and comparison of moments of intensity and interest from the city's fabric. Map by Eduardo Casteñeda.

at all scales. Not only does this film use varying scales well, it does so in a manner that applies to ecological thinking. This develops conversations about the micro-to-macro relationships intertwined in all cities. Cities do not operate at one scale, but all of them simultaneously, and variation of scales, through zooming in and out, allows one to test systematic relationships across scales.

Oscillating

Oscillating between general and specific conditions is similar to the act of varying to different scalar vantage points. However, this point relates more to content than it does scale. Inherent in these oscillations is the need to focus on the most pertinent data and omit information superfluous to the study. Through oscillation of content in this manner, one can determine which content is essential and related, while relegating the unimportant. This is assessed through the back-and-forth nature of the analytical oscillation. This could be analogous to empirical research studies where elements are added and subtracted carefully and individually in order to test composition and interaction. Such oscillations are also fruitful exercises for investigating non-hierarchical structures, where poles or components can be isolated in small sets for comparative means. By weighing parts against one another, one tests their relativity, but also understands their connectedness.

FIGURE 2.13 A series of maps depicting Dallas' urban canyons and their internal flows and connections. Drawn by Jonathan Brown.

30 Joshua M. Nason

Focusing

Focusing, here, specifically references the isolation and examination of urban components before returning them to their context. This focusing specifically examines contextual influences. While omitting, including, zooming, focusing, oscillating, and doing a host of other tasks in order iteratively studies the relationships within a data set, one must vigilantly remember the context in which each system (and decision) operates. However, to test the connection between the part and the whole, they must be examined both together and apart. Operating in a vacuum does nothing to test urban relationships. Focusing allows one to isolate and reintegrate to avoid such a trap. In fact, this error afflicts many studies that too eagerly simplify and isolate a multitude of urban ingredients in order to support pre-supposed conclusions of hierarchy or want a partial, cursory indication of pieces rather than the whole. Such studies, which fail to complete the reintegration, are not exercises in focusing. They ignore their responsibility to test direct relationships within the larger system, and fall short. Permanent isolation is shortsighted and insufficient.

Exposing

Lastly, exposing forces within the systems is crucial to understanding seemingly unpredictable and invisible influences acting as agents within an urban ecology. Such agents can be political, social, or cultural forces that are difficult to draw, but have tremendous influence in and on the city and must be accounted for. Certainly, making visible that which is not easily pictured is difficult. However, these must be drawn in order to test the potential causes, reactions, and interdependencies between elements of urban relationships. Simply because things are difficult to locate does not mean they have little influence on the form and/or fabric of the city. Through exposing such forces and elements within the city, one makes visible that which often goes ignored or unnoticed. For example, drawing political boundaries, such as voting districts, is simple, but digging into the household demographics at levels not apparent in common data sets is harder to accomplish. However, if drawn and placed over the voting districts and compiled with and compared to other related forces, a map can show direct influence on city form and culture. Many times, exposing is related to the drawing of cultural phenomena that go unrepresented otherwise.

On Forces and Traces

Many times, in order to chase the identity of the city through awkward mapping, one must go beyond drawing from a standardized cartographic

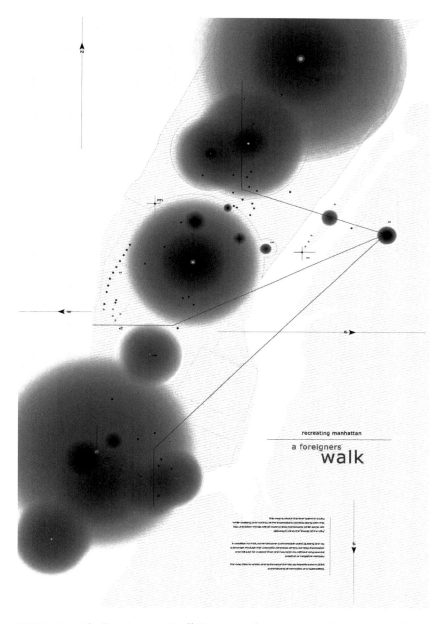

FIGURE 2.14 "A Foreigners Walk" maps the contrast between a visiting student's actual first-time experience in New York and the pre-empted city, one over-represented through tourist stereotypes. By Tobias Julinek.

toolbox. The awkward in a city can sometimes be discovered via detective work that investigates the systematic forces (input) and traces (output) that reveal patterns or outliers within the city. Some of the forces that can greatly impact a city are gravity, fugacity, mutiny, hierarchy, and codependency/reciprocity. In order to test these forces, one must look for traces of their existence within the city. While not always obvious, nor fail-proof, looking for traces of evidence can often lead the observer to the forces acting at the core of many ecological relationships within the system. Similar

FIGURE 2.15 Dallas' Design District is an underappreciated and rapidly evolving yet identity-giving part of the city. Map by Karis Bishop.

to Reyner Banham's identification of four architectures that are linked to the four urban ecologies of Los Angeles, each force has traces that exhibit their presence and influence.[24]

Gravity, Fugacity, Mutiny

In this case, gravity refers to the attraction of systematic elements to one another. If one element is pulled toward another, then there is a moment when they will collide. An example of this could occur when looking at a map examining levels of violent crime in comparison to levels of education. If there is indeed evidence of locational collision occurring, then gravity between those components may exist.

Fugacity—or instability—can be the product of many different things, but in order to test its presence, one must find evidence of such a force. Discovering vacillations within the urban fabric or habits can be traces of fugacity. In this case, vacillations are resonance or indecision. It is active stagnancy brought about by not knowing what should happen next. Many times, such vacillations can be difficult to define, and especially to draw. Instances where something is in definite need of attention, but sits and awaits change can be an example of fugacity.

Mutiny refers to a change in the balance of elements within the ecosystem, or possibly the system changing in its entirety. This can occur for many reasons, but when trying to determine where it may be happening, one could look for moments of evolution, both great and small. Such mutiny can be imposed either from the bottom up or from the top down. In many cases, it is evidence of a power struggle of some sort. Whether revolutionary or passive in nature, evolution occurs due to a need or desire for change. Many times, it is environmental conditions that instigate such change. An example of such forces existing within a city is evidenced in areas under directed gentrification or redevelopment efforts.

Each of these three forces is evidence of struggle or evolution within the city. If one can identify where these forces are occurring, one can determine places in the city where the identity is undergoing transformation. It is in these places where cities are redefining their identity. Such nodes house the awkward, both productive and otherwise. However, once recognized, these places can become opportunities for the cultivation of vital awkwardness within the city.

Hierarchy, Codependency/Reciprocity

More commonly understood, hierarchy is a systematic ordering or caste system that establishes what is most important or prominent within a system and that which is not. While hierarchies are more easily identified by trained designers, it still helps to look for traces of juxtaposition within ecology. Looking at the proximities, boundaries, and concessions between components of ecologies directly relates to the types of relationships within that ecology. Formal juxtapositions are the easiest to map when factors of height, volume, centrality, materiality, etc. are evidence of the pecking order. However, when other factors such as experiential reactions and processional arrangements are considered closely, one can begin to understand invisible hierarchies of individual and social natures.

Lastly, synchronism occurs when things seem to be related, but lack sufficient evidence to prove how or why. Such interpreted relationships can actually be traces of larger forces, such as reciprocity and/or codependency. Colloquially, one could say, "Where there's a spark, there's a fire." While not always the case, many times the appearance of synchronistic linkage is a trace of some related duality where two or more component ecological parts are tied together in some form or fashion. This goes beyond mere assumption, and stops shy of causality. It is essentially a mutually beneficial relationship of integrated parts such as two bordering areas within a city that seem to be linked economically or culturally in some way. In reality, it could be a third piece that connects them, such as a specific business or sub-group that has transcendent influence over both communities.

By identifying such forces within ecology, one can begin to understand some identifying characteristics within that system. Once identified, the complex interrelationship of the many factors influencing the city in superimposed and integrated ways can be made known through analytical awkward mapping. Once fruitful opportune places within the city are located, they can be capitalized upon or preserved. Chasing moments in the city to reinforce its awkward beauty and potential for authenticity may be difficult, but is worth it as we help to build cities that we associate with and that transform us as citizens.

In Conclusion

Clearly, the complex urban environments in which we operate frame our understanding of each component and their interrelatedness. It is imperative that we understand how to engage our cities through flexible analytical models of identity research, rather than containing them in hyper-specific element classifications that can ill afford to bend and sway with the changes occurring in our cities and merely reflect the continuation of stereotypical analysis of stereotypical city elements. We no longer operate in sacrosanct, purely identifiable systems (or maybe we never did). Our urban environments are concoctions of natural and synthetic ingredients mixed to near indistinguishability, garnished with the singularities and idiosyncrasies of place and culture most effectively manifested through the vitally awkward places within our cities. These compounds comprise contemporary ecologies, demanding every designer's responsible observation and inclusive operation and cooperation. In order to do so, we must understand each individual city as an identity-hopeful place. Analytical drawings such as specific, projective, and pleasantly awkward maps expose systematic, contextual interdependence, but also explore the emergence of the integral, yet idiosyncratic, moments that give cities their character.

As designers fighting the faceless banalities of stereotypical city-making, we can no longer rely on the tools—analytical and procedural—that bring uniform results. Through focusing on the vitally awkward moments in the city, we can fold back into our urban environments the very qualities that we appreciated in the first place. Award mapping doesn't just draw what breaks suit, it exhumes from fabrics the best they have to offer—their most authentic selves, even if those selves are not idealized. Awkward mapping is, in its purest form, a process of Chasing the City. It chases the city where it is, in search for what it is, hoping to find among the flaws and issues an entity crafting its own beautiful, awkward self.

Notes

1 Sanford Kwinter and Cynthia Davidson, *Far from Equilibrium: Essays on Technology and Design Culture* (Barcelona: Actar-D, 2007).
2 Norman Thrower, *Maps and Civilization: Cartography in Society* (Chicago, IL: University of Chicago Press, 1996), p. 245.
3 Gilles Deleuze and Felix Guattari, *A Thousand Plateaus: Capitalism and Schizophrenia*, trans. by B. Massumi (Minneapolis, MN: University of Minnesota Press, 1987), p. 12.
4 James Corner, "The Agency of Mapping: Speculation, Critique and Invention," in *Mappings*, ed. Denis Cosgrove (London: Reaktion, 2002), p. 215.
5 "Awkward," Definition 1, https://en.oxforddictionaries.com/definition/awkward (accessed June 29, 2018).
6 "Awkward," Definition 2, www.dictionary.com/browse/awkward (accessed June 29, 2018).
7 George Ritzer, *The McDonaldization of Society* (Thousand Oaks, CA: SAGE Publications, 2007), pp. 14–15.
8 Kevin Lynch, *The Image of the City* (Cambridge, MA: MIT Press, 1960), pp. 6–12.
9 Mario Carpo, *The Alphabet and the Algorithm* (Cambridge, MA: MIT Press, 2011), pp. 28–34.
10 David Grahame Shane, *Recombinant Urbanism: Conceptual Modeling in Architecture, Urban Design and City Theory* (Chichester: Wiley Academy, 2007), pp. 148–150.
11 Fumihiko Maki, *Investigations in Collective Form* (St. Louis, MO: University of Washington St. Louis School of Architecture, 1964).
12 Thom Mayne, *Combinatory Urbanism* (Santa Monica, CA: Stray Dog Cafe, 2011).
13 Reyner Banham, *Los Angeles: The Architecture of Four Ecologies* (Oakland, CA: University of California Press, 1971, 2009), p. 3.
14 Ibid., pp. 217–226.

15 "Aleatoric," Definition, https://en.oxforddictionaries.com/definition/aleatory (accessed June 29, 2018).

16 "Meronym," Definition, https://en.oxforddictionaries.com/definition/meronym (accessed June 29, 2018).

17 Kevin Lynch, *The Image of the City* (Cambridge, MA: MIT Press, 1960), p. 84.

18 "Anomalous," Definition, https://en.oxforddictionaries.com/definition/anomalous (accessed June 29, 2018).

19 "Anomalies," Definition 1, *Oxford English Dictionary*. Web (accessed June 29, 2018).

20 "Anomalous," Definition 1, *Oxford English Dictionary*. Web (accessed June 29, 2018).

21 Libero Andreotti and Xavier Costa, eds. *Theory of the Dérive and Other Situationist Writings on the City* (Barcelona: Museu d'Art Contemporani de Barcelona and Actar, 1996).

22 Guy Debord, *The Society of the Spectacle* (New York: Zone Books, 1994), pp. 27–45, 64–72.

23 Ray Eames and Charles Eames, *Powers of Ten: A Film Dealing with the Relative Size of Things in the Universe and the Effect of Adding Another Zero* (Santa Monica, CA: Pyramid Films, 1978).

24 Banham, *Los Angeles*, pp. 19–216.

3

CHASING #ANTIDRONE

Derek Hoeferlin

Introduction

It is imperative we collectively prioritize *water-based challenges* as a 21st-century design agenda in regard to cities' engagements with their resources and ecologies. More broadly, both climate change science and water resources funding allocations are now at risk given the current political climate, along with a foreseeable future of deregulation and lack of state oversight, and potentially at a global scale. When we assess this environmental and political decoupling with funding cuts that parallel delayed maintenance of failing 20th-century infrastructures, the prospects of future multi-purpose infrastructure and design projects are precarious.

Current political- and capital-driven models of urban and regional planning promulgate "sustainability," "resiliency," and "adaptation" as the go-to buzzwords for contemporary design solutions. These models tend to continue a 20th-century modernist tradition of idealistic utopian visions. And as a result, these buzzwords struggle to be implementable due to current, yet outmoded, funding procurement practices that are not structurally designed to enable such aspirations for "integrated" design.[1]

As described by Rem Koolhaas:

> [Bigness] implies a web of umbilical cords to other disciplines whose performance is as critical as the architect's: like mountain climbers tied together by life saving ropes, the makers of Bigness are a team . . . . Beyond signature, Bigness surrenders to technologies; to engineers, contractors, manufacturers; to politics; to others.[2]

However, it is now time for design disciplines to re-emerge as *proactive* agents of design, cognizant of contemporary *water* issues that sail way beyond Rem Koolhaas' 1995 manifesto of Bigness. In hindsight, Koolhaas' provocation now seems minuscule and maybe an obvious fact of life, only just over two decades later. Maybe that was the common-sense point?

More specifically, central to negotiating the future of cities' resources and ecologies will be the need to designate *water* as a primary, organizational design directive for the evolving city of tomorrow—in any city context, whether it be water-rich, water-poor, or in many instances, water-polluted. To be fair, copious amounts of inspiring work have been written and speculated on similar integrative water-based design, such as the design-research of Anuradha Mathur and Dilip da Cunha, or the integrated water management advocacies in New Orleans by Waggonner & Ball's *Dutch Dialogues* efforts, among others.[3] But few concretely offer implementable solutions in light of our rapidly changing socio-political contexts. As such, it remains a challenge to implement these ambitions, especially in regard to cities' anticipation of unforeseen water-based challenges. Thus, the design disciplines (architects, artists, landscape architects, urban designers, and others) will need to develop, deploy and disseminate alternate methods to engage physical conditions and their corresponding communities—and explicitly in relation to water. Such methods will need to: (1) negotiate themselves within contrarian interest groups, (2) self-sustain themselves within absent funding streams, and (3) broadcast themselves within multiple contexts, scales, venues, and disciplines.

Koolhaas suggests that this kind of complex work needs to be collaborative with—and even surrender to—other disciplines outside architecture and design. Going a step further than Koolhaas, not just collaborative with disciplines that are outside architecture and design, more importantly, the work should engage multiple users and voices with methods and tools that, in and of themselves, collectively require a team to operate, striving for collective outcomes. This is what is defined as **#ANTIDRONE**. The work advocates for a method of "Chasing the City" with multiple agents, not by the singular author. Simple enough, collaboration is needed now more than ever to address urgent design quandaries. As an alternative, this, albeit uncertain, integrative model for collaborative water-based design for the future of cities ultimately includes larger distributive contexts of watershed territories. The first section of this chapter, on *Way Beyond Bigness: A Watershed Architecture Manifesto and Methodology*, presents an overview of evolving water-based design research. The second section highlights a particular project of the methodology: a collaborative, and intentionally low-tech, investigative aerial photography mapping effort, the *Public Lab River Rat Pack*. Understood together, the two aspire for an #ANTIDRONE future for design.

Way Beyond Bigness: A Watershed Architecture Manifesto and Methodology

This research recalibrates the role of an architect, and by extension, advocates for other architects to be better equipped to *enable* design to avoid future crises (design as foresight), rather than to *rely* on design to react to crises (design as hindsight). In line with the framework of this volume, the work is indeed anti-utopian. It is not seeking a singular answer. It promotes pragmatism. It operates in a network. And it certainly is not hopelessly idealistic.

Way Beyond Bigness: A Watershed Architecture Manifesto and Methodology has resulted more out of self-critique, from many years working within the milieu of the post-Hurricane Katrina disaster context of New Orleans, collaborating with a broad network of academics and professionals. Since the unprecedented storm, many of us always seemed to be operating in reactionary modes of design.[4] As an alternate, *Way Beyond Bigness* builds upon work in the post-Hurricane Katrina context of the New Orleans region that focused on collaborative network engaged in *water-based design*.[5] It is an ad hoc advocacy network that emerged out of the post-disaster "plandemonium" context.[6] During this, we realized that water was the big elephant ironically absent from New Orleans' sinking room, both rhetorically and functionally—rhetorically, since water was frustratingly absent from the post-disaster planning efforts,[7] and functionally, since water had been drained from the urbanized areas of New Orleans for 20th-century development.[8] The scope of the architect's work needs to adequately meet the design challenges faced by post-disaster and rebuilding contexts, such as ones in New Orleans, "Way Beyond" an archaic definition for "architecture"—that is, one only relegated to the design of buildings. Rather, *Way Beyond Bigness* realigns architecture across: multiple scales (micro to territorial), multiple disciplines (ecologists to economists), multiple narratives (hyperbolic to pragmatic), and multiple venues (academic to professional)

This necessary realignment is defined as "Watershed Architecture," or [WA]. While the research first focused on New Orleans and its regional environmental deltaic context of the Louisiana Gulf Coast, it since has scaled up to understanding cause-and-effect circumstances up and down the entire Mississippi River Watershed.[9] Then, too, the Mississippi Watershed research situates itself within a comparative, collaborative, networked study of other global deltas and watersheds, particularly the water-rich watersheds of the Mekong and Rhine, and more recently, the water-poor watersheds of the Colorado and California.

[WA] posits a common-sense five-point manifesto for water-based design: (1) Water guides our shared lives—*since life and society depend upon water, understand that we must design proactively, not reactively.* (2) Water flows where water wants to flow—*since water may be the most politicized commodity on earth, understand that water ultimately is apolitical.* (3) Water starts far upstream—*since design exists within much larger distributive contexts of watersheds, understand the need to design at multiple scales.* (4) Water provides a mutual resource—*since fundamentals do matter, understand that water is the foundational component of the actual ground we occupy.* (5) Water is why you are where you are—*since designers are optimists, understand how the management of water prioritizes our design decisions.* [WA] deploys a four-part integrative methodology consisting of: (1) Document + Mobilize [D+M], (2) Compare + Analyze [C+A], (3) Speculate + Synthesize [S+S], and (4) Engage + Catalyze [E+G].[10]

Method 1: Document + Mobilize [D+M]

The first category is field documentation. Document + Mobilize [D+M] foregrounds aspects of living with water across multiple river basins. The primary methods of documentation mobilized are: geo-referenced photography, stationary video, and aerial photography via balloons and kites. The documentation is then curated and imported into open-source mapping platforms.[11]

To get closer to an integrative understanding of water, it is critical that the subsequent categories of the methodology (comparisons, speculations, engagements) are underpinned by rigorous, legible, and accurate field documentation, to best prepare for the forthcoming work. Much of this need for legible graphic representations of complex sets of information has to do with a diverse array of intended audiences, and with the fact that cause-and-effect conditions across river basins are complicated and change rapidly. Often the audience is meant to be multiple disciplines outside design, and ultimately for public dissemination. In other words, documenting cannot be just for design's sake. Additionally, issues being documented are not necessarily regarded as design per se. Rather, the documentations are indicative of conditions typically regarded outside design—such as agriculture, industry, infrastructure, and water issues.[12]

Method 2: Compare + Analyze [C+A]

The second category is river basin-based taxonomies. Compare + Analyze [C+A] articulates issues of living with water, primarily within the Mekong, Mississippi and Rhine river basins. The themes compared among these three river basins serve as a framework for additional analyses more particular to other global river basins. The structure and content are intentionally simple, utilizing didactic info-graphics, two-dimensional and three-dimensional spatial mappings and animations to legibly narrate very complicated themes across the river basins for multiple disciplines and user groups to access. The work is organized as a taxonomy around themes including territories, governance, population, terrain, agriculture, biodiversity, salinity, water quantity, water quality, sea level rise, subsidence, seasonal cycles, flooding, dams, and industry.

FIGURE 3.1   Compare + Analyze [C+A]. Part 2 of the methodology compares and analyzes multiple global river basins, primarily the three river basins of the Mekong, Mississippi, and Rhine, through a series of diagrams, info-graphics, and animations. Image by Derek Hoeferlin.

Building upon these taxonomies are a series of short videos that synthesize multiple themes into three key uber-themes: population/territories, water quality/quantity, and river control. The animations allow the work to be represented in both space and time—for example, how dams and navigation issues have developed in the past century in each of the river basins. Once again, simple use of info-graphics, spatial mappings, and axonometric diagrams is utilized in the animations.[13]

Method 3: Speculate + Synthesize [S+S]

The third category of [WA] proposes water-based design futures. Speculate + Synthesize [S+S] stimulates debates and long-term possibilities for multi-scaled river basin issues. Much of the discussions across entire river basins, in their current form, are predominantly rhetorical, rarely propositional, and other than a few noteworthy examples, unfortunately without input from the design disciplines.[14] The [S+S] work ranges from the hyperbolic to the pragmatic. One form of speculation cannot exist without the other.[15]

An example of "hyperbolic" speculation is the author's proposal *from the BLIGHTY MISSISSIPPI to the MIGHTY MISSISSIPPI*, a watershed-scale design future informed by cause-and-effect issues affecting the entire Mississippi River basin, with direct impact up and down the river system, and more specifically, for the degrading Louisiana Delta and its sinking urbanism of New Orleans.[16]

Project Description

No longer a natural river system, the Mississippi River watershed has become a controlled conduit system facilitating massive agriculture, commerce, development, and industrialization by prioritizing navigation and the barge industry to deliver it.[17] There have been great economic and resource benefits from such river control. But adverse ecological byproducts and de-industrialized regions have resulted as well, along with natural resources challenges and major stresses on flood and drought management.[18] In other words, ecologies, resources, industries and river control measures are inextricably linked along the Mississippi and its tributaries. While the Mississippi River basin's namesake is the main stem, just as important economically and environmentally are its two predominant tributaries—the Missouri and the Ohio Rivers. The Missouri River supplies the river basin's majority of sediment. The Ohio River, and by extension the lower portion of the Mississippi River, supply the majority of water volume. In current form, two of the main negative environmental and economic impacts from development of the Mississippi River watershed ultimately manifest in the

Chasing #Antidrone 43

delta of south Louisiana and the Gulf of Mexico: *wetland loss and the dead zone*. Both of these pose interconnected environmental and economic threats to not just the Gulf Coast and New Orleans region, but also ultimately the United States at large.

Accepting that the Mississippi watershed will not return to a network of natural rivers, the speculation retrofits the Mississippi's existing infrastructures and ecologies, at the river basin scale, into a networked eco-industry toolkit that holistically reconsiders cause-and-effect relationships, both

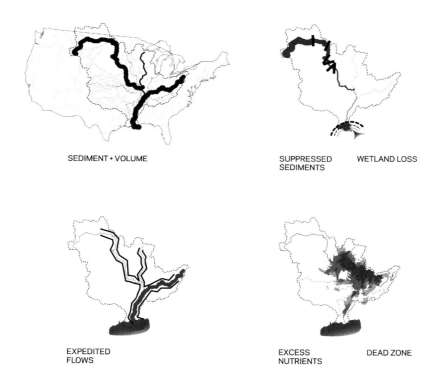

FIGURE 3.2 Mississippi River basin causes and effects. The diagrams, clockwise from top left, delineate overarching issues impacting the Mississippi River basin: (1) the Missouri River supplies the majority of sediment and the Ohio River supplies the majority of flow; (2) six major dams in the upper reaches of the Missouri River trap significant amounts of sediment, which in its natural sense assists in maintaining the Louisiana Delta; (3) the majority of rivers are leveed, in turn increasing the height and flow rate of the rivers; and (4) the excess levels of nutrients due to agricultural run-off, compounded by the expedited flows, significantly contribute to the Dead Zone phenomena of the Gulf of Mexico. Image by Derek Hoeferlin.

44 Derek Hoeferlin

environmentally and economically, over the next hundred years and beyond. The intertwined toolkit proposes: filtering nutrients, collecting sediment, farming algae, refining algae fuel, distributing sediment, and distributing fuel. To achieve the toolkit, the Mississippi River basin will be mighty once again by collecting, transforming, and distributing two important resources of the watershed that are currently mismanaged: excess nutrients and suppressed sediments. The speculation proposes physical engagement with existing locks and dams and their proximate under-utilized de-urbanized spaces and varied land uses along the Upper Mississippi and Missouri

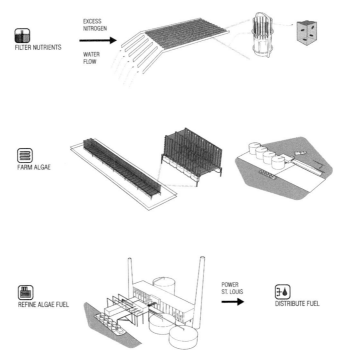

FIGURE 3.3 Algae bio-fuel process. The proposed process of transforming nutrient overloads in the Mississippi River to algae fuel includes: (1) extracting nutrients through bacterial filters in underwater barrels to be used as plant food for the algae farm; (2) farming algae into biomass in detachable photo-bioreactor units strung together on pontoons; (3) transporting biomass via barges to retrofitted industrial sites along the river to refine algae fuel; (4) distributing algae fuel for local alternative energy supplies. Image by Hoeferlin, Compadre, Mendez, and Stitelman.

Rivers. By extension, it is pragmatic to bundle this proposal with the backlog of maintenance to the locks and dams, a concern repeatedly expressed by the US Army Corps of Engineers.[19] Rather than allowing the excess nitrogen and phosphorus to contribute to the algae bloom Dead Zone in the Gulf of Mexico, a series of stations could be placed at each of the locks and dams in the Upper Mississippi River (north of the confluence of the Mississippi and Missouri Rivers). These stations will filter the nutrients into

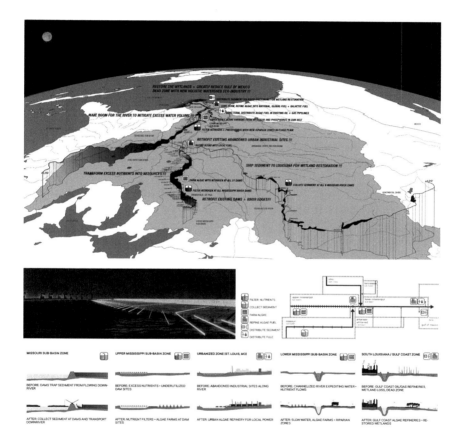

FIGURE 3.4 From the blighty Mississippi to the mighty Mississippi. The design proposes an ecological industry toolkit for the future of the Mississippi River basin, one that harnesses the existing cause-and-effect challenges confronting the basin in more integrative ways, such as transforming excess nutrients into algae fuel and harnessing mismanaged sediment sources for wetland restoration projects. Image by Hoeferlin, Compadre, Mendez, and Stitelman.

algae biomass that then can be transported to de-industrialized sites along the Mississippi River (such as North St. Louis or East St. Louis, Illinois) to be refined into bio-fuel for local power use.

This could create a massive new eco-industry that adapts to climate extremes such as floods and droughts, and retrofits existing infrastructure networks. In the long term, the algae fuel will be an alternate source of energy for the Mississippi River basin as the United States moves towards an alternative energy future, since the finite oil and gas resources from the Gulf of Mexico ultimately will become obsolete. Simultaneously, the proposal sequesters the sediment that is being trapped by the dams along the Missouri river and releases it to be utilized as a needed resource for the current and future wetland restoration projects of the Louisiana Delta. The continued coastal wetland loss certainly is an issue of national security for the future commerce of the entire Mississippi River basin, and for the local safety of New Orleans and coastal communities in the face of climate change, sea level rise, and tropical storm surges. Thus, long-term interventions far "upstream" in the Mississippi River watershed can generate a new hydro-region economy that has local environmental and economic benefits throughout river communities and cities in the river basin, and also will help remediate two of the main threats to the New Orleans deltaic region: wetland loss and the Dead Zone.[20]

Method 4: Engage + Catalyze [E+C]

The fourth category of [WA] sets the stage for collaboration and engagement across multiple disciplines, interest groups and venues. [E+C] advocates for designers to engage strong collaborative multidisciplinary networks by utilizing their skills from the first three categories (documentation, comparison, speculation). [E+C] succeeds when the speculative, complex river basin-scale work gets real, when it is proactive and projective, and by its very nature, inclusive with the design disciplines.[21] One such example of [E+C] is the *Public Lab River Rat Pack* (PLRRP), a project working with colleagues, research assistants, and students to document several sites along the Mississippi River and its tributaries. The work creates a highly visible understanding of the critical importance of intertwined, complicated, cause-and-effect relationships with the Mississippi River watershed.[22] Public Lab is a non-profit "community where you can learn how to investigate environmental concerns . . . using inexpensive DIY techniques, we [Public Lab] seek to change how people see the world in environmental, social, and political terms."[23]

Borrowing from Public Lab, the organization's mission prioritizes three objectives:

> 1) The Problem: Communities lack access to the tools and techniques needed to participate in decisions being made about their communities, especially when facing environmental hazards; 2) The Collaboration: We are an open network of community organizers, educators, technologists and researchers working to create low cost solutions for monitoring air, water and land. Discover, collaborate on, and contribute to locally important matters with the support of a global community; and, 3) The Solution: Join us today, as we work together to build and inspire a community of DIY activists and explorers using simple tools to build a growing body of data about our local environments.[24]

FIGURE 3.5 *Public Lab River Rat Pack* fieldwork. Images of various moments of collaborative fieldwork documentation with balloons and kites, along the rivers in the St. Louis region. Image by Derek Hoeferlin, *Public Lab River Rat Pack*, Washington University in St. Louis.

Utilizing Public Lab's DIY Mapping Kits, to date, the PLRRP has taken over 35,000 photographs above sites in the Mississippi River watershed, specifically in the St. Louis region and the Louisiana Delta. This is accomplished via camera rigs attached to big red balloons (and sometimes kites if too windy). The documentation has been curated and distilled into photographic and diagrammatic analyses of each site for comparative purposes, along with being imported into Public Lab's open-source website for dissemination.[25] The work is ongoing, and we will continue our collaboration with Public Lab and with others in the St. Louis region, the Mississippi River watershed, and beyond.[26]

By design—and in the spirit of #ANTIDRONE—the big balloons and documentary rigs require a *team* to operate, unapologetic in their embracing of trial and error, and by extension, promoting a hybridized analogue-digital approach to fieldwork. The balloons are expressive, highly visible objects in the sky. People easily see them. People ask questions about them. People tend to trust them, and even ask to participate in the teamwork. In other words, the balloons are the antithesis to drones. Drones have serious stereotypes for communities they document, and often for the communities they even target. By design, drones are inconspicuous, thereby conveying suspicions of surveillance, and as such, are mostly disengaged from the contexts they are actually documenting. Then, too, it typically takes just one person to operate a drone, usually in a solitary method of engagement. Obviously, an expensive and sophisticated network of infrastructure is required to back up this solitary operation. This exacerbates the potential suspicions among the communities being surveyed. Additionally, to operate drones, a person may be required to have a pilot's license. And their operation can even be conducted from halfway around the world.

Aside from the suspicions and difficulties for certain communities to have access to such sophisticated equipment and infrastructure, there are more practical reasons for deploying balloons in lieu of drones. Since the balloons are under a certain diameter, and their corresponding payloads of lightweight cameras are under a certain weight, and maybe most importantly, since the balloons are tethered to the ground by people with strings, the balloons are not subject to Federal Aviation Association regulations.[27] Drones are often subject to such regulations. In simpler terms, the balloons legally are considered toys. *Seriously, the balloons are just toys*—toys that happen to have cameras strapped to them, and can sway thousands of feet up in the sky, all the while taking thousands of photos, or hours of video, of what is below. Differences in time and logistics are important too. Current battery life of drones typically is under 30 minutes. Drones' firmware constantly has to be updated. A balloon can fly for hours. All a team needs is to rent a tank of helium, blow the balloon up, remain

FIGURE 3.6 *Public Lab River Rat Pack* engagement. Unlike drones, the balloons are big, red, and obvious in the field. As such, river dwellers and others become interested in the fieldwork and usually want to join the collaborative effort. Image by Derek Hoeferlin.

cognizant of physical obstructions such as transmission lines, and let it fly for as long as needed. The event is deliberate, requires patience, and is quite experiential. The team can conduct other fieldwork and activities while the balloon is swaying with the light winds, high above.

The following are descriptions of a selection of five sites documented with PLRRP colleagues and my Washington University in St. Louis students during 2014–2016.[28] The sites are along the Mississippi River in the St. Louis region and the Louisiana Delta, and each attempts to make highly visual time-specific understandings of sites related to the speculation, *"from the BLIGHTY MISSISSIPPI to the MIGHTY MISSISSIPPI."*

Specifically, documentations include: (1) a locks and dam structure as a potential site for future algae farm, (2) a large navigation canal to facilitate barge traffic up and down the river, such as a future need to transport algae and sediment, (3) a de-urbanized area along the river with potential for new industrial retrofits such as algae refining, (4) a current staging area for industrial use and transport, and (5) a river crevasse currently being modified as a wetland restoration project.

Each condition attempts to highlight the varying conditions of the actual water at each site as well, such as the radical difference between high and low river stages that can occur in short timeframes. To do the latter, the PLRRP quickly mobilized on January 1, 2016, at the peak of the third highest flood stage in recorded history for the Mississippi River in the St. Louis region. Over the span of just four months, the Mississippi River fluctuated up, then down, and then up again within a range of over 30 feet, from major flood stage to normal river stage. (low river stage would have needed to be another 10–20 feet lower).[29] In other words, the Mississippi River at St. Louis can fluctuate over an astounding 50 feet in height. This not only poses problems for flood and drought management, it also poses significant challenges to river access and the navigation industry.

Site 1: Melvin Price Locks and Dam

This site is on the Missouri State side of the Mississippi River, about 17 miles north of St. Louis.

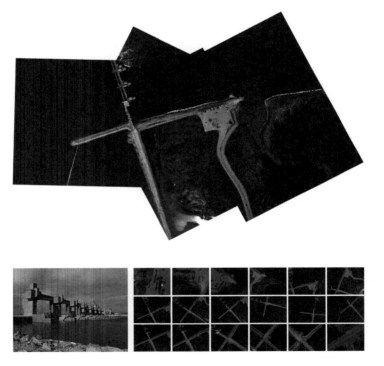

FIGURE 3.7 Melvin Price Locks and Dam. The top image is a stitched-together series of photos taken with the balloon, from approximately 1,000 feet in the air, highlighting the relationships between the Mississippi River, the locks and dam, levees, and land. The bottom left image is the series of tainter gates of the locks and dam. The bottom right series displays the rotation of the swaying balloon, in turn capturing different effects and angles of the flight. Image by Derek Hoeferlin, *Public Lab River Rat Pack*, Washington University in St. Louis.

Documented conditions include: the intersection of major river infrastructure (Melvin Price Locks and Dam) with ecological restoration (Audubon Center at Riverlands), including pooled and free-flowing river conditions resulting from the dam infrastructure.

The US Army Corps of Engineers (USACE) built the Melvin Price Locks and Dam in 1978 as part of the *9-Foot Channel Project*, a large effort by the USACE to maintain navigability along the Upper Mississippi River. South of here, the Mississippi River is free-flowing, unimpeded all the way to the river's mouth at the Gulf of Mexico. Critics of locks and dams have pointed out that these structures, while enabling low-emission transport of materials via barges, harm the river ecologically and exacerbate flood damage in the long term. By constructing a dam, the river moves from a free-flowing path to an "artificial slack-water reservoir habitat."[30] As a result, the chemical and physical properties of the water change, causing undue stress on the native fauna. The "pooled" water at this point is also high in nutrient content, specifically nitrogen from big-agricultural run-off to the north, as explained in the above [S+S] speculation *from the BLIGHTY MISSISSIPPI to the MIGHTY MISSISSIPPI* proposal that proposes algae farms at such nutrient-rich locations. Additionally, the dams trap sediment, thereby altering the flow of the river. The site of the Melvin Price Locks and Dam is at the intersection of another USACE partnership: the Audubon Center at Riverlands. The surrounding land is a restored prairie marsh and managed wetland network, providing important habitat for birds migrating along the Mississippi Flyway.[31]

Site 2: Chain of Rocks Canal

This site is on the Illinois State side of the Mississippi River, at the north confluence of the Mississippi River and Chain of Rocks Canal.

Documented conditions include: the 500-year levee with levee road and bike path, a parking pad at the canal's edge, the canal, erosion control along the canal, and the northern tip of Choteau's Island.

In 1953, as part of the *9-Foot Channel Project*, the USACE constructed an 8.4 mile-long canal with a 600-foot lock for ships and barges to bypass a unique natural navigational impediment, an exposed limestone dam that forms the "Chain of Rocks," rendering navigation through a stretch of the Mississippi River impossible during low river stages. This project's main aim was to facilitate barge traffic, primarily for petrochemicals and agricultural products up and down the river system. To mitigate erosion, the USACE constructs rock embankments known as "rip-rap," ubiquitously implemented up and down the river system. This infrastructure prevents soil from scouring and ensures canal depth remains stable. However, a downside to this practice is the lack of a fluctuating riparian-edged habitat

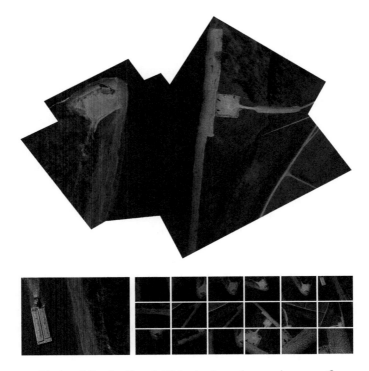

FIGURE 3.8 Chain of Rocks Canal. This site is at the northern confluence of the Chain of Rocks Canal and the Mississippi River. The canal was constructed by the US Army Corps of Engineers as a bypass to the natural limestone formations in the adjacent river that impeded efficient boat and barge traffic. Image by Derek Hoeferlin, *Public Lab River Rat Pack*, Washington University in St. Louis.

for the surrounding fauna and migratory birds, along with an undesirable edge condition for recreation, accessibility, and public amenity.

Site 3: North St. Louis Riverfront

This site is on the Missouri State side of the Mississippi River, just north of downtown St. Louis, Laclede's Landing, and the Gateway Arch. Documented conditions include: the 500-year floodwall, high and low water river stages, a bike path along the floodwall, and abandoned land and buildings. This is a large de-industrialized site, with a significant number of abandoned buildings and large open spaces within and surrounding it. The large concrete wall seen at this site is a floodwall—a large structure used to maintain the navigation of the river channel and to constrain floodwaters during high

FIGURE 3.9 North St. Louis riverfront. Both images were taken during two different balloon flights at approximately the same location, just six weeks apart. The top image highlights a more or less "low" level of the Mississippi River, and the bottom image highlights a "high" level of the Mississippi River, the third highest level on record, approximately 30 feet higher than the top image. Image by Derek Hoeferlin, *Public Lab River Rat Pack*, Washington University in St. Louis.

flow conditions. Floodwalls are typically used when levee construction is not possible, most often in cities where space is at a premium or in areas where bank access is necessary for commercial use. The photos in Figure 3.9 were taken just six weeks apart, first during the December 2015–January 2016 flood when the river stage crested at 42.3 feet, the third highest on record. Six weeks later, the PLRRP documented the river stage over 30 feet lower. The flood was of particular interest because its duration was much shorter than usual and because floods of this magnitude tend to happen during the spring, and very rarely during the winter months. Another point of interest here is the notion of public access to the river. Of note is the submerged bike path on the riverside of the floodwall during the high river stage.

54 Derek Hoeferlin

Several utopian visions have been proposed over the years to revitalize the area, ranging from urban farms to even a failed attempt to build a new National Football League stadium. Most recent is the vision affectionately referred to as the "North Riverfront Open Space and Redevelopment Plan," designed by Forum Studio.[32] According to the client, Great Rivers Greenway: "the overall goal ... is to promote economic revitalization of the North Riverfront by transforming vacant property along the Mississippi River into public parks and recreation amenities as well as encouraging private enterprise." And for this currently abandoned site, there is a proposal for an "Innovation District ... [a] live-work space to create a community of innovation, all organized, around a collaboration park, which is designed to recall and celebrate the historic Osage Nation mounds that once existed around this location." In other words, the district reflects both nostalgic guilt and a vague live-work economic future. In particular, the proposed Innovation District design does not address the current status of, or propose an engagement with, the floodwall, the bike path, or the radically varying river stages, each of which exhibits design potential by promoting economic, environmental, and recreational connections to the river.

Site 4: South St. Louis Riverfront

This site is on the Missouri State side of the Mississippi River, just south of downtown St. Louis, Choteau's Landing, and the Gateway Arch. Documented conditions include: the 500-year floodwall, high and low water river stages, a pumping station, an active staging area for various industrial uses, and a submerged ship. As with the North St. Louis Riverfront, areas south of St. Louis were historically a vibrant industrial district, and home to thousands of immigrants. Today, on first investigation, the site exhibits large areas of abandonment and de-industrialization. But there is more than meets the eye. The photos in Figure 3.10 were taken on the same days as those of the North St. Louis Riverfront, documenting the river stages varying over 30 feet. The flooded conditions show the river water up against the floodwall, and in fact, higher than the protected city-side of the wall. Piles of raw building material, equipment, and industrial byproducts that sat unprotected on the riverside of the floodwall were completely submerged, increasing pollutants in the river. While the floodwall served to protect the St. Louis downtown area from the rising Mississippi, it simultaneously concealed from the public's view the adverse effects happening just on the opposite side. When we documented the site in normal river stage, we found out from the workers at the site that it currently serves as the staging area for making concrete for the current renovations to the Gateway Arch grounds, just to the north of this site, so it

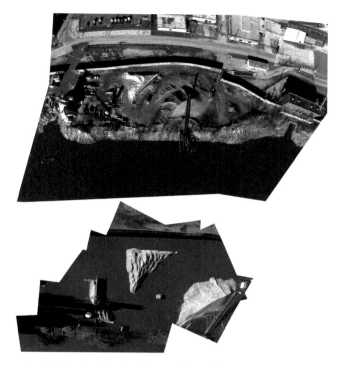

FIGURE 3.10   South St. Louis riverfront. As with Figure 3.9, the two images highlight the low and high water condition of one site, this time just south of downtown St. Louis and the Gateway Arch. At the time, this site was a staging area for mixing concrete for the renovations to the Gateway Arch grounds. Image by Derek Hoeferlin, *Public Lab River Rat Pack*, Washington University in St. Louis.

is in fact a very active, working riverfront. Also of note in the documentation is a pumping station, crucially important for stormwater management of the city to the west. Barely noticeable in the bottom-left corner of the normal level photo is a portion of a sunken World War II German U-boat. This boat used to be moored at the base of the Gateway Arch as a tourist site. The great 1993 flood, the highest on record, knocked the boat off its moorings, only to be submerged just south, at this mostly unknown location. Finally, at this particular section of floodwall is a "legal" graffiti wall, where the city-side portion of the floodwall becomes a canvas for a yearly international graffiti art and hip-hop festival known as *Paint Louis*.[33] This section—which has become a destination point for locals and visitors alike—encourages public engagement and acknowledgement of an otherwise solely industrial riverfront.

Site 5: Louisiana Delta

This site is on the east bank of the Mississippi River in the Louisiana Delta, south of New Orleans, in Plaquemines Parish, near the river's mouth at the Gulf of Mexico. Documented conditions include: a crevasse in the Mississippi River and a constructed marsh restoration project. The final site is far south of St. Louis, close to where the Mississippi River's mouth meets the Gulf of Mexico. A crevasse is a breach in a river, usually caused by a flood, when a river in a delta decides to alter its course. At this particular site on the east bank of the Mississippi River there is no levee. There is a levee on the opposite west bank of the river that protects the developed land and assists in maintaining the navigation channel. However, the river has been allowed to spill over at this location. This site was the first one documented with the balloons, and Public Lab and the Gulf Restoration Network, along with a local boat operator, joined and supported the effort, allowing access to the site. The boat operator along

FIGURE 3.11 Louisiana Delta. Taken at approximately 3,000 feet in the air, highlighted is a stitched-together panorama that documents a marsh restoration project south of New Orleans in the Plaquemines Parish. Image by Derek Hoeferlin, Derek Hoeferlin, Public Lab, Gulf Restoration Network, *Public Lab River Rat Pack*, Washington University in St. Louis.

with others have taken it upon themselves to construct this marsh restoration project, on their own terms, and without outside support. Locally
harnessing what is left of the sediment from the river crevasse represents
a grassroots effort by doing one's part to incrementally build land. It is a
simple design. Mound up soil from below the water's surface to be just a
couple feet above the water. Construct a gridded network of channels to
let the water flow with sediment, and saline-friendly marshes and grasses
then naturally grow. Because we were so off the grid, we were able to fly
two balloons, one at 1,000 feet and the other at 3,000 feet. Figure 3.11
reflects the 3,000-foot flight.

Conclusion

All of the documented sites represent challenging conditions for cities
like New Orleans and St. Louis in relation to water and the threats of
climate change, especially when understood in relation to regional and
watershed-scale forces. For example, despite the noble efforts of the marsh
restoration project in Louisiana, there is a distinct probability that the site
will not exist in the future, and as a result, the city of New Orleans is more
at risk as well. Current and projected sea level rise, land loss projections,
and storm surge scenarios put this site underwater during this century,
even if the proposed restoration projects of the Louisiana Coastal Master
Plan are implemented. The sites in the St. Louis region represent various
regional challenges for the city, ranging from the future status of major
infrastructure projects such as locks, dams, canals, levees, and floodwalls
to the speculative future of what large-scale industry will be in the region.
But these challenges are not insurmountable, as long as we begin to propose different attitudes towards how we engage, as designers, in innovative
efforts of "Chasing the City." *Way Beyond Bigness* and the *Public Lab
River Rat Pack* offer such flexible templates to reimagine the Mississippi
River Watershed as an integrated and collaborative design effort.

Notes

1 See D. Hoeferlin, *New Orleans: A Model 21st Century Cross-American Water
City?* (Santiago, Chile: ACSA International Conference Proceedings, 2016),
where Hoeferlin argues that current funding procurement strategies in the USA
still operate in silos, and are not designed for "bundled infrastructure projects."
2 R. Koolhaas, "Bigness, or the Problem of the Large," in *S,M,L,XL* (Rotterdam:
010 Publishers, 1995).
3 Several publications have investigated design in relation to water. Examples
include: three noteworthy publications by A. Mathur and D. da Cunha:
Mississippi Floods: Designing a Shifting Landscape (New Haven, CT: Yale
University Press, 2001); *Design in the Terrain of Water* (San Francisco, CA:
Applied Research + Design, 2014); *SOAK: Mumbai in an Estuary* (New Delhi:

Rupa & Co., 2009). Others include, but are not limited to: B. Busquets and F. Correa, *New Orleans: Strategies for a City in Soft Land* (Boston, MA: Harvard University Press, 2005); B. Meulder and K. Shannon, *Water Urbanisms* (Amsterdam: Uitgeverij SUN, 2008); T. Metz and M. van den Heuvel, *Sweet and Salt: Water and the Dutch* (Rotterdam: NAi Publishers, 2012); A. Acciavatti, *Ganges Water Machine* (San Francisco, CA: Applied Research + Design, 2015); S. Dunn and M. Felsen, *Urban Bowling* (San Francisco, CA: Applied Research and Design, 2017); H. Meyer, D. Morris, and D. Waggonner, *Dutch Dialogues: New Orleans/Netherlands: Common Challenges in Urbanized Deltas* (Amsterdam: Uitgeverij SUN, 2008).

4 See D. Hoeferlin, "Architectural Activism through Multiple Scales, Venues, Programs, and Collaborations," in *New Orleans Under Reconstruction: The Crisis of Planning*, ed. C. Reese, M. Sorkin, and A. Fontenot (London: Verso, 2014), which chronicles Hoeferlin's community-engaged professional and teaching design work in New Orleans during 2005–2011, responding to a specific set of crises.

5 The network includes: Washington University in St. Louis faculty and students (led by Derek Hoeferlin), University of Toronto faculty and students (led by Elise Shelley and Jane Wolff), Waggonner & Ball Architects, Public Lab, Tulane University School of Architecture (John Klingman, Dan Etheridge, Carol Reese, Richard Campanella, and Byron Mouton), Royal Netherlands Embassy in Washington, DC (Dale Morris), TU Delft (Han Meyer), landscape architect Robbert de Koning, Bosch-Slabbers landscape architects (Stijn Koole and Steven Slabbers), LSU Coastal Sustainability Studio (Jeff Carney), H3 Studio, Inc., STUDIO MISI-ZIIBI, Elizabeth Mossop, Ripple Effect, Longue Vue House & Gardens, and the Hollygrove neighborhood. Since Hurricane Katrina in 2005, the author has held design leadership roles on multiple water-based design projects in the New Orleans region, including *Gutter to Gulf: Legible Water Infrastructure for New Orleans* (2008–2012), *Dutch Dialogues* (2008–2010), *The Greater New Orleans Urban Water Plan* (2011–2013), *The Unified New Orleans Plan* (2006–2007), *St. Bernard Parish Framework Plan* (2006), and *Changing Course: Navigating the Future of the Lower Mississippi River Delta* (2013–2015).

6 For a thorough critique of the post-Katrina planning process, see Christine Boyer, "New Orleans under Reconstruction: A Crisis in Planning and Human Security," in *New Orleans under Reconstruction: The Crisis of Planning*, ed. C. Reese, M. Sorkin, and A. Fontenot (London: Verso, 2014).

7 See D. Hoeferlin, "New Orleans Needs a Water Plan," *St. Louis Post-Dispatch*, August 30, 2009.

8 For more information on the man-made reasons why New Orleans is subsiding and now partially below sea level, see "Why Is New Orleans Sinking?" *Gutter to Gulf*, http://guttertogulf.com/Why-is-New-Orleans-sinking (accessed June 29, 2018).

9 The Mississippi River watershed is the fourth largest in the world, extending from the Allegheny Mountains in the east to the Rocky Mountains in the west. The watershed includes all or parts of thirty-one states and two Canadian Provinces. The watershed measures approximately 1.2 million square miles, covering about 40% of the lower forty-eight states. Source: National Park Service, https://www.nps.gov/miss/riverfacts.htm (accessed June 29, 2018).

10 See www.watershed-architecture.com (accessed June 29, 2018)—Derek Hoeferlin (Principal Investigator), Alexander Agnew and Andy Lee (Research Assistants), and Washington University in St. Louis students.

11 See http://deltas-watersheds.com and https://publiclab.org/notes/gkdavis/09-11-2014/balloon-mapping-bayou-plaquemines (accessed June 29, 2018).

12 See http://watershed-architecture.com/document-mobilize-1 (accessed June 29, 2018).

13 See http://watershed-architecture.com/comparing-the-mekong-mississippi-rhine (accessed June 29, 2018).

14 Groups such as America's Watershed Initiative, America's Wetland Foundation, and the Nature Conservancy are developing venues for trans-boundary policy discussions across the entire Mississippi River Watershed. And these particular initiatives have begun to understand the importance of including the design disciplines as part of the discussions.

15 See http://watershed-architecture.com/speculation (accessed June 29, 2018).

16 Design Team: Derek Hoeferlin (lead designer), Lilia Irene Compadre, Allison Mendez, and Jonathan Stitelman.

17 From the US Army Corps of Engineers Mississippi Valley Division website: "The Mississippi Valley Division's navigation responsibilities include planning and constructing navigation channels, locks and dams, and dredging to maintain channel depths of the harbors and inland waterways within its 370,000-square-mile boundary. The division operates and maintains 4,200+ miles of navigable channels, 59 locks, 51 shallow-draft ports and seven deep-draft ports. In partnership with local port authorities, MVD personnel oversee dredging and construction projects at numerous ports and harbors." www.mvd.usace.army.mil/Missions/ (accessed June 29, 2018).

18 For a thorough explanation of the US Army Corps of Engineers' management of the nation's water resources, see "National Water Resources Challenges Facing the U.S. Army Corps of Engineers," https://www.nap.edu/read/13136/chapter/3 (accessed June 29, 2018).

19 For information regarding US Army Corps of Engineers infrastructure costs for maintenance and improvements, see Jordon Golson, "It's Time to Fix America's Infrastructure: Here's Where to Start," *WIRED*, January 23, 2015, https://www.wired.com/2015/01/time-fix-americas-infrastructure-heres-start/ (accessed June 29, 2018).

20 Edited portions of text for Methods 1, 2, and 3 were previously published in D. Hoeferlin, "*Hey Delta Urbanisms!!! Don't Forget the Watersheds!!! Advocating for Watershed (Not Just Delta) Urbanisms* (Delft, The Netherlands: EAAE/ISUF International Conference Proceedings—New Urban Configurations, 2012).

21 See http://watershed-architecture.com/#engage-catalyze-section (accessed June 29, 2018).

22 *Public Lab River Rat Pack* members: Derek Hoeferlin (Principal Investigator), with Washington University in St. Louis students: Spring 2016—Xiaoxin Cao, Molly Chaney, Nicholas Gentile, Katheryn Haas, Nina Lang, Rachel LeFevre, Amanda Malone, Xiaoqing Qin, Jinghan Shi, Micah Stanek, Rory Thibault, and Jessica Vanecek; Fall 2014—Alexander Agnew, Paige Bergmeier, Cristina Clow, Grace Davis, Shira Grosman, Taylor Halamka, Kayla Kroot, Andy Lee, Jennifer Rokoff, and Amy Sun; additional ad-hoc members: Michael Allen, Emily Chen, Allison Mendez, Elise Novak, Jonathan Stitelman, Fred Stivers, Tiffin Thompson, and Natalie Yates; partners: Public Lab; support: US Army Corps of Engineers St. Louis District, and Audubon Center at Riverlands; funding: Washington University in St. Louis.

23 See www.publiclab.org (accessed June 29, 2018).

24 Ibid.

25 See https://publiclab.org/notes/derekhoeferlin/05-09-2016/public-lab-river-rat-pack-st-louis-exhibition (accessed June 29, 2018).

26 Special thanks to: Public Lab (Shannon Dosemagen and Stevie Lewis); a 2015/2016 Washington University Sam Fox School of Design & Visual Arts

Creative Activity Research Grant for equipment, exhibition and research assistants; the US Army Corps of Engineers St. Louis District (Charlie Deutsch and Lane Richter) for permission and access to sites; Audubon Center at Riverlands (Julie Watson); Gulf Restoration Network (Scott Eustis); Stan Strembicki for printing access; and others, for their time and support.

27 See https://publiclab.org/wiki/balloon-mapping-regulations (accessed June 29, 2018).

28 Portions of text descriptions of documented Sites 1–4 in this chapter are revised versions generated by Washington University in St. Louis students, primarily by Molly Chaney, under the direction of Derek Hoeferlin and his Spring 2016 seminar *Public Lab River Rat Pack*.

29 The record high for the Mississippi River gauge at St. Louis is 49.98 feet (August 1, 1993) and record low is –6.20 feet (January 16, 1940), a 56.18 feet differential. For river stages, see the National Weather Service Advanced Hydrologic Prediction Service: http://water.weather.gov/ahps2/hydrograph.php?wfo=lsx&gage=EADM7 (accessed June 29, 2018).

30 See https://www.internationalrivers.org/environmental-impacts-of-dams (accessed June 29, 2018).

31 See http://riverlands.audubon.org/audubon-center-riverlands-0 (accessed June 29, 2018).

32 See http://greatriversgreenway.org/mississippi-greenway-master-plan/ and https://nextstl.com/2015/07/north-riverfront-vision-offers-ideas-with-or-without-nfl-stadium/ (accessed June 29, 2018).

33 See https://www.stlpaintlouis.com (accessed June 29, 2018).

4

CHASING THE LOGISTICAL CITY AND ITS SPATIAL FORMATIONS

Clare Lyster

FIGURE 4.1 Logistical logos. Assembled by Clare Lyster.

Introduction: The Logistical City

The logistical era is predicated on the expeditious flow of goods and information, rendering the city less an aggregate of objects and more a vessel for communication. At no point in our history has there been so much movement of bits and bytes from here to there, so the logistical city is first and foremost a fluid entity. To this end, there is evidence of how logistics is catalyzing new urban configurations in the present era, and many of the following examples have been documented by other scholars in recent years; nonetheless, it is worth cataloging them here as context for this chapter.[1]

Special Economic Zones (SEZs) are uniquely created districts for the packing, assembly, and processing of goods for export that lie adjacent to many manufacturing zones and container ports in cities all over the world, from Panama to Shenzen. Derivative of international production

FIGURE 4.2 UPC A-encoded barcode symbol. Drafted by Clare Lyster.

FIGURE 4.3 CenterPoint Intermodal Center, Joliet, Illinois. Satellite image, downloaded from Google Pro, November 6, 2014.

protocols, lax labor laws, tax incentives, and real estate formulas, these apolitical enclaves either emerge as new ground-up urban areas or are formed within existing urban contexts. Operating as mini-cities, with their own rules and regulations outside the nation state in which they find themselves, they nimbly foster trade flows and attract investment.[2] Deborah Cowen highlights Dubai Logistics City, a large SEZ, as follows:

> The emergence of the logistics city is significant. It marks a fundamental transition in the global space economy wherein the design and management of supply chains has become so critical to just-in time- production and distribution that there is now an urban form named in its honor. In the logistics city, urban space is conceived for the singular purpose of securing the management and movement of globally bound stuff.[3]

Global capitals such as London and Paris that are the nexus of financial trade and banking are logistical cities because they are sites where international markets and their affiliated services aggregate. These are the places, sociologist Saskia Sassen writes, "where the stuff of globalization" gets done.[4]

Backstage cities like ports such as Newark, New Jersey, and Oakland, California or Memphis, Tennessee and Louisville, Kentucky in the US, which are home to sorting and storage facilities for large shipping networks (for example, FedEx and UPS respectively), highlight that logistics, in the form of freight flow, is an active catalyst for urban development.[5] In order to be close to the FedEx World Hub for last-minute shipping and receiving, Memphis has emerged as a prime site for warehousing and packing, while UPS Worldport at Louisville International Airport accepts packages as late as 1:30 a.m.[6]

Technopoles, from Silicon Valley to Tel Aviv, illustrate how IT industries combined with institutional research and venture capitalism deploy logistics as an entrepreneurial ecosystem, currently manifested through urban gentrification (previously undesirable areas of cities that become "tech hubs") or the construction of new corporate tech campuses from the Googleplex to the imminent Apple campus.[7]

Logistic landscapes, from the Pearl River Delta in southeast China to Mumbai, exemplify how logistics—in this case, the procedures of transnational manufacturing and business—is responsible for the restructuring of existing urban configurations and the emergence of new ones at the regional scale. The area adjacent to Quincy, Washington State, has become the center of data storage (you could call it the capital of the Cloud) because of its adjacency to PC landings and cheap power courtesy of the damming of the Columbia River.[8]

Yet these categories of logistical urbanism, while offering up valuable examples of urban space in the commercial realm (the sites listed above are all trading and/or distribution centers of one form or another, and this is no surprise, since logistics is synonymous with the flow of goods and information) are one-sided encounters. When it comes to understanding the range of spatial formations in the city, they only offer scenarios designed around efficiency and economic exchange. They do not render a complete picture of the material impact (and potential) of logistics in the more quotidian spaces we experience in the city on a regular basis.

My recent book, *Learning from Logistics: How Networks Change Our Cities*, tries to correct this by citing a series of spatial transformations directly resulting from logistics invading the city.[9] Some of these are summarized as follows.

First, the city is no longer metrically determined (geo-spatially quantified by distance), but instead measured according to time. Logistics is a temporal construct. Evidence of this ranges from how FedEx, the US and now global shipping company, receives, sorts, and transfers packages within hours to satisfy priority delivery around the world to how financial trading networks build infrastructure to minimize transmission lag. I cite a 825-mile fiber-optic cable installed by Spread Networks in 2010 that connects New York to Chicago in 13 milliseconds.[10] One might say that logistics shrinks the gap between time and space to the point that we are only left with time. Space has been superseded.

Second, logistics has finally severed the relationship between the place of production and the site of consumption. While this decoupling has been widening over the last 250 years since the first industrial revolution, nonetheless, in denying place and territorial adjacency, the logistical city is an a-geographic concept.

Third, in relying in equal measure on virtual (soft) infrastructure as well as physical space, logistics expands the notion of the city beyond what was traditionally possible. Urbanity is a hybrid space akin to a platform—that is, a fusion of hard and soft space that allows us, the urban subject, access to a range of collective and social experiences (from online shopping to social media).

FIGURE 4.4 FedEx Memphis World Hub. Courtesy of FedEx.

Chasing the Logistical City 65

FIGURE 4.5 Constant Nieuwenhuys, "Vergelijkende plattegrond New Babylon," Amsterdam. Collection Gemeentemuseum Den Haag. Photographer: Tom Haartsen © Constant/Fondation Constant c/o Pictoright Amsterdam 2017.

Fourth, since logistics relies on infrastructure (communication systems through which flow is concentrated and optimized), the architectural object (building) is no longer the primary integer of urbanism. The irrelevance of architecture in organizing the city is having an enormous effect on the discipline by shifting attention from objects to systems. While systems thinking has been brought to the forefront of urban thinking in different eras (the Futurists in the early 1900s to the radical projects of the 1960s to landscape processes as a trope for planning in the 1990s and 2000s), today the emphasis on infrastructural connections has expanded to a range of "strata." Including ground (transportation flow and embedded conduits), air (bandwidth, drone and airline travel), and sea (container shipping and fiber), the logistical city is a super-striated thick field. This may be due to the corporate players (Amazon to Uber) continually stretching their dominion over multi-scales of territory as well as our work and domestic lives.

Subsequent to writing *Learning from Logistics*, other fallouts have crystallized. The dominance of logistical corporations, especially the larger ones (in 2017, Apple's cash in hand of $178 billion is equal to the GDP of New Zealand[11]) provides a startling glimpse of corporate power in the urban environment. Their bigness might be convenient for us, but it is also predatory. The logistical city is the latest incarnation of capitalism, and this has major pushback on its political underpinnings. The "gig" economy might be a hip space for some, but in lacking many of the fundamental social structures of the welfare state, it can also be discriminatory and unfair. Some companies avoid responsibility to their employees by not offering insurance and worker compensation. Freelancing or contract work (for example, as a self-employed Uber driver) offers no job security, and benefits are slim, if not non-existent.

Furthermore, questions regarding the form of the logistical city still remain. The spatial formations of the city in previous eras are well documented. Concentrated (medieval), radial (industrial), and sprawl (early post-industrial) settlement patterns prove that urban morphology is derived from the spatio-temporal networks of a given era, or put another way, that the shape of the city is directly impacted by the shrinking of time and space.[12] However, in contrast with previous eras, the time–space networks that now define how and where we live are not all physical, nor do they incite actual spaces, but instead they are temporal and hidden. So while the canals of the 17th century had a distinct configuration in the landscape, as did the railroads a century later, and the highway after that, today contemporary communication networks (that is, logistics) are less legible on the built environment. However, finding the moments when their presence is visible helps us articulate formal concepts. For example, the logistical city is a real place, but not a whole composition. It is made of fragments that erupt here and there throughout the fabric of the urban environment. The logistical city is at the intersection of two streets or in a building lobby, because that's where a FedEx box is located. It's in a parking lot where we find Zipcar. It's on our doorstep where our Amazon deliveries are stacked. It's in our kitchen when we receive a food delivery. It's on the sidewalk when we call for an Uber. It's in a Seven Eleven where we find an Amazon pickup location. It's in an ex-urban environment at the location of a warehouse where goods are stored. It's at a port terminal where container ships of international shipping are processed. It's at a train station when you rent a DVD. It's at the site of a PC landing or the location of a data center, and it's in your home when you order goods online. The logistical city is everywhere, but it is not continuous, it manifests itself as intense junctures in the landscape that are connected to each other.[13] Who would think that something so ubiquitous could be so unpronounced? Moreover, it crosses over many disciplinary realms, industrial design (boxes, phones, machines, and distribution devices) to architecture (large attendant spaces of logistical systems) and infrastructure (airports, port terminals, cables, bandwidth), all of which merge together as a large connected web of actions. The logistical city is a polyvalent net.

However, is there a way to expand the definition of the logistical city beyond these narratives, to one that foregrounds material formations that allow logistics and its effects to be expressed in other ways beyond efficiency, optimization and the proliferation of neoliberal behavior (none of which make particularly good subjects for architecture)? True, there are already examples of this. While logistics is synonymous with excessive consumption and neoliberal ideology in the west, the agency of mobile technologies and smarter governance protocols in large African cities without reliable municipal infrastructure is evidence of a more ethical use of logistics.[14] And we find an increasing presence of medical drones and micro-financing in rural and underserved regions.[15] Also worth noting is the use of technological systems in the design and maintenance of natural ecologies, and drones to combat wildlife crime.[16] Yet these uses are episodic, not to mention that their material implications remain unclear. Instead, it might be more productive to move beyond logistical operations to the study of their broader cultural effects. What is great about logistics is not only the systems themselves, but more significantly, the new worlds (good and bad) that are made possible by them.

Logistics and the Space of Desire

We live in an era when global mobility and systems of flow have become central to how we work and live. We now think nothing of dropping a priority package in a drop box in Chicago at 9:30 p.m. knowing it will arrive in Los Angeles by 7:30 a.m. the next morning. Talking in real time with a friend in a remote location via video-telephony is taken for granted, using nanosecond transmission signals is fundamental in the financial industry, while ordering groceries with a phone application and having them delivered later the same day is now commonplace. Every day we become more enticed by the convenient yet increasingly abstract actions of post-Fordist production and its associated delivery systems. Many of us shop via Amazon.com as well as a wide range of other online retailers and have products delivered directly to our home, sometimes within hours of ordering.[17] Courtesy of apps, we can have food cooked by willing chefs to match our culinary desires and, at a whim, have it delivered to our table. We can stream movies and games from media networks via high-speed fiber. We can send a document around the world via priority shipping within forty-eight hours and track every moment in its trajectory. We upload millions of videos and images in servers in large data centers so that others can download them in micro-seconds, and we can video-chat with a friend in real time despite being 5,000 miles apart. We can arrange for a driver to pick us up, meet up with a stranger, share a car, live in someone else's apartment, rent books, and borrow bikes. The almost simultaneous delivery of a plethora of services and experiences to fulfill every whim and fancy we might have induces new phenomena that merit further scholarship, for example cultures of desire, some of which are described below.

A recent feature by the BBC highlights the power of Facebook's algorithms, specifically how "likes" can be used to know more about users. You may think clicking the "like" icon is just a means for you to express your agreement with or support for something; well, Facebook is collecting and archiving your innocent input in the hope of leveraging it to influence you at a later date. With just nine likes, Facebook can predict your character as well as a co-worker would, with sixty-five likes as well as a friend, with 125 likes as well as a family member, while 225 likes, the average number of likes of a person on Facebook, can almost predict your personality with the accuracy of a spouse. Facebook as well as other powerful logistical players are writing code to potentially use psychometric theory to influence people, particularly when it comes to purchasing habits and political views. Your "likes," or to use another word, your "desires," are not neutral, they are its currency.[18] Leveraging desire is the modus operandi of logistical networks, especially social media.

The hyper-capitalist underpinnings of online commerce are also based on unlocking desire. That Amazon offers over 480 million products online, delivered in expedited timeframes, as soon as one hour in certain situations, allows you to have what you want when you want and wherever you want. Logistics is all about meeting your cravings.

Desire is also clearly demonstrated in the food industry, where we are witnessing major transformations in the movement and distribution of food. In a 2005 article, author John McPhee familiarized us with the complex and time-sensitive distribution of fresh lobsters from the North Atlantic via the UPS Worldport in Louisville, Kentucky, but since then, new food delivery systems from GrubHub, to DoorDash provide even more access to a range of food courtesy of a food app.[19] Other delivery systems offer home-cooked meals, such as Josephine (San Francisco, 2015) to connect busy, hungry people with chefs who prepare alternative home-cooked meals in their own homes for pickup or delivery. Meal kit systems, such as Blue Apron and Hello Fresh, drop portioned food off directly on the doorstep. These provide subscribers with fresh ingredients and recipes to cook meals at home. All of these systems work in tandem to create new relationships around food. For example, crowdsourced food networks match desires, and in so doing, bring strangers together to enjoy home-cooked meals. Cooking and hosting the public in your own home is one of the fall-outs of food logistics, and this is flipping boundaries between public and private space. Your studio kitchen is now a restaurant.

In tandem with this, increased automation and sophisticated software—from digitally controlled assembly lines to technological services in the office and home (door-to-door delivery and the plethora of smart devices that replenish inventories)—are eliminating work and allowing us more free time. (Peapod means you no longer have to do grocery shopping.) By extension, the traditional spatio-temporal routines associated with work and domestic chores disappear. In this context, desire can be expressed as having more free time to do something else, something more pleasurable.

Suffice to say that logistical desire and convenience are producing new social situations. So the question is: what new spatial formations are emerging from logistics' cultures of desire? Fortunately, there are some precedents.

New Babylon

Constant Nieuwenhuys' *New Babylon* (1956–1974) has been the subject of much scholarship; however, it is worthwhile exploring it again here under the lens of the logistical city since it was presented as a model for a new time–space regime, a phenomenon that is the primary tenet of logistics. In particular, the project arose out of the promises of automation, in that technological systems could handle all the actions of life (work, shopping, cooking), so the urban subject would no longer be limited or contained by occupation or place. In a world where complete technological agency is possible, architecture (and urbanism) is removed from efficiency and function, thus allowing design to be catalyzed through other criteria. In the case of *New Babylon*, this was desire. Without work as the defining motivator of subjectivity, the urban subject (Constant used the term *Homo ludens*) is presented as an artist, making his or her own life and the conventions by which one would live. In the absence of work, art would become the primary occupation of the urban subject.[20] The organization of the proposal reflects this.

Presented across multiple media formats—texts, models, posters, lectures, paintings, audiotapes, and slides—the project is more a theoretical framework than a project proposal, despite having encompassed nineteen years of Constant's life from 1956 to 1975. In fact, Constant was careful not to call it an urban plan, but more a way of thinking about the future. Excerpts from lectures given by Constant that relay the context for the project seem far more articulate and engaging than the actual work documents, which come across as fragmented, inaccessible, and vague.

The project comprises large urban units (sectors) made of space frames and suspended on columns that are linked via connector bars to form a large, continuous floating megastructure. In between sectors, pockets exist for open space, nature, agriculture, or urban context (the proposal was often superimposed over existing cities, such as Rotterdam and Amsterdam). Such an archipelago of patches and connections is reminiscent of the psychogeographic maps produced contemporaneously by Guy Debord and Asger Jorn, such as the *Naked City*, an alternative map of Paris that crops out zones of atmospheric intensity which are linked together by arrows and lines. Each sector of *New Babylon* (akin to a very large building with an area of 5–10 hectares) is identified by colors or formal type, and some comprise as many as four levels, floating 16 meters over the ground, which is dedicated to traffic flow, nature, and monuments with automated industries and factories underneath. This is not unlike Nicholas Shoffer's *Ville Cybernetique* (1969), which had an automatic

FIGURE 4.6   Constant Nieuwenhuys, "Mobiel ladderlabyrint I." Collection Gemeentemuseum Den Haag. Photographer: Tom Haartsen © Constant/Fondation Constant c/o Pictoright Amsterdam 2017.

distribution center to supply residents' daily needs. The rooftops of the sectors host airports for rapid travel across longer distances. Sector floors are open-plan and flexibly organized, while labyrinths of planes and partitions subdivide others. Each sector has a hotel where citizens momentarily rest (no houses or ownership of property in *New Babylon*). Large interiors are conditioned to allow for a range of climatic options that can be controlled by the public. Artificially lit interiors and atmospheres also support a range of preferences and demands.

Without work or any purpose in life, users wander through and navigate the different labyrinthine fields to reshape their lives. Constant writes: "The increasingly traumatized inhabitants have to take over the shaping of their own spaces to recover the pleasure of living"—in other words, with nothing to do, one must intervene within the fundamentals of the space as a way to find oneself, as it is through interaction with the elements in the sectors that self-expression and self-awareness are achieved.[21] A range of labyrinth types provide for endless interaction, or "endless drift," to use a term from the Situationists International, the avant-garde group of artists and designers co-founded by Constant and Guy Debord in 1957, some of which were later modeled at full scale at subsequent exhibitions. Other sectors are subdivided by changing mobile elements from bridges to stairs to furniture to planes. Without class or social hierarchies that are the fallout of a society defined by labor, and with the freedom that comes with no work, the dynamic landscape is the means for the citizens of *New Babylon* to invent their own way of being in the world, for one's desire is now a creative self-fabrication.

Architectural theorist Mark Wigley has already linked the project to the notion of desire by describing it as a vessel for play (the subtitle of his 1998 book on *New Babylon* is *An Architecture of Hyper-desire*). Here, through the analogy of the playground, desire is presented as choice and formalized by game-like changeable environments and atmospheres, a predominant trope of the radical architects of the 1960s. However, in the case of this project, it was enacted to provide continuous stimulus and spaces that could shift to match one's mood. Constant believed in a hyper-mobile life where one experience is automatically eroded and superseded by another. He writes: "24 hours may offer more experiences and more sensations than a long journey in any former period in history."[22]

Constant admits that the project contemplates a world after work, and that mobility (nomadism) is a consequence of traditional temporal rhythms (cycles, tempos, and routines) disappearing because the structuring effect that labor has on society is eliminated. On the one hand, the eradication of work was an equalizer of sorts, a labor-free existence was no longer the privilege of the upper class or the aristocracy (as in the 18th and 19th centuries), but an option for all. Furthermore, since one's position in society

72 Clare Lyster

was no longer characterized as an instrument of production, labor was no longer the sole defining characteristic of the subject. No doubt Constant was reacting to the increased automation of the post-war era, and the subsequent changes in social relations with the corresponding shift in work and labor routines. *New Babylon* is a model for a world where the subject no longer has anything to do. Desire is freedom. He writes:

> In a society where structural unemployment takes on such a permanent character that large sections of the workforce no longer participate in the production process at all, in what is for many to all intents and purposes a dead-end situation, it is no longer possible to think about urban planning from the utilitarian perspective of the Athens Charter with its four work-based functions. Planners must at least theoretically, start looking at alternative forms of urbanization.[23]

Desire as a Vehicle for Contemporary Planning

Contemplating a society without work is now plausible due to the increased automation as well as the time-saving and convenient accouterments enabled by logistics. At no point in our history has technology come so close to taking over every aspect of our work and personal lives. As economist and social theorist Jeremy Rifkin points out, it's not just the possible elimination of work completely (some of us still work very hard), but the overall decrease of the workforce worldwide. Over the last 200 years, technological advancement has continued to increase productivity, shrinking the work week, and further efficiencies and optimization strategies courtesy of logistical systems and their attendant software and spaces (robotics to SEZs) will only further decrease the workforce as we move forward. In addition, further drops will also result from a more equal distribution of labor so that more people can remain employed, as well as from those currently employed who will welcome reduced hours (despite lower compensation) for a more balanced lifestyle.[24]

Moreover, with the promise of commercially produced driverless cars in 2020, robots in industrial realm are already the norm, but domestic robots are also now available; delivery drones and autonomous cargo-bots are being tested (with one very nicely designed by an architect), and artificial intelligence (AI) is exploding.[25] Amazon allows one to talk to a device as if it was a human being (Echo), and order merchandise to be delivered within an hour.[26]

What Will We All Do?

Re-reading *New Babylon* from the perspective of the logistical city illustrates how the effects and consequences enabled by contemporary mechanisms of fulfillment might be more productively considered. The design community is struggling with how to get a grip on logistics in society and their implications for the future of our cities, which makes Constant's lessons particularly relevant.

Desire as Collective

Of significance in *New Babylon* is that contrary to the super-individualization that was predicted as the fallout of an automated world, technology could instead serve to collectively fashion the spaces of the city. In his 1998 book *The Situationist City*, urban theorist Simon Sadler points out that *New Babylon* becomes a medium for collective interaction (presumably everyone is struggling to navigate the labyrinth together), so desire is less defined as unbridled individualism and personal demand, but more through communal interaction and goal-setting. And this is a very important lesson in the logistical era, whose mantra is all about customization, niche markets, cult followings, and atomized culture. It is comforting to know that we can still reclaim a collective project in a world of hyper-singularity.

Desire as Multi-scale Environments

New Babylon ignores the particulars of context by taking over the world (a feature that was also highlighted in other radical projects in the 1960s and 1970s). In other words, it was conceived as large-scale in the knowledge that the effects of the new regimes of industrial production would be widespread. The continuity exhibited by the megastructural form (no distinction between center and periphery) presents the idea of a shrinking world space (McLuhan's global village)—that is, a state of complete urbanization in which we are all connected physically and emotionally. Such scalar extents are a useful precedent for the logistical era, which posits a similar ambition. Its domination over geography (FedEx ships to 95% of the world in forty-eight hours; Amazon delivers in one hour, Facebook has over a billion participants worldwide) through conquering extreme distances quickly with communication systems (from glass fiber to satellite technology) erodes boundaries to offer the appearance of a singular space accessible to all. At the same time, *New Babylon*'s focus on the individual subject (most of the interior sketches illustrate human-scale interaction within the spatial elements) highlights that while Constant conceptualized the project at the territorial scale, he was also aware of the interface of the body within this new world order. This emphasis on individual experience instructs us toward an equally responsible consideration of the logistical citizen in the all-encompassing space of contemporary time–space regimes.

Desire as the Surreal

Moreover, *New Babylon* promoted surreal encounters—strangers bumping into each other in the playful landscapes and then moving on to the next encounter is a physical corollary of the interactions made possible by social media apps from *Meet Up* to *Peoplehunt* to *Nearify* that promote new friendships and match strangers. Sharing protocols allow a range of new social spaces, as do the new metabolic typologies (from pickup stations to tool libraries). Desire is a mechanism for new types of social life and collective space within the fantastic and boorish world of logistics. All promise to enact chance happenings and reclaim an extraordinary way of inhabiting the city.

Desire as Infrastructure

New Babylon was a city for the people, built by the people, and in the increasing DIY world of logistics, this is now entirely possible. Algorithms are increasingly used as a planning mechanism in the attendant spaces of logistics and other realms of planning—for example, the zoning of an Amazon fulfillment center is an algorithmic act.

The formal and material features of *New Babylon* were pretty abstract. Models were fabricated from acrylic, metal, lines, and wires, with an overall lightness devoid of traditional forms of representation. The models

FIGURE 4.7 Amazon Fulfillment Center, Madrid, Spain. Photo by Álvaro Ibáñez.

look more like industrial design artifacts than architectural documents. Sketches and renderings of possible interior conditions accompanied these. In the open field-like qualities of the space, undefined and a-formal spaces (you don't see buildings and figures, just elements and effects), the project is remarkably tuned to the reality that urbanity would increasingly be produced not by objects, but by a mélange of technological devices, software and communication networks—a spatial platform. Sounds like a prologue for the logistical city!

Desire as Abstraction

To be sure, repeated negotiation and manipulation of the formal elements in the sectors of *New Babylon* might eventually cause frustration rather than fulfillment, and furthermore, the urban nomad might suffer some degree of alienation within the abstraction of *New Babylon*'s interior. However mesmerizing this would have been, the theme of abstraction is very relevant here. For when one looks at the interiors of the large attendant spaces of logistics, such as warehouses and sorting centers, with their infinite repetitive fields of shelving and pallets and robots, taking direction from algorithmic printouts and other abstract numerical coding systems from RFID tags to QR codes, one recognizes that abstraction is the language of logistics. In this way, *New Babylon*, despite the uncomfortable world it envisions, is a precedent for thinking critically about how the increasing abstraction of contemporary culture can be materialized in space.[27]

Yet one cannot ignore that *New Babylon* is also a dystopian concept. Constant had to defend the overtly mechanic and technocratic attributes of the project when the research was represented in The Hague in its entirety in 1974 and subsequently criticized as nothing more than a permanent vacation resort. Desire here is nothing short of decadence. To this point, Simon Sadler cites Herbert Marcuse, who argued that in the absence of work, the body would instead become an instrument of pleasure (one structuring regime is substituted for another). Marcuse also muses that with technology as the new hegemony, the public would become bored and uninteresting. Later in life, Constant seemed to concur with the ambivalence that might set in, despite the earlier promise of abundant creativity.[28] Perhaps it was this that motivated his later renderings for the project, which depicted more erotic scenes and events, leading one to wonder if desire was instead a mere conceit for debauchery and self-indulgence.

Constant hides industry from *New Babylon*'s public as if to say that it was of no concern. Such isolation from how things are produced and the social and political context of production is of concern here, just as it is today, given logistics has successfully severed the relationship between production and consumption. Desire should not mean ignorance. The instant gratification (and public ignorance) promised by the hyper-efficiencies of logistics, now being even more distantly rendered by AI technologies, is ultimately unproductive for society. In fact, recently, scientists and theorists under the title of "facile externality" are rallying against the seamlessness of logistics by arguing for more friction in contemporary mobility systems and questioning if the convenience provided by some new technologies is really necessary.[29] This means learning to put up with, or even embrace, hassle and slowness in the rendering and delivery of services and goods as a way to reclaim value and meaning in production.

Concluding Remarks

Logistics as Alibi

An investigation of logistics allows us to speculate on new social constructs that could have significant ramifications on the form and culture of the city. If, as Marx believed, work is central to society and how we explain our existence, then what happens when its elimination brings about a major realignment. If Constant reclaimed a surreal way to inhabit the city in the mid-1950s, then the logistical networks of the 21st century allow it to happen. In allowing choice, desire, abundant possibilities, and free time, *New Babylon* was a rehearsal for the logistical city.

Yet it is important to note that Constant's project was born out of larger socio-political motives in the aftermath of World War II, when many artists and architects used their skills to present new worlds. This ideological motive of a new (and better) society is absent in today's era of personal desire and consumer fulfillment. In this context, one must be careful in referencing Situationist theory, since its agenda was to critique the very values that are now espoused by logistics. Its role, instead of being to map an alternative city, was one that was anti-capitalist and critical of commodification. So, too, one must acknowledge how desire is currently expressed as a mechanism for planning, most notably as themed environments (Disneyfication) or as entertainment districts in the downtown districts of many urban centers in the US.[30] However, more conceptual precedents exist, for example *Delirious New York*, where capitalism and entertainment merge to produce cultures of desire that in turn organize the metropolis. Here, massive interiors, new technologies, and the abstraction of the urban grid were the spatial tropes for the cultivation of desire as a social space (a culture of congestion) in the city.[31]

New Babylon is a most useful precedent for urbanism in the logistical era because it provides a glimpse of the spatial formations possible when technology replaces every human function. For good or bad, it accepts technological determinism as context for the project, but uses it as an alibi to focus on what was of real concern: not the technology, but how the human subject would be occupied and fulfilled in this new world. And this is an important lesson. While logistics is about warehouses and goods, software, and communication systems, it is the real cultural fallouts enabled by logistics, not the systems themselves, that provide much more robust opportunities for the design community, offering new criteria for city-making beyond efficiency, ethics, therapy, and nostalgia.

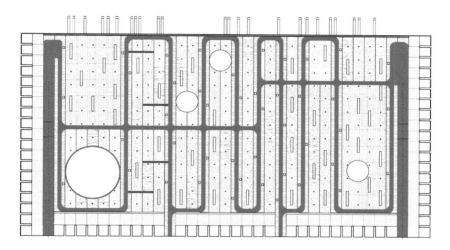

FIGURE 4.8 "Urbanism in Disguise," plan view, 2013. By Clare Lyster, CLUAA.

FIGURE 4.9 "High-tech Hot Tub," 2013. By Clare Lyster, CLUAA.

FIGURE 4.10 "Urban Lounge," interior perspective, 2014. By Clare Lyster, CLUAA.

Notes

1 It would be foolish to argue that the logistical city is a new phenomenon. Many cities in history stand out as paradigms of communication and flow, from Rome in the ancient world, with its emphasis on military surges, onward. Coastal cities, such as Venice in the Middle Ages, were known for their central role in the flow of goods between east and west, and Chicago, in the industrial era, stood out as a logistics hub for grain, lumber, and meat, while its concentration of railroads made it the sorting and distributing hub of the nation, if not the world.

2 Keller Easterling, *Extrastatecraft: The Power of Infrastructure Space* (New York: Verso, 2014), pp. 25–69.

3 Deborah Cowen, *The Deadly Life of Logistics: Mapping Violence in Global Trade* (Minneapolis, MN: University of Minnesota Press, 2014), pp. 163–195.

4 Saskia Sassen, *Cities in a World Economy* (Newbury Park, CA: Pine Forge Press, 1994), pp. 1–8.

5 Susan Nigra Snyder and Alex Wall, *Emerging Landscapes of Movement and Logistics, Architectural Design Profile* 108 (1994): 16–21.

6 "UPS Breaks Ground on Louisville Centennial Hub Expansion," August 25, 2016, https://www.pressroom.ups.com/pressroom/ContentDetailsViewer.page? ConceptType=PressReleases&id=1472127665826-590 (accessed June 29, 2018).

7 Alexandra Lange, *The Dot-Com City: Silicon Valley Urbanism* (Moscow: Strelka Press, 2015). See also Kelsey Campbell-Dollaghan, "How the Tech Industry Is Quietly Changing the Face of American Cities," *Gizmodo*, June 18, 2013, http://gizmodo.com/how-the-tech-industry-is-quietly-changing-the-face-of-a-513266451, and Steven Levy, "One More Thing: Inside Apple's Insanely Great (or Just Insane) Mothership," *WIRED*, May 16, 2017, https://www.wired.com/2017/05/apple-park-new-silicon-valley-campus/ (accessed June 29, 2018).

8 Mason White, "Farm Cloud," in *New Geographies# 07: Geographies of Information*, ed. Ali Farad and Taren Meshkani (Cambridge, MA: Harvard Graduate School of Design, 2015), pp. 67–75.

9 Clare Lyster, *Learning from Logistics: How Networks Change Cities* (Basle: Birkhäuser, 2016).

10 Michael Lewis, *Flash Boys* (New York: W.W. Norton, 2014), p. 22.

11 Adrienne LaFrance, "Apple Is Basically a Small Country Now," *The Atlantic*, February 11, 2015, https://www.theatlantic.com/technology/archive/2015/02/apple-is-basically-a-small-country-now/385385/ (accessed June 29, 2018).

12 Alan Berger and Charles Waldheim, "Logistics Landscape," *Landscape Journal* 27(2) (2008): 219–246.

13 Henri Lefebvre used the term "the mesh" to describe contemporary patterns of urbanization, and one could appropriate the term here to describe the logistical city. As a continuous interwoven fabric, the mesh was for Lefebvre an analogy for the proliferation of horizontal urban development—or what he called complete urbanization. But Lefebvre's mesh was not of uniform thickness. It had holes as well as thin areas. In the case of the logistical city, we can also think of the city (the built fabric of the city) as an uneven mesh, with the nodal intensities as the moments where it tightens. However, the mesh-net of the logistical city is constantly shifting—tightening, flattening and then tightening again—depending on the activity of the nodes. In this manner, it's also worth referencing Richard G. Smith's analogy of the crumpled handkerchief that he uses to explain how globalization is impacting urban territory. For more information, see Henri Lefebvre, "Right to the City," in *Writings on Cities*, trans.

by and ed. Eleonore Kofman and Elizabeth Lebas (Malden, MA: Blackwell Publishers, 2000), Part II, and Richard G. Smith, "World City Topologies," in *The Global City Reader*, ed. Neil Brenner and Roger Keil (London: Routledge, 2006), pp. 400–408.

14 "Big Data and Mobile Technology Reshapes One African City," *IBW21.ORG*, December 26, 2013, https://ibw21.org/editors-choice/big-data-and-mobile-technology-reshapes-one-african-city/ (accessed June 29, 2018).

15 I cite Zipline and Kiva as logistical systems operating in less affluent and rural areas. For more information on this, see Rohini Nambiar, "How Rwanda Is Using Drones to Save Millions of Lives," May 27, 2016, www.cnbc.com/2016/05/27/how-rwanda-is-using-drones-to-save-millions-of-lives.html, and Jessi Hempel, "Peer-to-Peer Site Kiva Is Finally Offering No-interest Microloans in the US," *WIRED*, December 9, 2015, https://www.wired.com/2015/12/peer-to-peer-site-kiva-is-finally-offering-no-interest-microloans-in-the-us/ (accessed June 29, 2018).

16 Bradley Cantrell, Erle Ellis, Kristina Hill, and Laura Martin, "Ecology on Autopilot," *Landscape Architecture Magazine* (June 2017): 106–119, and Gerry Moriarty, "Drones Being Used by PSNI to Protect Birds Like Red Kites and Peregrines," *Irish Times*, May 22, 2017, www.irishtimes.com/news/environment/drones-being-used-by-psni-to-protect-birds-like-red-kites-and-peregrines-1.3092452 (accessed June 29, 2018).

17 "Most Popular Retail Websites in the United States as of December 2017, Ranked by Visitors (in Millions)," www.statista.com/statistics/271450/monthlyunique-visitors-to-us-retailwebsites/ (accessed June 29, 2018).

18 "How Powerful Is Facebook's Algorithm?" *The Inquiry, BBC iPlayer Radio*, www.bbc.co.uk/programmes/p04zvqtx (accessed June 29, 2018).

19 John McPhee, "Out in the Sort," *New Yorker*, April 18, 2005, www.newyorker.com/magazine/2005/04/18/out-in-the-sort (accessed June 29, 2018).

20 The emphasis on art as a substitute for work emerges from two grievances. First, it addressed Constant's frustration with the decline of the artist in a corporate economy; second, the idea that everyone was now an artist removed the traditional association of elitism with art. Art was the fundamental structure of society, and not a commodified enterprise.

21 Mark Wigley, *Constant's New Babylon: The Hyper-architecture of Desire* (Rotterdam: Witte de With Center for Contemporary Art/010 Publishers, 1998), p. 9.

22 Ibid., p. 215.

23 The categories of planning in the Athens Charter were work, rest, recreation, and transportation. Laura Stamps and Mercedes Pineda, eds., *Constant: New Babylon. To Us, Liberty* (Berlin: Hatje Cantz Verlag, 2016) p. 220.

24 Jeremy Rifkin, *The End of Work: The Decline of the Global Labor Force and the Dawn of the Post-market Era* (New York: Penguin, 1996), pp. 221–235.

25 "Driverless Car Market Watch," December 25, 2014, www.driverless-future.com/?page_id=384; Bob Tedeschi, "The Year in Robots," *New York Times*, December 24, 2014, https://www.nytimes.com/2014/12/25/garden/10-home-robots-to-lighten-your-domestic-chores.html; Leo Kelion, "CES 2015: The Robots Moving in to Your House," *BBC News*, January 8, 2015, www.bbc.com/news/technology-30708953; Lora Kolodny, "Why Piaggio Built Gita, a Cargo-carrying Robot, to Follow in Your Footsteps," *TechCrunch*, January 31, 2017, https://techcrunch.com/2017/01/31/why-piaggio-built-gita-a-cargo-carrying-robot-to-follow-in-your-footsteps/ (accessed June 29, 2018).

26 Jamie Condliffe, "What's Next for AI Home Assistants," *MIT Technology Review*, February 16, 2017, https://www.technologyreview.com/s/603672/whats-next-for-ai-home-assistants/ (accessed June 29, 2018).
27 David Zielnicki, "Fulfillment," *Harvard Design Magazine* 43 (Fall/Winter 2016): 83–89. I would also like to publicly thank David Zielnicki for sharing his utterly fantastic drawings of an Amazon fulfillment center with me when we met at the Harvard Graduate School of Design in November 2016.
28 Simon Sadler, *The Situationist City* (Cambridge, MA: MIT Press, 1998), p. 153.
29 "The Case for an Efficiency Tax," *The Economist*, March 30, 2017, www.economist.com/news/leaders/21719799-it-time-recognise-value-bit-hassle-case-efficiency-tax (accessed June 29, 2018).
30 The term "Disneyization" is also used when describing the overall shift in land use in our cities from industrial production to commercial and themed environments. For more information on this, see Alan Bryman, "The Disneyization of Society," *Sociological Review* 47(1) (1999): 25–47.
31 Ellen Durham-Jones, "Rem Koolhaas and the 1990s," in *Architecture and Capitalism, 1845 to the Present*, ed. Peggy Deamer (London: Routledge, 2014), pp. 153–155.

PART II
Resource

5

CHASING AND REWIRING RESOURCE TERRITORIES

Neeraj Bhatia

Privileging Future Productions

In the context of South America, resource extraction and its associated logistical infrastructures have played a central role in organizing the territory. In many cases, the framework these infrastructures have inscribed on the land has been appropriated by future developments, and even turned into cities, such as Ciudad Ojeda and Nueva Loja. As posited by Felipe Correa, "The metrics of the oil camp have become the template for a new type of post-oil city, one that is a direct byproduct of the oil extraction process itself."[1] This eventual second production is arguably contingent upon the *permanence* of the infrastructures and the territories they established—the logic of one system *inadvertently* forming the template for a future system of development. Yet, while these energy infrastructures were robustly built, the resources they extract, transport, and refine oscillate with global market forces, often leaving these infrastructures abandoned long before their material lifespan.

What if the design and organization of logistical infrastructures anticipated their presumable second production? This becomes a critical question when considering that the physical artifacts, machines, and infrastructures of extraction—offshore rigs, jack pumps, pipelines, tank storage farms, refineries, transfer ports, etc.—will long outlive the resources they are exhausting. While the current lifespan of the global oil industry is estimated to be between forty and fifty-three years, geographically specific infrastructures will be used for a fraction of that time, as in the Brazilian context where this estimate drops to approximately twenty-five years.[2] The most recent wave of extraction over the past ten years has been the most technologically advanced—reaching horizontally into distant geographies and vertically to enormous depths—making this final push for resources a costly venture. Yet, despite this, new infrastructures are being deployed at a faster and faster rate in service of this limited resource. Recognizing the sheer amount of infrastructure that is estimated to be constructed and the limited duration of its use, we must question how these processes and infrastructures could be organized to account for their future production(s)—a production that could comprise a more holistic set of cultural, political, ecological, and economic factors. This is to say that current extraction infrastructures not only Chase the City—attempting to feed the metropolis' energy needs—but they also build the city, with their physical residue acting as a catalyst for future forms of urbanism. The organizations and urbanisms that emerge from these infrastructures are perhaps more predictable than we imagine, yet, as designers, we have failed to seize the opportunities present in their design and deployment. Assuming the role of spatial detectives, we can leverage how these infrastructures and their future affects might be steered to more equitably benefit socio-economic and ecological systems. This would position extraction infrastructures as the *proactive* framework for new urban organizations.

We could say that the major spatial formats of logistics consist of *surfaces, containers,* and *conduits.*[3] These formats have colonized vast swatches of hinterland environments, and operate at a scale that is closely aligned to global and regional logistics. *Surfaces* are planes of mediation that typically function at a territorial scale as they are primarily implicated in a form of harvesting or collection. *Containers* are architectural shells of enclosure often sited between the formats of surfaces and conduits—for storing, refining, or distributing a particular good. The *conduit* as a type is tasked with interfacing between the scale of the territory and that of architecture. Conduits are used to transfer matter and energy across vast distances, cutting through local settlements, political boundaries, and ecosystems, and connecting to both containers and surfaces. Conduits have a particular significance in logistical systems as they allow for the spatial separation between extraction, processing, manufacturing, and consumption. Forming a physical network across the globe, conduits ensure access to resources that are spatially remote—making them one of the primary technological artifacts for capitalist expansion and consumption. Pipelines are one of the most under-studied conduits within the design disciplines, yet despite their inconspicuous nature, they are highly prevalent in our daily lives. The ability to be within the domestic realm and have water and energy supplied with the flick of a switch or turn of a knob is because of pipelines. More abstractly, the ability to tap into cheaper labor markets or geographies of specialization is enabled by pipelines. Currently, there are five million miles of pipeline in operation around the globe, which, if connected end-to-end, would wrap the equator two hundred times.[4] Given the pipeline's prevalence, permanence, and capacity to form networks, an opportunity arises if we privilege its future production to form new relationship between resources, cultures, and economies once fossil fuels are depleted.

Dissociated Technology

Energy pipelines are large infrastructural conduits used to transport oil or gas, deployed primarily between points of extraction and refining. Pipelines are desirable because they are able to move energy in a more efficient, reliable, and safe manner than tanker trucks or rail tanker cars.[5] Beyond safety, the pipeline was a critical invention in making energy an abstract commodity by separating sites of extraction from those of consumption; operating almost invisibly with little human interaction.[6] This enabled the environmental costs of oil extraction to be highly removed—allowing those who benefited from cheap energy to not have to confront the consequences of its extraction. These consequences range from environmental contamination to inequitable labor practices to the production of urban residue once resources are depleted. The abstraction fostered by spatial detachment has characterized the pipeline as a *dissociated technology*.[7]

As a dissociated technology, the physical tension between local conditions and the territorial deployment of the artifact can be witnessed both at the scale of the region as well as the detail. Regionally, pipelines are but one component in the larger linear infrastructure of the easement, a zone approximately 75 meters in width that is cleared to neutralize and tame the varied conditions that are to be navigated. The easement becomes the primary corridor for access, communication, maintenance, surveillance, and construction. Moreover, compared to the pipeline itself, the easement creates perhaps the most permanent condition of all—these zones are often deemed their own political-economic jurisdiction (free trade zone), a designation that attracts other infrastructures and activities that solidify particular characteristics within this vector. Accordingly, the rules governing these thickened lines are established through global concerns and rarely bring benefit to local communities or ecologies. At the scale of the detail, it is the technical engineering and properties of fluid dynamics that determine the internal specifications of the pipe—including the diameter, thickness, material selection, and fittings. Once these are determined, this cross-section is extruded endlessly across the territory. Although the outside of the pipeline inevitably interfaces with the external environment, these conditions are typically viewed as secondary to the internal specifications, and therefore addressed through mitigation techniques. What if the physical environment and its inhabitants played a larger role in determining the location, trajectory, and design of pipelines and their associated infrastructures? This would bring into consideration the settlements and ecologies that will ultimately inherit these infrastructures and potentially utilize them for differing means. This could reframe these infrastructures as *associative* technologies—moving resources to connect people and environments while also providing legibility to logistical processes and thereby reducing their abstract logic. Through clarifying once-abstract territorial processes, one is made cognizant of their effects (both positive and negative). Our contention here is that the capacity for someone to physically "read" the components and relationships within a logistical system is critical to an awareness of one's position within this territorial arrangement. This understanding has deeper affects on how one acts, is accommodated, and ultimately empowered within urban space—even when this space is organized at the scale of the territory.

The interdependencies between sites of oil and gas extraction, refining, and consumption have fostered a network of territorial conduits, which

FIGURE 5.1 Sites of oil and gas extraction as well as pipeline conduits in South America. By The Open Workshop/Cesar Lopez.

FIGURE 5.2   The MCC65 Pipeline and the geography it transverses in southern Brazil. By The Open Workshop/Cesar Lopez.

move through the South American hinterland, including its communities and ecologies. Attempting to shed light on the above questions *through* design, we focused our case study on the Uruguayana–Porto Alegre Pipeline (also termed MCC65), which will unify a series of separate energy pipelines developed over the past two decades into an "energy ring." Spanning over 3,100 kilometers and running through Brazil, Argentina, Bolivia, and Uruguay, this circuit will link northern regions to the southern cone once completed. The last remaining segment, MCC65, will transverse 570 kilometers across southern Brazil and terminate in Uruguay. This journey crosses vastly different conditions from the developed and industrialized coast to the agrarian hinterland. The following two case studies examine how industry, ecologies, local cultures, and economies can take control of these territorial artifacts.

Rewiring Hydrology

Hydroscapes is a proposal that leverages the territorial connectivity of the pipeline and its easement for a future production of sustainable water management; benefiting new subjects and making legible key components within the logistical process. Linking processes within a territorial scale, the study examines how local communities, economies, and ecologies would benefit from this network.

The lifespan of fossil fuels within the geographic context of central South America coincides with a tipping point in water availability and food scarcity.[8] Climate models anticipate that the isolated inland region known as the Gran Chaco—spanning from northwestern Argentina through western Paraguay and Brazil—is in a state of increasing desertification that results in reduced agricultural productivity. The Gran Chaco has been in a rapid state of decline since its very settlement in the late 19th century by colonizers exploiting the abundant hardwoods of the region and securing additional land for cattle grazing.[9] Nearly 3,000,000 hectares of forest have been lost from the Chaco between 1990 and 2011,

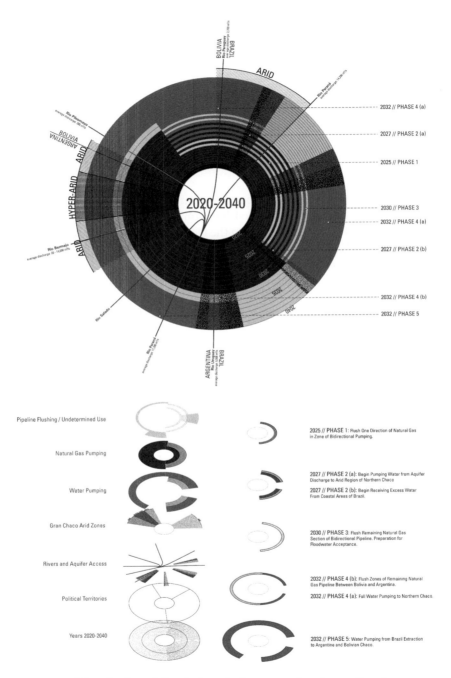

FIGURE 5.3 The phasing of South America's energy ring from oil and gas to fresh water pumping. By Blake Stevenson.

Chasing and Rewiring Resource Territories **91**

largely due to the expansion of irresponsible farming techniques that have precipitated soil erosion and groundwater *salinification*.[10] Moreover, the lack of infrastructural connections into this region has limited the economic output for the locally deprived inhabitants of the Gran Chaco. As a consequence, the already isolated Gran Chaco is suffering from a lack of agricultural productivity, making it fragile to cope with projections of drought. Conversely, along the eastern coast of Brazil and its string of coastal cities, climate change models are anticipating an increase in precipitation and unprecedented flooding as the watershed drains into the ocean.[11] The proposed pipeline not only traverses these complex ecologies related to both water scarcity and surplus, it provides new infrastructural access and connection into the hinterland. Re-operationalizing the pipeline by transitioning from fossil fuels to water transport and management has the ability to reconcile territorial water imbalances while leveraging this global infrastructure to benefit some of the most deprived citizens and damaged landscapes in South America.[12]

Spanning between and below these diverse regions is the world's second largest groundwater source—the Guarani Aquifer. This aquifer contains nearly ten times more water than the Ogallala Aquifer in the American Midwest, a critical resource activating the American agricultural economy. Although the Ogallala has a low recharge rate and is swiftly diminishing, the Guarani has a heavy recharge rate and can maintain a volume of water to supply fresh drinking water to the present population for up to 1,600 years.[13] The potential of the Guarani Aquifer lies in its ability to saturate the arid soils of the Gran Chaco, yet historically this region has lacked appropriate management to ensure it avoids over extraction and salinification. *Hydroscapes* utilizes the pipeline in combination with the aquifer to establish a sustainable water management system—balancing extraction and recharge. The aim of *hydroscaping* the larger territory is not to simply reverse climatic trends, but rather to empower local economies in the hinterland that might benefit from the pipeline. Additionally, the project seeks to reduce the abstraction of these infrastructures through an architecture that celebrates an increasingly scarce and volatile resource, creating legibility at the scale of the individual and territory they belong to. The proposal consists of critical nodes linked to specific geographies of the energy ring—*collection* and *remediation* along the Atlantic coast through the re-operationalizing of pipelines and easements, *water banking* and *aquifer recharge* on the coastal interior in former mine quarries, water *extraction* and food logistics along the western edge of the aquifer, and finally *surface recharge* sites that interface with natural rivers.

The primary region for capturing water exists along eastern portions of the energy ring, spanning the Brazilian coast and crossing the Atlantic watershed of southern Brazil. By redeveloping the pipeline's easement as a phytoremediation wetland and detention basin, this vast linear territory would capture, cleanse, and hold the increased predicted water runoff while mitigating flood threats to coastal cities. Water would then be moved by culverts into the main pipeline and pumped westwards to regions of water scarcity. This collected water would primarily be utilized to ballast aquifer extraction, recharging the groundwater with remediated runoff. These sections of the pipeline and easement on the eastern edge of the energy ring could transition resources as soon as 2030, after the pipeline is absolved of fossil fuels.

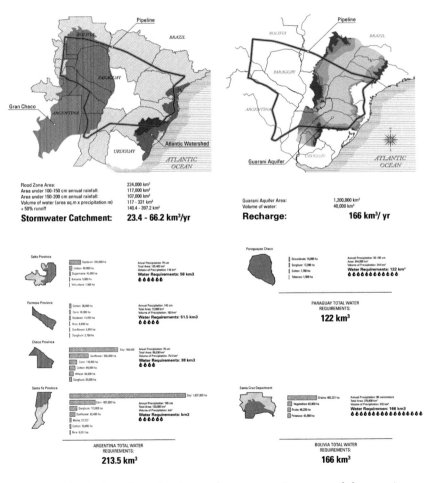

FIGURE 5.4 Agricultural production and water requirements of the provinces and districts through which the pipeline transverses. By Blake Stevenson.

Chasing and Rewiring Resource Territories 93

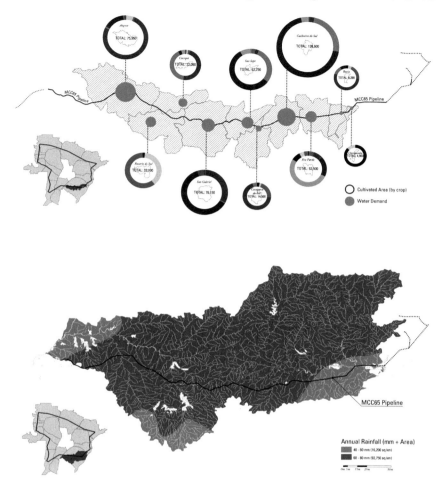

FIGURE 5.5 MCC65 municipalities of influence, their agricultural area, water requirements, and annual accumulated precipitation. By Blake Stevenson.

Water banking would take place on the coastal interior in areas above the aquifer, and employ former mining sites as recharge points. Passing through Brazil's hinterland in Rio Grande do Sul, the MCC65 pipeline encounters a series of settlements that economically depend on the extraction of coal, copper, gold, and stone to support local labor. Massive pits in the earth produced by these processes descend toward the Guarani Aquifer beneath. These resources, like fossil fuels, are quickly being exhausted and are threatening the vitality of local economies that are confronted with adaptation and diversification of markets to persist. For instance, between 2020 and

94 Neeraj Bhatia

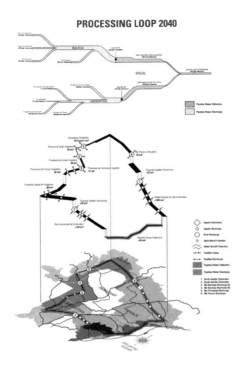

FIGURE 5.6   Master plan of the pipeline energy ring, including moments of pipeline interface and water volume. By Blake Stevenson.

2025, the mines of Cacapava do Sul that sit along the pipeline's path will be obsolete and the lands of its settlement, currently with a population of over 30,000 people, contaminated. By remediating these mining pits, these sites could be leveraged for water banking and aquifer recharge. This would shift the cultural and economic identity of the settlement from one dependent on global resource extraction to one rooted in local ecotourism and recreation, which is an emerging economy in the region. Already, natural attractions such as the Pedra do Segredo (Stone of the Secret) and Cascata do Salso (Salso Waterfall) attract local and national tourists.[14] Introducing cultural and ecological programs to these formerly hidden sites invites local subjects to engage with the territorial systems that surround them. Further, it would create moments of territorial visibility using architecture at the key point of water transfer between the pipeline and aquifer, offering a legibility to the past and present processes running through the site. Both of these tactics reduce the abstraction of these infrastructures and allow local residents to find opportunity by locating themselves within the logistics of the territory.

FIGURE 5.7 Mining sites at Cacapava do Sul recharging the Guarani Aquifer. By Lujac Desautel.

FIGURE 5.8 Ecotourism and recreation potential of remediated mining sites. By Lujac Desautel.

FIGURE 5.9 Moments of cultural interaction with remediated mining and water banking sites. By Lujac Desautel.

FIGURE 5.10 A moment of territorial legibility at an interaction point between the pipeline and a former mine. By Lujac Desautel.

Moving deeper into the interior of South America by the western edges of the aquifer, a series of water extraction sites are selected which tap into the aquifer and transport its water further inland to the Gran Chaco. One such site is in the city of Uruguayana, located along the Brazil–Argentina border. Uruguayana is one of the most infrastructurally connected cities in the Brazilian hinterland; a series of highways and rail lines converge in the city to feed the largest dry dock in South America and third largest in the world. Acting as a critical node to gather and move agricultural products to the eastern coastal cities, the logistical hub and transfer station have a direct relationship to the suffering agricultural regions that benefit from extracting groundwater at this site. The compressor station for energy transport is easily retrofitted into a pumping station for the distribution of water to the east. This extraction point would also be designed to house the region's largest food distribution center and public marketplace. Overflowing seasonally with the consolidated products from the Gran Chaco such as cotton, sorghum, sugarcane, soy, maize, beans, and rice, this exchange point will be visible at great distances from the infrastructures that gather at this node.

Once extracted from the aquifer, water exits the MCC65 section of the pipeline and enters the larger energy ring, moving towards the Gran Chaco and is eventually being discharged into four natural rivers—the Rio Bermejo, Rio Pilcomayo, Rio Paraguay, and Rio Parana. Each of these rivers acts as a conduit for surface recharge—irrigating the desertification of soils in the six

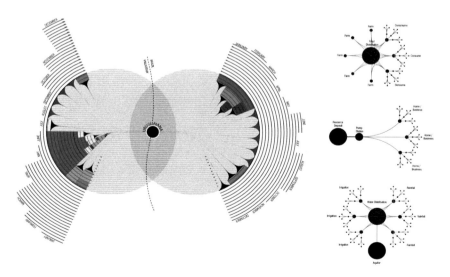

FIGURE 5.11 Uruguayana's role within the processes of food, natural gas, and water distribution, and the city's relationship to seasonal rainfall and crop harvest on both sides of the Argentina–Brazil border. By Lujac Desautel.

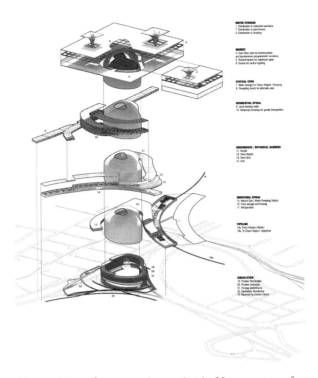

FIGURE 5.12 Guarani Aquifer extraction point in Uruguayana, featuring a food distribution center, public marketplace, and housing. By Blake Stevenson.

FIGURE 5.13 Uruguayana extraction point and its interface with ground and rain water sources. By Blake Stevenson.

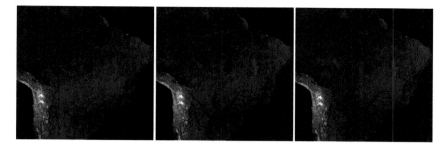

FIGURE 5.14   Major rivers reinvigorated after interaction with the pipeline. By Blake Stevenson.

provinces in Argentina, Brazil and Paraguay lying within the Chaco territory. The point of discharge—the intersection between natural hydrological systems and the pipeline that reinvigorates them—is punctuated in the proposal with architectural form, celebrating a critical infrastructural point of transfer.

Rewiring Ecology

The insertion of oil and gas pipelines across a vast landscape introduces a range of ecological issues. This is primarily caused by the large area of the easement, which is clear-cut across the territory to enable access, maintenance, and surveillance. Issues from pipeline construction alone can instigate the loss of native vegetation species diversity, loss and fragmentation of habitats, alteration of drainage patterns, introduction of invasive species, as well as new human access to previously undisturbed areas.[15] One of the most pronounced concerns is the fragmentation of biomes. Fragmentation refers to "a reduction of the initial area covered by a natural habitat in a landscape, and an alteration of the habitat structure, where the remaining habitat is divided into smaller and more insulated portions."[16] As pipelines and their associated easement cut through a biome, they destroy habitats for interior species, and create more areas for edge species.[17] Edge species and their associated habitats thrive on the boundary or interface between two biomes or landscape elements. To the inside of this edge exists the ecotone, or a zone of transition between two adjacent ecosystems. Biodiversity is generally higher along the edge due to the gradient of conditions. In several instances, however, these species penetrate inland, where they compete with interior species. Interior species exist in more stable environmental conditions within the biome. One of the ramifications of pipeline fragmentation is the disruption the typical food web, which introduces new predatory species and transforms migratory patterns of species. Within this third space of the easement, new migration paths are formed, which create unique hybrid food webs between species that are able to move more fluidly between biomes.[18] *Migratory Ecologics* is a proposal that asks how this unique ecoweb within the third space could be made more robust while strengthening the interior of the biomes. Chasing transformations to the ecological network, the project opportunistically reframes the easement as a zone for the confluence of ecological, economic, and recreational systems.

One of the most effective stewards of the interior landscape in South America is eco-tourism. Studies have shown this to be particularly true when the industry is small-scale and locally operated and owned.[19] Local inputs of stakeholders in the planning, development, monitoring, and management of ecotourism help ensure that firsthand knowledge of the environment is privileged and that locals benefit economically from the industry. Local knowledge and management are ideally complemented by regional frameworks of policy to secure best practices. Operating this industry in a sustainable manner positions nature as the central element of the tourist experience, and therefore adequate mechanisms to assure low impact on the natural resource are paramount.

The spatial experience of ecotourism typically involves descending into a particular location, and using this point as a base point for daily hiking. Instead of the hub–spoke model, *Migratory Ecologics* examines how the easement can be designed to allow for the co-existence of migratory species as well as eco-tourists. In this way, the tourist experience of the landscape is not framed as an experience within the day, but rather continual, with tourists moving through and inhabiting various landscape systems. In this manner, eco-tourism is set up as a series of trails that leverage the extraordinary cross-sections through the South American landscape. Variable hierarchies of pumping stations are coupled with different rest-stops for hikers. These pump stations already contain access to energy and water, requiring modest economic investments for the

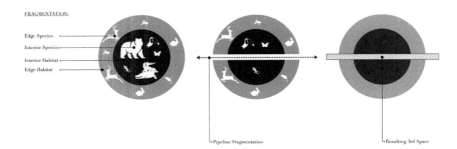

FIGURE 5.15 The third space created by the pipeline's easement. By Jill Chao and Enrique Justicia.

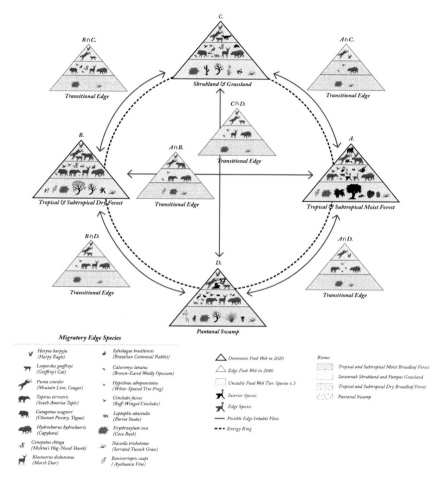

FIGURE 5.16 Example of a new food web created within the third space through the adapting migration/predatory patterns of edge species. By Jill Chao and Enrique Justicia.

rest-stops. The economic gains by introducing eco-tourism through this third space are used to manage, conserve, and protect the surrounding landscape. Within this third space of the pipeline's easement, the surreal confluence of migrating species, tourists, local operators, and energy find a surreal resonance.

Different nodes along this super-ring of pipelines are developed into areas for rest, research, or ecologic choreography. *Eco-Junction* is sited where the introduction of the pipeline fragmented the Atlantic Forest biome into a series of islands that privileged zones for edge species, but reduced the interior habitats. Strategically located as an inter-habitat bridge for interior species that typically do not migrate, the project examines how to create artificial interiors of biomes that are able to cross the fracturing easement of the pipeline and connect between these islands. This transverse corridor connection between interior habitat patches has been studied and modeled in other parts of the globe, such as California.[20] These crossings allow for the co-existence between tourists and particular species that remained undisturbed by human presence.

Conceived of as a rest-stop/research station along the pipeline's route, the *Eco-Hut* proposal plugs in to the energy ring as a secondary node. Making reference to tribal building traditions in the area, the structure embeds itself in its surroundings, concealing its presence from the animals as a way of minimizing its physical and visual impact. The allocation of the program forces interaction between the researcher and the tourist by organizing the guest rooms and research labs around a collective space that is supported by smaller common areas. Through these moments of engagement, the tourist

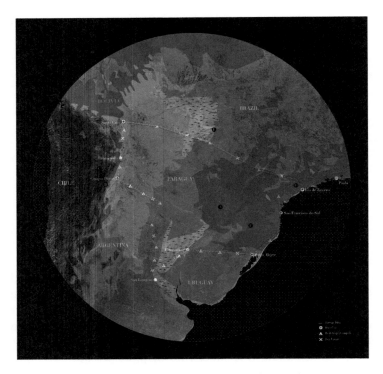

FIGURE 5.17   Master plan of eco-tourist ring along the pipeline's trajectory with a coupling of pump stations and rest-stops. By Jill Chao and Enrique Justicia.

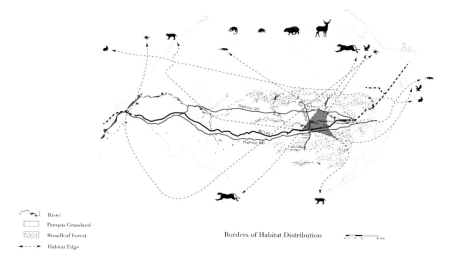

FIGURE 5.18   Mapping specifies flow and biome limits to site-opportune *Eco-Junctions*. By Jill Chao.

acquires a deeper understanding of the local flora and fauna and the impact of pipeline infrastructures on natural ecosystems. For instance, observing how particular species hover adjacent to the microclimate produced by the pipeline clues us into the anthropogenic forces species have adapted to. These ramifications—whether positive or negative—are no longer abstract and dissociated; they teach us as much about natural systems as they do about human influences. Ultimately, *Migratory Ecologics* studies how to leverage new mutant ecologies produced by large-scale infrastructures as a way to protect and conserve untouched landscapes as well as promote new forms of human interaction, engagement, and learning.

Phasing the South American energy ring into an aqueduct or hiking trail does more than simply combat the negative effects of climate change—it challenges the existing methods of land and water management, suggesting instead a system of adaptation through infrastructural reuse. This exploration into retrofitting fossil fuel infrastructure attempts to rewire the relationship between conduits, economies, local communities, and resources. Establishing a second production that finds opportunity in territorial imbalances, it bestows the benefits of these differences to strengthen local communities and ecologies. The vast scale and abstract nature of these relationships are clarified and made legible through discrete moments of architectural form. The transition from the dissociated technology of globalized logistics to an associative and empowering technology that links and makes visible local inhabitants' relationship to water, ecosystems, as

FIGURE 5.19 *Eco-Hut*, an architecture that occupies the easement and acts as a research vessel. By Enrique Justicia.

well as each other, is ultimately a socio-political question of design. By bringing these otherwise background infrastructures to the foreground, new subjects become implicated in what was previously a top-down system of resource management and engineering. This enables a more complex discourse on climate change that goes beyond technological advancement to include new subjects that form a cultural project.

Project Credits

Hydroscapes: Blake Stevenson and Lujac Desautel

Migratory Ecologics: Enrique Justicia and Jill Chao

Acknowledgments

The author would like to thank the design-researchers Blake Stevenson, Lujac Desautel, Enrique Justicia, and Jill Chao for their research assistance in the production of this chapter.

Notes

1 Felipe Correa, "Afterlife Strategies: The Other Post-oil City," *Volume* 29 (2011): 130.
2 Lydia Smith, "World Energy Day 2014: How Much Oil Is Left and How Long Will It Last?" *International Business Times*, October 22, 2014, updated February 11, 2016, www.ibtimes.co.uk/world-energy-day-2014-how-much-oil-left-how-long-will-it-last-1471200 (accessed June 29, 2018).
3 Neeraj Bhatia et al., "Formatting Contingency," in *Pamphlet Architecture 30: Coupling* (New York: Princeton Architectural Press, 2011), p. 8.

4 Thomas O. Miesner and William L. Leffler, *Oil and Gas Pipelines* (Tulsa, OK: PenWell Books, 2006), p. 213
5 Morgan Downey, *Oil 101* (New York: Wooden Table Press, 2009), p. 257.
6 Christopher F. Jones, "Pipelines and Power," in *Routes of Power* (Cambridge, MA: Harvard University Press, 2014), p. 143.
7 Ibid., pp. 143, 144.
8 Ximena Loza, "Paraguay: The People's Tenacity Revives El Chaco," *World Food Programme*, September 30, 2013, https://www.wfp.org/stories/paraguay-people%E2%80%99s-tenacity-revives-el-chaco (accessed June 29, 2018).
9 Fernando Riveros, "The Gran Chaco," Food and Agricultural Organization of the United Nations, http://archive.is/FVhp (accessed June 29, 2018).
10 J. Walcott, J. Thorley, V. Kapos, L. Miles, S. Woroniecki, and R. Blaney, *Mapping Multiple Benefits of REDD+ in Paraguay: Using Spatial Information to Support Land-use Planning* (Cambridge: UNEP-WCMC, 2015).
11 Jan Rocha, "With Climate Change, Brazil Faces Drop in Crops," *Climate Central*, September 8, 2013, www.climatecentral.org/news/with-climate-change-brazil-faces-drop-in-crops-16439 (accessed June 29, 2018).
12 A precedent of this transition can be witnessed in parts of the TransArabian Pipeline. See Aaron Wolf, "Water for Peace in the Jordan River Watershed," *Natural Resources Journal* 33 (1993): 797–839, and Neeraj Bhatia, "Harvesting Urbanism through Territorial Logistics," *The Petropolis of Tomorrow* (New York: Actar Publishers, 2013), pp. 284–285.
13 "Guarani Aquifer," *World Heritage Encyclopedia*, http://cn.worldheritage.org/articles/Guarani_Aquifer (accessed June 29, 2018).
14 For Ecotourism evaluation of the region, see S.M. Degrandi and A.S. Figueiró, "Patrimônio Natural e Geoconservação: A Geodiversidade Domunicípio Gaúcho de Caçapava do Sul," *Revista Brasileira de Ecoturismo, São Paulo* 5(2) (2012): 173–196, www.sbecotur.org.br/rbecotur/seer/index.php/ecoturismo/article/view/315/285 (accessed June 29, 2018).
15 Marilyn Neville (Graminae Consulting), *Best Management Practices for Pipeline Construction in Native Prairie Environments: A Guide for Minimizing the Impact of Pipeline Construction on the Native Prairie Ecosystem* (Edmonton: Alberta Environment and Alberta Sustainable Resource Development, 2002), pp. 23–24.
16 Linnéa Johansson, "Conservation Aspects for a Fragment of Araucaria Moist Forest in Southern Brazil: Regarding Species Composition and Diversity of a Small Fragment of Araucaria Moist Forest Embedded in a Matrix of Pampas Grassland," (Bachelor of Biology thesis, Halmstad University, 2013), p. 4.
17 Ibid., p. 6. See also Maíra Taquiguthi Ribeiro, Flavio Nunes Ramos, and Flavio Antonio Maës Dos Santos, "Tree Structure and Richness in an Atlantic Forest Fragment: Distance from Anthropogenic and Natural Edges," *Revista Árvore* 33(6) (2009): 1124.
18 Ibid, pp. 6–7.
19 R. Hearne and A. Santos, "Tourists' and Locals' Preferences toward Ecotourism Development in the Maya Biosphere Reserve, Guatemala," *Environment, Development and Sustainability* 7(3) (2005): 303–318, and T. Hinch, "Ecotourists and Indigenous Hosts: Diverging Views on Their Relationship with Nature," *Current Issues in Tourism* 1(1) (1998): 120–124.
20 W.D. Spencer, P. Beier, K. Penrod, K. Winters, C. Paulman, H. Rustigian-Romsos, J. Strittholt, M. Parisi, and A. Pettler, *California Essential Habitat Connectivity Project: A Strategy for Conserving a Connected California* (Sacramento, CA: California Department of Transportation, California Department of Fish and Game, and Federal Highways Administration, 2010), p. 125.

6
CHASING MILITARY LOGISTICS IN THE URBAN VOID

Jeffrey S. Nesbit

FIGURE 6.1　US Federal Shipyards map. By Haecceitas Studio/Lucas Flint.

As early as 1767, the United States Navy manufactured landscapes in order to properly fabricate and maintain the various fleets, keep up with technological upgrades, and sustain military agendas. Today, with only five remaining active sites, the majority of the original shipyards have been turned over to the local municipality. Ironically, due to relentless excavation of ground, the sites are left as huge voids in the now ever-expanding urban metropolis. This research theme examines the history of the shipyard processes and their territories of influence in order to generate questions on the future ecological performance within the continuous potentiality of a productive void.

Production

In the city, the productivity of ground has been adapted many times over, leveled and re-leveled. Post-modern cities are inherently systems of ecologies, manipulations of productivity, and scenes of developmental and economic forces at work, all leading to hyper-differentiated states. It is not the products of capitalistic development, but the process leading to such outcomes, such as fragmentation and demolition, which can reveal and describe the reality of our urban landscape. The strategies here define processes of leveling and re-leveling in the city as critical participants in generation for designing urban evolution.

Post-industrial Paradox

Described by Carol Berens in her work *Redeveloping Industrial Sites*, "these original locations shaped land-use patterns and thwarted further development or revitalization of many cities. These defunct industrial sites now occupy some of the potentially best urban sites, whether on the waterfront or in other critical locations."[1] Berens claims many cities contain symbolic references—as an "advertisement for a city"—through internationally acclaimed buildings within such places of reclamation. For example, Sydney and Bilbao, both showcased by singular artifacts of contemporary architecture in the city, position themselves on the global stage by way of repressed former industries. She continues, suggesting: "these projects can create a second center for a city, refocusing activity and energy from its traditional center to the edges."[2] In Berens' collection of case studies on industrial projects, such as Mill City Museum in Minneapolis, the work enables a kind of cultural integration, producing exhibits and showcasing activities, demonstrating processes in the factories from the past. The "exposed ruins keep history palpably alive" in the series of artifacts, acting as interpretive centers for a public audience.[3] This is a compelling argument. On one hand, the city's economy has been energized many times over through the increase of tourism—by way of an opera house, in Sydney, and museum, in Bilbao. On the other hand, the public investments move from the previous "traditional centers" and cause an abandonment in terms of both cultural and physical voids. The author clearly advocates for the ruin as cultural artifact participating in an ongoing educational process on historical impacts of place. Yet it remains artifact—a monument caricaturing a productive past.

The Bilbao spectacle activates global tourism while supposedly rejecting a traditional center, and the Mill City artifact integrates into its cultural fabric, hoping to successfully fill an abandoned central void. In both cases, the abandoned voids have been plugged—and the implications of industrial productions exaggerate broken reference or stage characterizations of historical production. Thus, here we encounter a dilemma, perhaps a paradox. If our cities re-organize themselves structurally based on political, economic, social, and environmental climates, then it is safe to suggest that the refocusing efforts in development impact behavior in other locations, which may result in the formation of new unpredictable voids.

In the notoriously sprawled city of Houston, Lars Lerup uses "stim and dross" to explain a foundation of such behaviors in contemporary urban form. Lerup carefully denotes the behavior of sprawl as a behavior, not as the typical illustration of sprawl depicting negative impacts on our urban realities. He marks the city full of stimulated locations "precariously pinned in place by machines and human events," while the other reciprocal space defines populations of "the dross—the ignored, undervalued, unfortunate economic residues of the metropolitan machine."[4] Therefore, we are left with the reductions of activities occurring in singularities, isolated by the other impurities of unclaimed design outcomes. It is under this premise, the space of differentiations, that the Bilbao spectacle or Mill City artifacts are allowed to take shape and become "space as value, as locus of events, as genius loci" distributed outside the voided, uncertain milieu.[5] The porosity, gaps in the urban fabric, between fluctuations of activity to void, or stim to dross, cleverly mark new territory in the understanding of place. This is especially useful in our pursuit of intellectually advancing the value and meaning of the post-industrial paradox.

Let us consider the definitions of impact within the adverse models above to articulate the paradox further. Findings in inactive shipyards may shed some light on the consequences of such modes of urban practice—particularly moving from mechanized synthetic landscapes and into environmental and global unpredictability. A total of fifteen shipyards were constructed in the United States by the federal government. Only four remain as active yards for the building and maintaining of the US military fleet. Seven of the inactive sites have been turned over to the local municipality. As these properties are turned over to municipal control and released for development plans, developers and planners quickly find themselves linked to conversations of brownfield remediation and redevelopment.

To introduce the role of inactive shipyards in contemporary urban planning trends, let us begin at the end and briefly review a site undergoing revitalization efforts. The size and immense spread of land that the shipyards occupy is astonishing, even after their closure. The Navy Yard in Washington, DC offers a glimpse into development undertakings funded through public-private collaborative financing. Currently, the site is converting into a highly dense mixed-use project made up of 475 residential units, 400,000 square feet of retail and cultural space, 1.8 million square feet of office space, and 700 parking spaces. The project also considers 1.72 acres of park and 5.87 acres of new open space. Developer Forest City teamed with the urban planning firm Lee and Associates and civil engineering consultants Greening Urban to manage the design of the substantial revitalization project. The Washington Yard has been advertised as emphasizing sustainable approaches for low-impact development. These approaches are specifically described through four methods—"a tree trench infiltration system to absorb water slowly from storm events, vertical recharge shafts that deliver runoff directly to the natural underground water table, smart irrigation and gray water systems for water recycling, and flow-thru planter boxes."[6] The challenge of low-impact urbanism should not be solved exclusively through strategies of engineered systems, for the same reasons the practice of architecture is not handled by structural engineers. The discrepancy here between engineered systems of check-boxed LEED (Leadership in Energy and Environmental Design) credit sustainability and the formal articulations of buildings and landscape outcomes sets the pace for our design challenge.

Leading to this point, we have introduced edges of the post-industrial paradox and outlined trends for capitalistic redevelopment. If we are to fully understand the implications of such robust places of productivity, we must revisit the generations before us. Critically evaluating necessary processes is crucial before consideration of redevelopment, enabling a drift toward sustainable engineering. We must acknowledge these shipyards as places—landscapes tied to a broader cultural, physical, and political coextensive contextualization. The porosity of the city must be considered. The desire for completely autonomous density and economic stability is unrealistic, and suggest a naïve understanding of how the city operates. As we know, the city is complex and ever-changing. The remainder of this chapter outlines themes in favor of the generative porosity, the fluctuating context of a growing polycentric urban behavior. Two primary topics inform the basis for such a view: the shipyard productivity, systematic operations in use, and the shipyard void, processes of inactivity and memory.

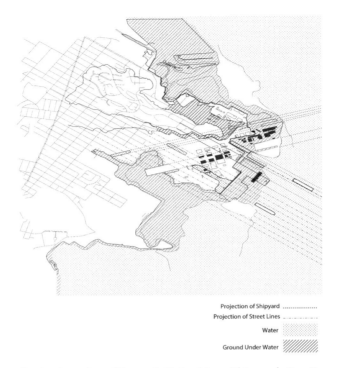

FIGURE 6.2 Projective edges, Hunter's Point Navy Shipyard, San Francisco, CA. By Christina Booher and Nazanin Modaresahmadi.

FIGURE 6.3 Bremerton (Puget Sound), Brooklyn, Charleston, Philadelphia, and San Francisco (Hunter's Point) Navy Yards, 2016. By Haecceitas Studio.

Territory

Beyond the conditions expanding the federal footprint of naval operations on the shipyard landscape, we find three dimensions of expansion. First, the scope of economic influence in the landscape extends into development, production, and consumerism, all of which are tied to the civilian community adjacent to such military activities. In every instance, the naval complexes have immediate impacts on economic successes—or declines during non-productive periods. In Brooklyn, the neighborhoods of Williamsburg and Dumbo, particularly the legacy of Vinegar Hill, have been and still remain greatly shaped by the existence of the yard. The yard cultivated the development and establishment of new shops, business incubation, and redevelopment properties, which often reside along the periphery of the former federal boundaries. In San Francisco, due to oscillations in production, ownership, and tenants, the Hunter's Point yard constantly changed boundaries, both at the water's edge and in the Bay View neighborhood to the east. From production efforts of shipbuilding and naval radiological research to social and cultural transformations, the geographical territory radically blurred community activity and economic instability. Physically, the activities in the yard alter the territory, including the economic growth of nearby neighborhoods.

Second, the United States Naval Shipyards uniquely act as absorbers of raw materials, such as steel (and wood for early construction). In Philadelphia, the shipyard had been built on an island in the Delaware River south of Center City. As production requirements demanded more real estate, soil was shipped into the area ultimately leading to the manufactured grounds transforming the boundaries from island to peninsula. Along with ground for expansion, new materials, such as steel, were shipped in or brought to the site by railway. During the peak periods of production, the Philadelphia Naval Shipyard demanded a massive influx of steel. The majority of the extraction sites for iron ore focused on filling orders to be sent directly to the shipyard in Philadelphia. Major state and national railway systems contributed to the shipyards' production success through infrastructurally connecting the extraction of resources from our landscapes to territories reaching as far as distant state lines.

The United States Navy yard constructed federal property boundaries outlining its so-called "regulated operations" even though evidence indicates regular boundaries change, indicating their unfixed nature. Additionally, we know production in the yard impacts neighboring economies, directly influencing social and cultural factors, and vice versa. As demands for military tactics in naval operations require new and retrofitted vessels to be constructed, monopolized extraction sites increase removal and distribution of raw resources within and across state lines. The third dimension of expansion includes a range of influence uniquely extending geographical and political territory. It is here, within the shipyard landscapes, that marks the geographical nodes for military deployment. This geopolitical territory is expansive and powerful, as demonstrated by President Roosevelt's "Great White Fleet," debuted as evidence of the US as the pre-eminent global super-power. As an aggressive political message to North Korea, in April of 2017 under President Trump's administration, the United States Navy dispatched the 97,000-ton USS *Carl Vinson* to the East Sea, escorted by a missile cruiser and destroyers. Such positioning, regardless of whether an act of war, expands the boundary of the shipyard manufacturers into the seas of political territory. The decision to move the powerful naval fleet off the coast of the Korean peninsula demonstrates a message both visually and politically. According to a CNN news report, "the deployment is a military show of force, signaling to North Korea that the US military can operate at sea in area where the regime might engage." It also suggests that an actual engagement of war would require a much larger call to action by the United States military forces.[7]

Even after these fleets are utilized for varying tactics in military warfare, the ships are then dispersed to other locations. Known as the mothball fleets, decommissioned ships are repurposed as holdings of the National Defense Reserve. Primary sites populate the coastlines for containment and are expended once again. Although inactive, these ships are considered capable of becoming reactivated in a time of national emergency. However, often these fleets are scrapped for other purposes. The National Defense

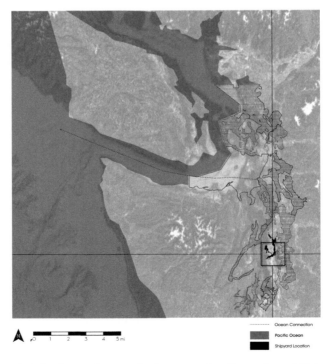

FIGURE 6.4 Sub-basins and watersheds connecting Puget Sound Shipyard to the Pacific Ocean. By Velina Paneva and Bradley Singletary.

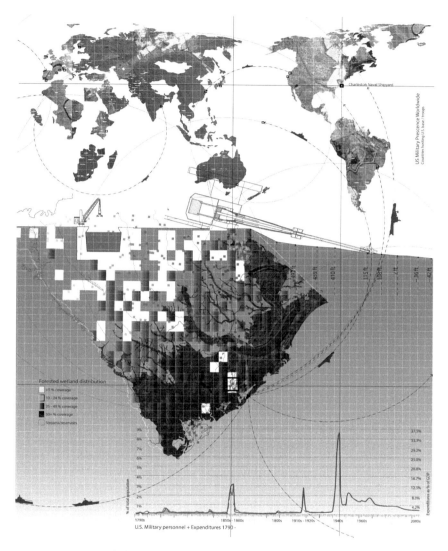

FIGURE 6.5 Expanded territory: South Carolina Wetlands and world map. By Haecceitas Studio/Robby Stubbs.

Reserve Fleet in Suisun Bay, northern California or other mothball fleets, including transport ships and twelve minesweepers in Beaumont's reserve on the Texas coast, house many of the ships. As figurative extended islands of productive ground, the reserve fleets become anchored and tethered to one another in the shallow tidal estuaries of the United States coastline.

114 Jeffrey S. Nesbit

If the vessels are not consigned to the mothball fleets, they are fully discharged and recycled. Primarily responsible for the recycling of nuclear submarines along with other battleship deconstruction, the Naval Inactive Ship Maintenance Facilities in Bremerton, just outside Seattle, use the materials in two ways. If materials do not contain high levels of radioactivity, they are deconstructed for other military uses. On the other hand, if too dangerous for reuse, materials, including submarine reactors, are disposed of. In 1982, Congress passed the Nuclear Waste Policy Act, mandating the proper disposal of nuclear waste. Deep in burial trenches, the permanent disposal facilities house the last remains of vessel waste and geologically embed themselves deep in the trenches of the sub-ground storage.

The shipyard uses various types of extraction processes for raw materials, efficiently establishing manufacturing and maintenance productions in a domestic landscape. This leads to the deployment of vessels around the globe to project military tactics and logistical positioning, both physical and political. The geopolitical dimension of expansion rests in the hands of military defense systems and philosophies, all the while demanding the utilization of a working ground on a once profoundly different landscape. The landscapes themselves remain altered by absorbing varying degrees of influences from each condition of territorial domain. From raw extraction of geological resources to historically profound memories in our local communities and global politics, the shipyard leaves us with a stratification of ground, history, and geospatial territory.

Excavating Grounds

Level can be defined as a means for establishing a horizontal line and a measurement of difference between two points. Particularly related to the horizontal condition, the relationship between one position and another establishes the conceptual framework for this design research project. The idea of being *on level* can be thought of through multiple rhetorical exercises. Initially, the design study begins with *on level*, with regard to "level" as the agency for architectural inquiries, which ultimately establishes ideas defining objects paradoxically *on level*. The paradox here refers to the very fact that objects and locations *on level* are never truly the same; thereby constantly marking the difference between one tangent, point, or reference and the other. Gilles Deleuze, in his introduction to *Difference and Repetition*, asked: "what is the concept of difference—one which is not reducible to simple conceptual difference but demands its own idea, its own singularity at the level of ideas?"[8] From a Deleuzian perspective, we can infer that the essences of objects and their locations in space are to always be described through their non-level dimension— through their inherent lines of difference. This is precisely how managing the materiality of objects *on level* results in the accumulation of multiple measurable locations. The acceptance of difference coupled with the acceptance of a materialistic assumption allows for the range of relationships *on level* to be described.

If we anticipate *on level* to be an architectural reduction of precision, we find examples which demonstrate precisely an architecture that is not level. The Pantheon, built in 128 CE as a Roman Temple, is ordered through perfect geometries of the circle and sphere as a dome. The famous central oculus stretches light from above into the singular round space. Although the measurements of precision are almost flawless—and known for their otherworldly references, being dedicated to gods—the floor is not so pure. Level is a datum where locations are referenced, whereas flatness is an unattainable idealistic condition. The prominent pattern of alternating circles and squares exaggerate the ground in relation to the properties of water and illumination of perspective. The leveled floor is in fact not level. In order to eliminate standing water, the ground was distorted ever so slightly to move water coming in from the oculus to the edges of the circle. David Leatherbarrow's "Leveling the Ground" rightfully illustrates Alberti's strategy for "having a slope of 2 inches in 10 feet, to allow for rainwater to run off" and uses these particular measurements, which are commonly found throughout Roman practice.[9] Also mentioned by Leatherbarrow, the Campidoglio is yet another precedent for extending the differentiation of ground to be a working, operational tool. Prior to Michelangelo's renovation on the Capitoline Hill in Rome, the medieval site was considered to be unorganized, irregular, and a mask of governmental control through the papacy. It was then that the Church commissioned Michelangelo to improve the irregularity of the ground in order to restore the site to ordered geometry. However, again we find the symmetry and ground to not be level. The oval in plan occurs in section as well, making the statue of Marcus Aurelius to stand at the highest point, symbolically and physically, in the Campidoglio piazza. Leatherbarrow concludes: "to think of leveled land as flat is to wrongly project the vertical onto the horizontal, mistaking the second as a mirror image of the first, neglecting all the differences."[10] Being *on level* is no longer simply having zero slope, but rather a distinction between the relationship of horizontal and vertical—from earth to sky and back again.

Another notable characteristic of being *on level* includes the dimension of distance. If one considers two differentiated states, the position from one to another includes the difference of both horizontal and vertical. By the 17th century, a device known as the waywiser was developed in order to measure distance, marked by the circumference and degree of rotation of a wheel being pushed along the ground. This device, known today as an odometer, was used by surveyors to index the differences between one

116 Jeffrey S. Nesbit

location to another along the section of an area of land. The device was relatively accurate on smooth surfaces, but became extremely inaccurate when measuring ground which was not smooth nor level. This demonstrates the discrepancies between an instrument and the material ground plane. The degree of separation assumes lines of measurement on a non-level surface, thereby exaggerating its reality. In other words, we may now know the simple distances between points on the ground plane. However, the measuring device is unable to adequately describe those differences by oversimplifying objects as being *on level*. Fortunately, technological advancements are capable of more accurately capturing differences on the ground.

Based on the work of the National Oceanic Atmospheric Administration, we have three primary techniques for survey leveling: differential, trigonometric, and barometric.[11] Differential leveling is known to be the most accurate because it directly reads the difference in elevation between two points without cumbersome calculation, unlike the trigonometric method. Leveling rods are set into position to mark the points of locations, and with the instrument locked into position, calibration along the rods sets elevation markers, and the dimension by a vertical datum marks others. As early as 1895, German engineers had developed the first devices to capture such differential leveling through what is known as the surveying scope. This extremely intricate device allows for highly advanced measurements by dialing in on fixed points, making it much more feasible to document differences along a field of points.

Dedicating his life to water supply, in 1913 William Mulholland advanced the differential leveling tool to construct a major infrastructure in the western United States.[12] In a project that supplied water to the city of Los Angeles via access to the Owens Valley water bodies, Mulholland utilized the new technology in survey equipment to aid in the growth of one of the largest cities in the world. Mulholland's career work on water systems and supply emancipates our former geographical constraints and jurisdiction of municipal growth by intelligently, and synthetically, manufacturing water distribution to places otherwise deserted. This translation of geographical specificity, water supply, and the use of differential leveling plays a key role in our work on leveling. Ground is not flat, populations are no longer bounded by geography, and tools for understanding the differentiations of ground enable greater control over excavation and management.

Let us revisit the definition of level once more. The epistemological reference for "level" is derived from the Middle English noun *libel*, and in Latin, *libella*. *Libella* can be translated as the plummet line, level, or water level. To unpack this, we can reflect upon each. For level, we have already seen its behavior in points of differences, not being level. The other two defining elements here—plummet line and water level—have other characteristics. A plummet line describes a line which is to be plumb. Plummet can then be defined as something that weighs down, or to fall straight down and plunge. As another device for marking a measurement, plummet immediately has association with two features; indexing vertical dimension due to horizontal variance being zero and a reference to water, and to plunge. This leads us to the third *libella* definition, water-level. Here the direct reference to water includes gravitational force. Water falls to the lowest level it can possibly access. The relationship between the water volume and its limits below has associations with the gravitational force acting upon it and the ground containing it. This leads us to our operational tool—the relationship between differentiated level and water.

Topography is the collected differential levels and delineation of ground. Bathymetry, stemming from the Greek *bathus*, which means "deep," and *metron*, meaning "measure," marks its distinctive differences at the water level itself. We move from a topographic to a bathymetric measurement when crossing the water level. Our mark of zero in this framework is the water's edge defining the boundary of ground to water as water levels change constantly through tides, droughts, and rising sea levels due to climate change across the globe. The datum is no longer a fixed plane. As such, maintaining *level* demands continuously evolving measures to accommodate the relationships between points, or from one ground to another—all revealing the differentiations of ground.

The terrain of earth's surface is the physical manifestation of the ground's description of its own history of environmental influence. As the environment changes, such as the aforementioned changes in water level, the terrain registers its heritage in remarkable ways. Found across the globe in a variety of contexts, the fabric of the Earth's surface is the mark of our geographical and environmental ancestry. The stratification of geographical features, layer upon layer, helps describe time and ecological impact. Much like the dating of fossils in the stratified excavations of ground, the differences in horizontal and vertical position allow for readings of evolution and signify past memory. Dating from 4000 BCE, agricultural field systems have been excavated in Chuodun (modern-day Kunshan, China) along the Yangtze Delta.[13] This ancient artifact of ground symbolizes human ability to manipulate the leveling of ground in order to efficiently order productive means of living. It is not only the natural offerings of ground and resources, but also our human ability to cultivate and manipulate such levels. The famous rice field landscapes on the hillsides of China exaggerate the relationship between the natural terrain and human impact *on level*.

The leveling of ground through natural events, such as those in Utah with the astonishing registrations of erosion on the Hoodoos, or the underwater bathymetry maps of the Indian Ocean, indicates patterns of atmospheric impact. It is through these terrain patterns that we have

118 Jeffrey S. Nesbit

the ability to learn from the consequences of processes over thousands of years. This segment *on level* takes a perspective derived from materialistic philosophy. The shipyard evolutions mark our legacies of time. Throughout the remainder of this chapter, we utilize the nature of leveled lands as an operative tool for projecting into the newly developed and ecologically sensible shipyard legacy. Methodically we find the practices of manufactured and leveled grounds as a guide to operate physically as well as a framework for theoretical underpinning.

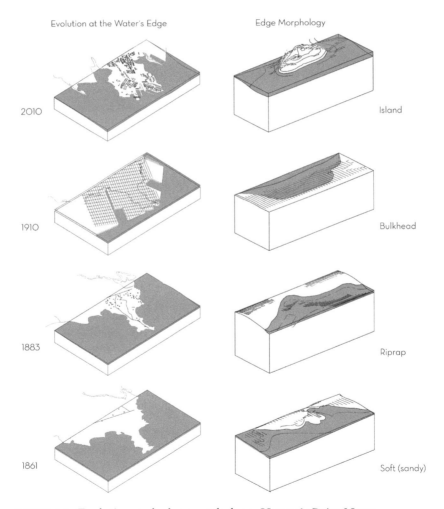

FIGURE 6.6 Evolution and edge morphology, Hunter's Point Navy Shipyard, San Francisco, CA. By Christina Booher and Nazanin Modaresahmadi.

Chasing Military Logistics in the Urban Void **119**

FIGURE 6.7   Charleston Shipyard transformations (1909, 1945, 1996, 2015). By Haecceitas Studio/Lucas Flint.

Military Production and Landscape

Mapping the Landscape

The processes in military tactics during wartime directly impact modes of manufacturing in shipyard landscapes. Corresponding increases in production inflate local economic fluctuations. Expanded production and employment, altered site configurations, and political consequences generate a stratified landscape. Historical and ecological stratification leave physical imprints on the globe—in this case, by ship assembly production and residue. However successful economically, the landscape of the former Navy Shipyard in Charleston, South Carolina has endangered its local coastal wetland ecology and continues to deteriorate its natural terrain. Contrary to dismantling a historical past and only harvesting a natural landscape, *LANDYards*, a design reserch project, seeks to paradoxically enrich the environment by manufacturing ecologies and enable design alternatives in a porous and unpredictable future.

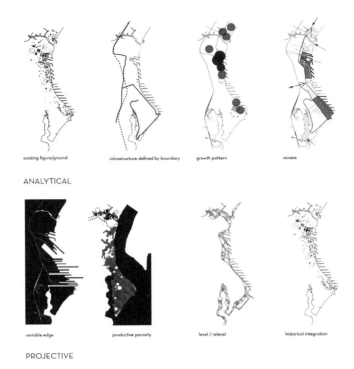

FIGURE 6.8 Analytical and projective mapping, Charleston Navy Shipyard. By Haecceitas Studio/Lucas Flint.

By 1907, the United States Navy had constructed a sixteen-ship fleet that toured globally as a deterrent to threats and a demonstration of American might under President Theodore Roosevelt.[14] Named the "Great White Fleet," this flagship fleet exhibited the far-reaching impact of the shipping industry, from local production to mobility in international waters. Military logistics and global politics participate in shaping the landscape beyond the means of a fluid boundary. In *Ecologies of Power*, Pierre Belanger describes the impact of military logistics as a "field of influence that consists of both the operational environment and the flows of operations."[15] Belanger clarifies this point by stating: "the contradictory and paradoxical double-entendre of 'landscape' [is] expressive of different media and modes of power, both operative and emergent, simultaneously fixed and fluid, inscriptive and descriptive, projective and receptive." This further illustrates a contradiction in our understanding and the role of territory and that of terrain, or ground.[16] This paradoxical enterprise of landscape marks a primary theme for this chapter—the inactive shipyards offer operational tools of systematic manufacturing and become catalysts for a dynamic topography.

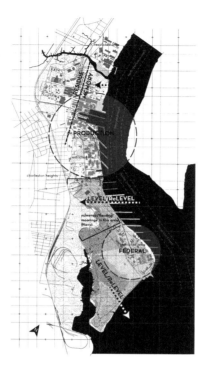

FIGURE 6.9 Impact on landscape, Charleston Navy Shipyard. By Haecceitas Studio.

As the US Navy evolved into the national first line of defense, shipyard construction proliferated, which in turn created fluctuations in local economies. Charles Waldheim's position on the industrial and post-industrial landscape argues: "these logistical zones are hardly recognizable as city forms, yet produce and provide a base to the economic activity that supports contemporary urban development."[17] The grounds of the inactive navy shipyards may be considered an expansion of Waldheim's speculation on post-industrial landscapes, where the ground itself becomes the currency influencing economy and productivity. More specifically, docks, outfitting wharfs, and assembly buildings become measures of growth and military development.

Rhizomatic Landscape

David Harvey's narrative on spatial fix becomes critical in our endeavor moving forward. Harvey outlines "fixed space" as a contradiction in development—not as fixed, anchored, or otherwise, but instead as a necessary evolutionary cycle "in its [capitalism] history only to have to destroy that space at a later point in order to make way for a new *spatial fix*."[18] The nature of the paradox in capitalism describes a territory of flux, a territory incapable to survive successfully. Harvey highlights three criteria, or possible evidences, of such behavior in the territory of capitalism: geographical expansion, innovations in transport and communications, and modes of dependent circumstances. To unpack these criteria, we can consider the situations marked and made on the landscape. First, as noted, capitalism would not be possible if geography was not capable of expanding beyond lines of demarcation. The very notion of acquiring and occupying neighboring real estate empowers the interworking of the capitalistic enterprise. This has the opportunity to expand beyond lines of property boundaries, and extends into new markets across the global domain. Second, developments in technology have allowed for such expansions to occur. The water canals becoming transportation routes, railways carving over terrain, and aviation and maritime routes with the inclusion of new technologies based on traffic algorithms and Geographic Information Systems expand our globe like never before. And third, the very modes of expanding our geospatial territory greatly depend on searching for new frontiers in markets, resources, and production. Therefore, capitalism's dependence is our paradoxical consideration in the physical boundary of place.

As explained earlier when describing poly-nucleated urbanism and in the descriptions of paradoxical urban holes, the ever-changing condition of ground is embedded in the premise that necessitates the urban machine to continue its progress. Investments in new production facilities, increases in new labor powers, or changes in political climates significantly impact the continuous alterations to process, all along the way from extraction to consumption. The dangerous characteristic of this "spatial fix" behavior indicates that all territories will be expanded and collapsed, vibrating intensively until reaching economic ruptures in the horizontal urban fabric. However precarious a system of instability may seem, we use strategies in the landscape to enable such fluctuations.

Situational considerations are employed through the internal logics of the so-called rules and relationships, or rather capacities and tendencies. More importantly, the populated distribution of development continuously locks into and dislodges from contextual anchoring. This negotiation process of historical memory, existing configuration, and future unpredictability is critical in order for systems of urbanism to assimilate successfully back into the already established historical landscape. Systems of analytical design processes enhance flexibility and become informed by existing behavior of the urban legacy, not simply by following formal aesthetics. As the singularities of form are distributed among the large-scale networked simulation, each criterion must abide by the neighboring consequences from one to the next, physical and historical adjacencies. When the unpredictable outcomes present situational and consequential relationships based not on formal states, but rather on the behavioral strategies, by nature, the urban fabric will continue to oscillate and negotiate.

The negotiation process is a search simulation, attempting to allow for unpredictable configurations. Systematically, the generative evolution positions for possibility space for extended growth and recessed elimination. Compared to the former master planning principles and strict orthogonal grid planning, the population distribution allows for such organizational tools to survive. Similar to biological processes, "as social agents we live our lives within spaces delimited by natural and artificial extensive boundaries" through an acknowledgment and understanding of flexible model simulation.[19] Zones of elasticity cultivate "boundaries of which are not defined by spatial limits but by critical thresholds." The "critical threshold" is precisely the kind of coding necessary for component logics to search and negotiate as optimal model sequencing. For example, in certain situations, a singular component may need to extend much further than its predecessor. The components are not to be thought of as references to the matrix platonic, but rather as in an elastic state. Operating similarly to a reference of internally influenced urban forces, the component multiplication does not have "beginning nor end, but always a middle," and distributes according to the principle of elastic extensity. As Deleuze and Guttari state, "the rhizome connects any point to any other point" and has the potential and, more directly, a milieu "from which it grows and overspills, [constituting] linear multiplicities."[20]

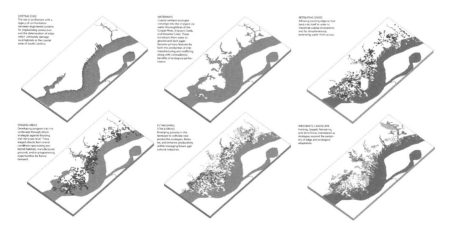

FIGURE 6.10 Rhizomatic landscapes, former Charleston Navy Shipyard. By Haecceitas Studio/Robby Stubbs.

Productive Residue

Throughout the last twenty years we have seen projects across the post-industrial landscape reconfiguring possibilities of re-use for a healthier environment, moving from the brownfield to images of greening landscapes. They originate alongside many substantial contributions through a tapestry of theses such as ecological urbanism, landscape urbanism, or even infrastructural urbanism.

Significant innovations and intellectual rhetoric between the disciplines of urban design and landscape cultivated a savvy 21st-century agenda capable of establishing public sensitivity to landscape recovery. However, many of these projects fail to recognize the necessary urban fragmentations and dismantled landscapes as participants for evolutionary growth. In order for such reclamation to occur, the materiality of our world rests on the premise of evolutionary behavior: transforming from one state to another. As such, we are seeing the processes of the city behave in a similar manner to that which we find in our so-called "natural environment." The ground becomes the palimpsest of productivity, moving from one stage of the process to another.

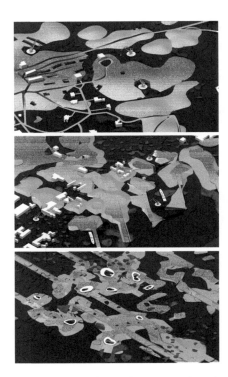

FIGURE 6.11 Speculations (historical, productive, and ecological), former Charleston Navy Shipyard. By Haecceitas Studio/Robby Stubbs.

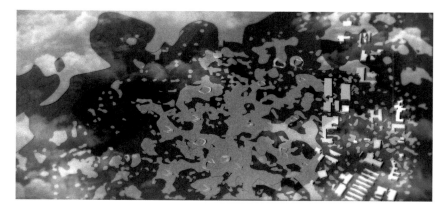

FIGURE 6.12   Speculation of Shipyard Creek and Shipyard residue, former Charleston Navy Shipyard. By Haecceitas Studio/Robby Stubbs.

For architects and urban designers, considerations of military logistics integrated with the operational landscape become fundamental in how we position design processes for future environments. Demolition, abandonment, construction, and landscapes of residue all fall into a category of productivity bounded by their counterparts of healthy and developmentally productive places. We have evidence of objects and their associated operational plane charging the horizontal fabric to stage its interworking behavior. Military logistics tend to maximize interruptions on the urban surface; however, the movement of ground should plan responsibly for the consequences of traversed ground. Just as biological models self-generate and adapt to circumstances in their environments, such as the clearing, grading, draining, and excavation of ground for military production, fragmentations of landscape processes continuously shape the urban fabric.

Notes

1 Carol Berens, *Redeveloping Industrial Sites: A Guide for Architects, Planners, and Developers* (Hoboken, NJ: Wiley, 2011), p. 115.
2 Ibid., p. 150.
3 Ibid., p. 160.
4 Lars Lerup, *After the City* (Cambridge, MA: MIT Press, 2000), p. 58.
5 Ibid., p. 58.
6 Kaid Benfield, "After Decades of Neglect, Washington Finally Fixes Its Waterfront," *CityLab*, January 19, 2012, https://www.citylab.com/design/2012/01/after-decades-neglect-washington-finally-fixes-its-waterfront/996/ (accessed June 29, 2018).
7 Tim Schwarz, Barbara Starr, and Zachary Cohen, "North Korea Issues Warning as US Strike Group Head to Korean Peninsula," *CNN News*, April 13, 2017, http://edition.cnn.com/2017/04/10/politics/us-aircraft-carrier-carl-vinson-north-korea-strike-capabilities/ (accessed June 29, 2018).

8 Gilles Deleuze, *Difference and Repetition* (New York: Columbia University Press, 1968), p. 27.
9 David Leatherbarrow, "Leveling the Ground," in *Topographical Stories: Studies in Landscape and Architecture* (Philadelphia, PA: University of Pennsylvania Press, 2004), p. 177.
10 Ibid., p. 181.
11 Christine Schomaker and Ralph Moore Berry, *NOAA Manual NOS NGS 3: Geodetic Leveling* (Rockville, MD: NOAA, 1981.
12 Catherine Mulholland, *William Mulholland and the Rise of Los Angeles* (Los Angeles, CA: University of California Press, 2000).
13 Chun-Hai Li, "Pollen and Phytolith Analyses of Ancient Paddy Fields at Chuodun Site, the Yangtze River Delta," *Pedosphere* 17(2): 209–218.
14 Mark Albertson, *U.S.S. Connecticut: Constitution State Battleship* (Mustang, OK: Tate Publishing, 2007).
15 Pierre Belanger, *Ecologies of Power* (Cambridge, MA: MIT Press, 2016), p. 25.
16 Ibid., p. 41. The term is used here to avoid the common confusions or overlooked complexities associated with notions of land, terrain, territory, and territoriality:

> To the military, territory is topographic features conditioning tactical and strategic considerations as well as distance or space to be played with; occasionally it is also resources in terms of local supplies. To the jurist, territory is jurisdiction and delimitation; to the specialist in international law it is both an attribute and the spatial extent of sovereignty. To the geographer, it is the portion of space enclosed by boundary lines, the location and internal characteristics of which are to be described and explained. To the specialist interested in political geography . . . territory appears as a material, spatial notion establishing essential links between politics, people, and the natural setting. Under a purely analytical approach, the notion of territory would break up and dissolve into a multitude of different concepts such as location, natural resources, population density, settlement patterns, modes of life, and so forth. The important aspect of territory as the unit in the political organization of space that defines, at least for a time, the relationships between the community and its habitat on one hand, and between the community and its neighbors on the other, has been little explored.

17 Charles Waldheim, *Landscape as Urbanism: A General Theory* (Princeton, NJ: Princeton University Press, 2016), p. 181.
18 David Harvey, "Globalization and the "Spatial Fix," in *Geographische Revue: Marxism in Geography* (Waake, Germany: Institut für Geographie, 2001), p. 25:

> Capitalism has to fix space, in order to overcome space . . . this leads to one of the central contradictions of capital: that is has to build a fixed space necessary for its own functioning at a certain point in its history only to have to destroy that space at a later point in order to make way for a new 'spatial fix' at a later point in its history.

19 Manuel DeLanda, *Deleuze: History and Science* (New York: Atropos Press, 2010).
20 Gilles Deleuze and Felix Guattari, *A Thousand Plateaus: Capitalism and Schizophrenia* (Minneapolis, MN: University of Minnesota Press, 1987), pp. 7–10.

7

CHASING LINES OF ENGAGEMENT

Edward Becker

Resource Exchange: Artifacts of Value

It is a warm evening in late June, sometime around 10 o'clock in the evening. A hum of conversation and clinking tableware floats over Teurastamo, its red-brick buildings glowing a soft, saturated orange in the low Nordic summer sun. The former abattoir of Helsinki is as alive as it has ever been, the soft sounds of laughter and the occasional ringing bike bell belying the grit and mass-slaughter that characterized the district upon its inception in 1933. This emerging magnet of the creative class in design-focused Helsinki contains an eclectic and refined food culture, a food culture of local specialization attracting a diverse clientele. Where money met ideas—the resultant now clothed in historic brick façades—culinary and contemporary urban cultures now intermix in a diverse array of specialized eateries. In establishments such as Flavour Studio and Tislaamo, tastes such as foraged sorrel from the wilderness with dill flowers or Lappish reindeer with handpicked lingonberries are complemented by spirits from Finland's first Helsinki-based distillery in over a century. With an alcohol content of 47% that is primed to soften the palate, the complexity, structure, and cemosensational hierarchy of Balkan juniper, Seville orange, Finnish lingonberry, and a pinch of rose petals, among other ingredients, collectively allude to the larger urban context within which the new culinary heart of Helsinki resides. Like this combination of ingredients, the contemporary city exhibits complexities, layerings, juxtapositions, hierarchies, and sensual engagements that result from a complex interplay of local and global forces.

Macro-scale urban influences such as infrastructure, energy, landscape, and socio-economic conditions spur the process of urbanization. This process,

128 Edward Becker

while encompassing in scale, can ultimately be reduced to a plethora of tactile value-based decisions. The web of value-based decisions that drive urbanization is constructed of threads, or "lines," of related logic. Thus,

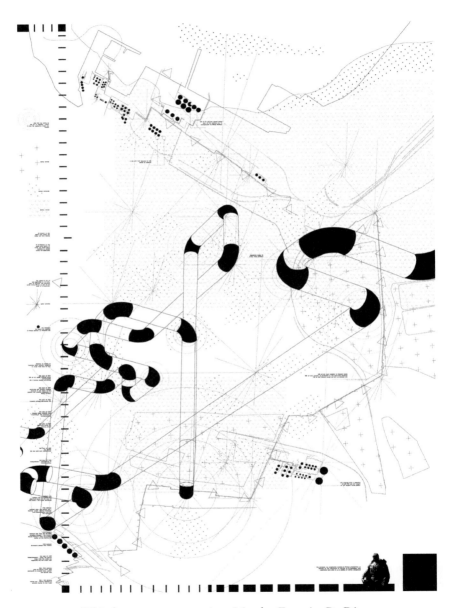

FIGURE 7.1 Oil infrastructure mapping, Mardu, Estonia. By Disa Reuterswärd.

Lines of Engagement can be defined as the malleable and fluctuating thresholds between opposing conditions of value in the built environment that are emblematic of the aforementioned social and economic systems at play. They are at once tactile because they have been manifested in some way, while also being concurrently metaphysical, relating to larger questions of origin and root purpose. Arguably, just as a group of young women finish off their spirits and pay the bill in Teurastamo, two small yet important transfers of value have occurred. The consumption of a product and a bill payment link the commercial establishment, and thus its larger economic network, to the urban inhabitant. Despite the seeming banality of the monetary exchange imbedded within an otherwise indulgent evening, such value transfers—and associated value-state changes—comprise the lifeblood of the contemporary city; the city being simultaneously both an instrument to understand, as well as a derivative of, value exchange. It is important to note that understanding of value should not be simply limited to financial value. A more encompassing concept of value may provide an enhanced reading of the urban realm, and thus a greater agency for design fields. *Lines of Engagement* expounds a conceptual value-based lens through which the city can be understood. By following the veins of value thresholds throughout the body of the city, one can dissect the city per the value-based lens of resource transference.

As a means to more cohesively comprehend and relatedly capitalize upon opportunities for increased design agency in the built environment, this chapter posits a value-based reading of the urban condition for use by architects, designers, and urbanists. A value-based process of inquiry can be pursued in supplement to primary modes of architectural or urban discourse that unpack the contemporary urban condition through more traditional methods of reading—including, but not limited to, historicity, architectural lineage, typology, and urban precedent. In its most pragmatic understanding, value-based thinking can result in more leverage at the table where the decisions are really made. This can open the eyes of the designer, architect, and urbanist to the possibilities for proactive impact.[1]

The Strained Evolution of Post-Fordist Cities

Since the earliest days of human congregation into structured communities and networked societies, the city has provided a platform for the exchange of goods and services while also providing various forms of protection—whether economic, social, or physical. At its most fundamental level, the city structures, frames, and supports the political, economic, and social systems of people. The city as organism is not a new idea in urban discourse. However, urban growth and consumption patterns stemming from "Fordist" thought have pushed global cities into new territory

130 Edward Becker

beyond society's own ability to effectively control and manipulate them. Though examples still persist of new, prescriptive "utopic" urban visions being implemented across the globe, we must question the relevancy of such rigid visions as cities become increasingly fluid, borderless, and multifaceted. In places such as Helsinki, often regarded as one of the world's most effectively planned cities, suburban sprawl and increased car usage threaten planning ideals. The urban visions of Eliel Saarinen's Plan for Greater Helsinki in 1918 and Heikki von Hertzen's original concepts for the garden city of Tapiola speak to the dynamics between "utopic" visions and their implementation in practice. On one hand, the ideals of the post-Fordist city still seem saturated in trends of Fordist consumption; on the other hand, the contemporary city seems to be thriving with novel opportunities for new forms of inhabitation, such as cost-sharing, flexible transit, and work economies engendered by novel digital technologies.

The interrelationships between consumption, the availability of capital, and policy, among other factors, drive the unfolding of the built environment at macro scales. Despite such dehumanizing scales of interaction, designers, architects, and urbanists could benefit by isolating instances of the aforementioned urban drivers relative to capital. Through such isolation followed by collective inquiry, "lines of engagement" emerge, leading to a play-by-play understanding of the fluctuations and dynamics of the post-Fordist built environment. In an attempt to study a dynamic built environment, questions such as "How can one begin to understand the language of the post-Fordist city with such rapidly changing and diverse conditions?" and associatively, "How can one make an impact or have design agency in the post-Fordist city?" may be more effectively answered via value-based methods of understanding.

Design Agency in the Post-Fordist City

In 2016, my business partner (a financial analyst) and I (an architect) cofounded the Finnish-American architectural office VÖR. Due not only to the massive capital expenditure associated with the recently completed Guggenheim Helsinki Competition—nearly \$8 million of free labor was "donated" by 1,715 entrants—but also to other disciplinary factors, including architecture's generally anemic state of agency in the built environment, our multidisciplinary practice began pursuing newfound opportunities to explore the role of risk and value-based thinking. Operating via a lean, slow-growth, investment-based business model, the office's ongoing architectural projects and research endeavors aim to both comprehend and capitalize upon value dynamics in the contemporary built environment. In practice, this means that despite being a more traditionally structured architectural office, we actively seek an equity stake in each of our projects.

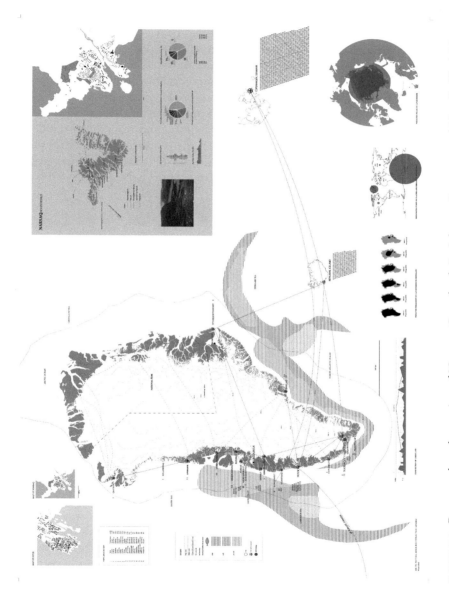

FIGURE 7.2 Resource-based mapping of Narsaq, Greenland. By Johanna Brummer and Natalia Vladykina.

132 Edward Becker

As opposed to a competition-based project acquisition model characteristic of other young practices, we proactively create proposals based upon what we see as value-based opportunities for engagement within the built environment. Not only does an equity stake allow for more leverage in value-based decision-making, but it also provides flexibility relative to organizational arrangements of project stakeholders and consultants. While speaking purely in terms of the office's business and agency-related perspectives, rather than a design-based standpoint, an emphasis on value-dynamics and value-based opportunities for proactive engagement within the urban realm may provide a critical path for design-related professionals as we attempt to effectively comprehend, analyze, and respond to rapidly changing spatial conditions in the global post-Fordist city. Identifying "lines of engagement" relative to value transfer may help designers and planners alike to illuminate the inner workings of the contemporary city.

Value Dynamics: Three States of Value

In terms of value-based decision-making, one must not only question what states of value exist in the built environment, but also how decisions are made relative to the underlying perceptions of those values in the global post-Fordist city. In an effort to both provide a model for increased design agency as well as to increase the possibilities for proactive impact, value is categorized into the following three primary states: *dormant*, *potential*, and *applied*. These states are inextricably linked to one another and are by no means static. The following paragraphs describe the proposed "value-states" and offer their conceptual application in decision-making processes as a means to proactively impact the contemporary city.

Dormant Value

Private property, or real estate, and the concept of ownership are closely linked to the concept of dormant value in the built environment. This particular type of value is described as dormant due to its faunal resemblance—in, or as if in, a deep sleep. Stemming from a systemic shift in the Middle Ages, real estate became inherently linked to private property with a designated owner embedded within common society. In the case of the nascent United States, the concept of ownership was particularly powerful, relating the opportunity to procure property to fundamental inalienable freedoms. It is logical, then, to relate the ownership of property to its use or economic value as the potential for self-sustenance, the most basic form of asset creation, as inherently tied to the products of that property. Self-sustenance, a key concept relative to land ownership in early America, is one example of dormant value.

As an owner maximizes the asset production capabilities of their specific property—growing beets or supplying hay to cattle—the property has produced some entity of economic value. However, if the owner has determined the property to support merely individual sustenance, the assets produced on the real estate, or its economic capability, are deterministically isolated from larger economic systems of exchange. The property contains value because it is capable of producing assets that have reciprocity within an economic system. However, it can be considered dormant because the entities containing actionable economic attributes are deterministically subdued. The assets can be considered off-market or frozen.

"A Room against Ownership" by Aureli provides another glimpse as to what dormant value may look like as a tangible concept. Hans Meyer's 1924 Co-op Zimmer is utilized in the text to demonstrate the opposing economic conditions of use and property.[2] Property, or an entity containing the possibility of owning the labor of people as described by Marx, has its origins in the means to control production and work. Logically, one would not claim to own anything unless it contains reciprocity within an economic system, meaning that it has economic value. Otherwise ownership would simply be irrelevant. Thus, relative to the concept of dormant value, ownership of an asset entails its involvement in an economic system. Ownership can therefore be understood as the inverse condition of use or sharing.

In spatial terms, the practice of use or using implies a lack of economically transferrable value to the lessee. The lack of reciprocity in an economic system for the lessee, due to the lack of ownership, provides opportunities to further exemplify dormant value. Like the Mendicant order of the Franciscans described in Aureli's text, a refusal to own as a means to nullify any possibility to exploit others illustrates the creation of dormant value in the built environment. In the case of the Franciscans, sharing the use of physical spaces and objects was a distinctly deterministic act of sharing, purposefully relinquishing control or power over a space or object so that it could be evenly shared. This self-imposed poverty is not distinctly different than the aforementioned example of self-sustenance. Both conditions could be considered a form of impoverishment, as the individual possesses nothing with reciprocity within larger social and economic contexts. Rather, a distinct intent to avoid catalysts of inequality and domination embedded within property or real estate positioned the monks outside the controlling system. Dormant value is economic value, yet as with the example of the Franciscan monks, this value is neutralized through actions and intent. If the institution of the Church or an individual Franciscan leader were to take control of the physical objects and spaces, even on behalf of the larger whole, the dormant value-state would then switch to a state of potential value. Possession is thereby inherently linked to systems of control and dominance.

134 Edward Becker

Potential Value

An asset can be deemed to have potential value so long as it is capable of catalyzing a transactional sequence. Potential value in the built environment is by far the most common value-state because, unlike dormant value, potential value involves some degree of ownership or possession. Through the process of deduction, the state of having possession introduces an additional asset-based relationship—that between the possessor and possessee. Described as the origin of inequality, the seminal relationship between the differing socio-economic classes has a lengthy and complex history in economics. However, in its most straightforward and ubiquitous form, money or currency can be understood as a repository of potential value. Attempting to deconstruct the properties of money and real estate as differentiated assets in the built environment may assist in the understanding of potential value's ecosystem of influences, thus uncovering an urban identity.

As described by Jacob in "Money: Time: Space," money is in some ways related to potential energy.[3] Money has the ability to catalyze transactions. Transactions would not commence without a trust in the relevancy of money. Money is referred to as being both the symbol and lifeblood of a structured economic system and monetary transactions as being essentially a form of bartering where a piece of paper or metal is a repository for applied value. There are many historical examples of the failure of trust in such structured systems. In these instances, the differentiation between money and potential energy is obvious. Unlike the inability of potential energy to evaporate or disappear within an isolated system, a property described by Newton's Law, the potential value in money can swell or shrink considerably with even just a simple qualitative change or shift in perception. Jacob describes money as being a form of imaginary energy while nonetheless having concrete effects on reality.

Money's potential value, or the potential of money to catalyze systems of exchange, is highly volatile and is time- and space-sensitive. A prime example is inflation, a condition where the purchasing power of money falls while the related costs of goods and services rise. Within standard economic systems, money's ability to accrue interest is one dynamic characteristic of its power potential. External factors, including demand, greatly impact the cost of goods and services, thereby relatedly linking the relative value of money to an unstable continuum. Money, an asset, is equivalent to other assets such as real estate, in that the potential value in real estate can also catalyze transactions. However, unlike real estate, money—synonymous in this case with currency—can be deemed a "proxy asset" due to its use-value stemming from relevancy to an economic system primarily based upon trust—this following the movement of many countries away from the gold standard during the 20th century. Real estate—synonymous in this case with property—is an asset that yields greater leverage for transactional brokerage, and thus power, due in part to its condition as a physically tangible entity. Both money and real estate hold potential value.

In a similar manner to the potential energy of money, real estate is two-faced, its value stemming from a physical product as well as an imaginary system of perception. As we are now a decade removed from the largest financial crisis in US history during the late 2000s, we can view the social phenomenon of the housing bubble as a glaring example of how dependent real estate value is on behavioral patterns, or as John Keynes and Robert Shiller have labeled the phenomenon, animal spirits.[4] This example can also illustrate how one might deconstruct the origins of potential value relative to single-family homes, an asset type particularly prone over the last decade to financial volatility. In regard to the aforementioned housing bubble, this singular contagion was not only emblematic of society's behavioral patterns relative to hope and fear, but it also frames the more general patterns of societal perception as Shiller has professed. In the case of the United States, society has placed a significant trust in the power of single-family homes to hold potential value.[5]

The greater the perceived potential value, the greater the desire for that asset. Thus, at least in the United States, the expanses of cookie-cutter suburban homes are indicative of society's value perception of this singular asset type. As Shiller describes, the Homestead Act of 1862 capped a lengthy period of evolution relative to the concept of ownership, and relatedly to the American Dream of owning one's own home. From the feudal period when modern land tenure practices first began to evolve to the end of the 18th century, the concept of home ownership has been intimately linked to ideas of freedom and power. The Homestead Act of 1862 furthered socio-cultural perceptions of freedom and power via property ownership by providing the policy measures to back those perceptions.[6] As such, a uniquely American system of checks and balances on real estate value emerged. This system of checks and balances impacts a loose societal framework of square footage, aesthetics, layout, and infrastructure. In addition, the system greatly influences what types of residential buildings are constructed and what types of residential buildings have the highest resale value. It can be labeled a circular system of perception and actualization.

While the potential value of the single-family home is a manifestation of perceptions driven by social and cultural norms, the single-family house is nonetheless an asset. The home cannot escape the law of supply and demand, with the only true value of the asset being what a perspective buyer is willing to pay. Thus, for this particular example of the American single-family home, and real estate in general, the potential value of the entity is never truly known until a transactional undertaking is completed. It is at the culmination of the transaction where one entity (such as real estate), and the other entity that has reciprocal agency (such as money), are exchanged so that the real estate shifts from having potential value to having applied value, relative to the original possessor. The possessee subsequently acquires an entity with only estimated potential value, because it is not until they in turn complete a transactional process that the applied value will be known. As such, existing assets linger in a state of potential value as long as they are possessed.

Applied Value

The third and final value-state to introduce is applied value. Applied value is dynamic rather than latent, and is proactive rather than reactionary. It contrasts the dormant value-state that has been defined as one in which an asset is off-market or frozen, whether due to the lack of integration into an existing economic system or due to a lack of ownership. Applied value-states also contrast potential value-states, or those that involve some form of ownership and are capable of catalyzing a transactional sequence. A future possessor may apply value to an existing asset by purchasing it or by transforming an asset they already possess. Thus, applied value is proactive and procedural, unlike potential value, which is fundamentally reactionary. Through the various processes that impact the asset, it may gain value via proper planning and decision-making, whereas the potential value-state relies solely on external factors. The applied value-state is proactive, because value can be applied to the asset regardless of pre-existing properties or conditions. As such, the applied value-state is open-ended, malleable, and perhaps most importantly, relative to predetermined market volatility.

Despite the clear financial advantages of operating in a proactive and procedural applied value-state rather than the contrasting, reactionary potential value-state, the applied value-state also arguably induces the emergence of capitalism's most undesirable byproducts, namely inequality. The logical output of a system receiving applied value inputs is a greater disparity between those that have and those that have not. As described by Ryan and Bello in "The Fiscal Topography of the Shrinking City," the global city's tall towers and financial returns are not only inverses to, but also direct causes of, poverty seen elsewhere.[7]

Chasing Lines of Engagement **137**

If we refer to the prior text regarding dormant value, applied value is diametrically opposed to the ideals of the Mendicant order of the Franciscans. The Franciscans chose to avoid ownership so as not to possess economic power, thereby exploiting others. At the other ideological extreme, the process of systematized market-driven restructuring, termed by various authors as "neoliberalisation," exemplifies the applied value-state's peak financial agency.[8] Neoliberalism as a philosophical doctrine relating to deregulation and "intelligence" of markets, can provide an effective lens through which we can study the dynamics and characteristics of applied value systems in the built environment.

The anti-statist or anti-institutionalist ideology of economic neoliberalism stems from its philosophic predecessor, economic liberalism—a system of economics based upon individual choice and a reduction of institutional influence. Based upon concepts originating from the Enlightenment era, people make decisions in their own self-interest, and generally, if such a laissez-faire economic philosophy is impeded by excessive regulatory oversight, then the social benefits that the economic liberalist engenders via free choice will be reduced. However, it should be stated that neither liberal nor neoliberal economics have ever occurred in a pure form, thus the outcomes of such systems should be understood as resultants of hybrid conditions. In a similar manner, the urban condition should also be understood as a resultant of hybrid conditions. The social concepts that accompany "utopic" visions become diluted by diverse socio-cultural interests and diverse economic perspectives. That said, one could still comprehend certain tendencies in the built environments of non-socialist societies that result from underlying liberal beliefs. *Fulcrum*, a student-led publication of the Architectural Association, presents a clear example of neoliberalism in economics as it related to applied value. *The Ingot*, a project published by *Fulcrum*, traces the wealth-distribution behaviors of a neoliberalist economy as the lessors of real estate value utilize loans in the form of mortgages to consign the lessee with perpetual conditions of debt.[9] *The Ingot* importantly outlines that neoliberal real estate decisions made in rational self-interest are drastically different than what would be commonly considered as socially progressive (we can generally term self-interest decisions economically rational, although research has demonstrated that this is not necessarily how behaviors result in practice). A lack of comprehensive or macro knowledge is a primary reason self-interest decisions may be irrational.

Like typical development models, a certain portion of the new construction only exist as a means to offload a debt burden, meaning to pass the building construction debt on to the lessees. The lessor's offloading of the debt burden to the lessee supports a compounding economic

138 Edward Becker

benefit for the lessor as rentable space is increased. *The Ingot* diagrammatically demonstrates that the more efficient the debt offloading of the lessor's fixed costs can become, the more opportunity the lessor has to maximize income. As such, a significant portion of the built environment exists primarily as a means to efficiently offload debt. As designers and planners, we must question the social impact of this practice and what opportunities may exist for systemic improvement. As rapid city growth arguably outpaces our own ability to effectively manage and respond, the development of systemic, incentive-based solutions that prioritize the urban inhabitant over individual debt concerns may exist via the uncovering of the "lines of engagement" that drive debt-based decision-making practices. The larger the buildings grow, and associatively the more value is applied to the assets, the greater a differential between those who are consigned to positions of debt and those who are not, namely the common urban inhabitant who holds vastly different perceptions about the use, value, and purpose of urban space. While applying value to an asset is logically the rational choice in financial terms, the tangential social ramifications for such intensified instances of value application are crucial to consider.

Arguably one of the greatest examples of value application in the history of urban development was the design of Frederick Law Olmsted and Calvert Vaux's Central Park in New York City. The Greensward Plan was constructed within a rapidly growing city in need of public park space and provided a butterfly effect of progressive impacts for the city. Perhaps its greatest accomplishment as a designed artifact—at least in economic terms—is its powerfully catalyzing effect on not only the immediately adjacent parcels of land, but also Manhattan as a whole over its lifespan. The park's decline in the late 20th century and improvement in the 1930s generally parallel the potential value-state of the urban asset. It is clear in the example of Central Park that intelligent design in combination with institutional support has resulted in an exceptionally large applied value-state to the City of New York that benefits all citizens regardless of economic intent or background.[10]

In summary, the dynamism of value in the built environment has been categorized into three primary value-states: *dormant, potential,* and *applied*. The fluidity of state-changes and interactions between the three entities comprises the economic landscape of the built environment in non-socialist societies. Whether one is buying a cup of coffee or designing new infrastructure for human-centered interactions, a complex interplay of fluctuating value-states is occurring within the spatial constructs that comprise our built environments. Value-based thinking can enhance the reading of how decisions are made in the built environment by deconstructing the logic of conflicting interest groups. This in turn can increase the agency of design professionals, as they are more capable of identifying value-add opportunities in practice and pursuing socially equitable outcomes. As one follows the veins of value thresholds or state-changes throughout the body of the city, one can dissect the contemporary city using the value-based lens of resource transference, thereby opening novel insights into the rationality of the urban realm. As global cities become increasingly more complex due to evolving technologies and rapid growth, among many other factors, framing the city through *Lines of Engagement* can uncover the complexities, layers, hierarchies, and sensual engagements of the extra-urban context, as well as providing agency for design professionals to speculate on the future city organization and development. Lines of engagement are metaphysical while also concurrently being tactile. Examples of the physical manifestations of this tactility and their encompassing metaphysical outlooks on contemporary society are provided in the following sections. The threshold conditions driven by the interactions between potential and applied value-states comprise the fabric of the post-Fordist city.

Projects

The processes of urbanization are constituted by a collective web of tactile value-based decisions while also being catalyzed by the availability of resources, infrastructure, and energy, among other factors. Such factors—intimately related to the processes of urbanization and the value-based decisions they support—were the subject of housing and urbanization studios taught at Aalto University in Espoo, Finland in Spring 2014 and Fall 2015. Over a four-week timeframe, the students examined the Nordic contexts of Norway, Sweden, and Finland, as well as Estonia, Greenland, and the northwestern territories of Russia relative to resource dynamics, instability, and associatively, risk. Urban research was initiated following the provision of resource-related topical areas to student groups. These included, but were not limited to, resource extraction, water, infrastructure, and energy. The groups subsequently engaged in a comprehensive issue-identification phase relative to their particular topic area within northern Europe before isolating specific conditions of the built environment. By isolating specific issues or conditions for further study, the students were able to research the topics at an in-depth level, thereby engendering a myriad of tangential observations, speculations, and related critical inquiries. This hourglass-shaped process supported the development of the following projects that approach the urban condition as a manifestation of an ecosystem of interactions catalyzed by fluid

140 Edward Becker

systems of value exchange and often-conflicting interests. Specificities of regional culture, climate, and landscape contextualized the projects. Project texts are paired with mappings illustrating value-state understandings and relationships in practice. Despite the apparent macro scale of inquiry, each project is rooted in the relatively small-scale, value-based decisions that involve resource exchange at scales of the individual and community.[11] Potential and applied value-states and associated "lines of engagement" were particularly formative in the uncovering and mapping of the following global territories. As illustrated by the following projects, infrastructure, energy, landscape, and socio-economic conditions spur urbanization, which in turn is comprised of a plethora of tactile value-based decisions. The following projects—*The Absolute Arctic*, *Aerotropolis*, *Watershed*, and *Arctic Natural Resource Extraction: Oil*— have each explored value-based relationships at a variety of scales and across geopolitical boundaries and cultures.

The Absolute Arctic

Fascination with the unreachable and unknown Arctic drove expedition after expedition seeking to claim uncharted territory. Monarchies and nation states competed for the honor of sponsoring the first navigators. During the Cold War, Arctic airspace was the shortest distance between the USSR to the US—missiles pointed north in both countries. As nations make overlapping claims to the Arctic territories, geopolitical economic and political interests have the potential to become increasingly conflicted.

The romanticized, harsh Arctic environment is losing its inaccessibility as anthropogenic global warming and the intensifying exploitation of the Arctic Ocean bring dramatic changes to both the regional culture and environment. Cross-border infrastructural developments related to global shipping and oil, mineral, and gas extraction are severely disrupting a unique ecosystem. Indigenous peoples in the Arctic countries are already struggling to maintain their traditional lifestyles dependent upon seasonal hunting and fishing. Cultures historically tended to rely on predictable ice conditions. The interface of how such different cultures can coexist in the future is unknown as natural borders slowly melt into extinction. As the ecology of the Arctic lines diminishes, the territory will gradually lose its romantic identity. Only the abstract geographic and astronomic position of 66°33'44"N of the Arctic Circle will remain. This research focused on global shipping and port infrastructure, along with the related biological contaminants that shipping brings to the Arctic region. The opposing macro conditions of value

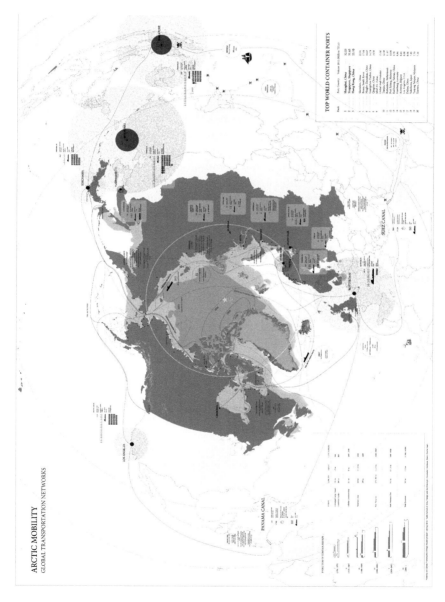

FIGURE 7.3 Arctic mobility: global transportation networks. By Heini-Emilia Saari and Anastasia Laki.

between geopolitical economic interests and localized biological diversity are symbolized through the design of Arctic mobility mappings (Figure 7.3).

Aerotropolis

A series of extremely isolated Soviet military settlements with standardized urban plans are located along Russia's Arctic coastline. The typologically unique Soviet settlements are indicative of both the macro geopolitical interests of the Soviet state as well as the socio-cultural factors of the communist system from which the settlement patterns were derived. Each extremely isolated settlement of study is comprised of related Soviet-era communal housing, air, and port facilities, and common spaces, and is disconnected from all road and energy infrastructure. The decaying, standardized housing blocks that still display Soviet iconography sit in stark contrast to the beauty and diversity of the Arctic coastal landscapes upon which they have been placed. This example of a replicated "urban" plan in the isolated north exemplifies the geopolitical values of the Soviet system and indicates a unique type of urban condition stemming from socialist value-based decisions.

The distances between settlements to three different continents, Asia, Europe, and North America, are relatively short. As such, the distance between time zones is comparably shorter than anywhere else in the world. This advantageous global proximity was a seminal reason why the Soviet state originally established military settlements with airfields along the Arctic ocean, and it is also an important design factor in the project *Aerotropolis*. The proposal extends the logic of this type-based urban condition to the present day. Existing Soviet airfields and advantageous global

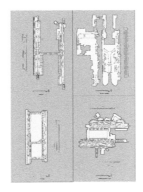

FIGURE 7.4 Arctic-to-global airport scales. By Ron Aasholm, Xudong Yan, and Martins Smilts.

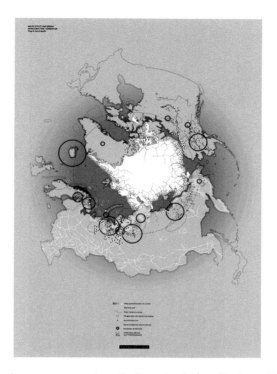

FIGURE 7.5 Arctic energy mapping. By Ron Aasholm, Xudong Yan, and Martins Smilts.

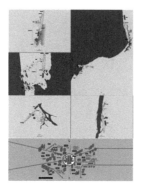

FIGURE 7.6 Soviet Arctic urban development. By Ron Aasholm, Xudong Yan, and Martins Smilts.

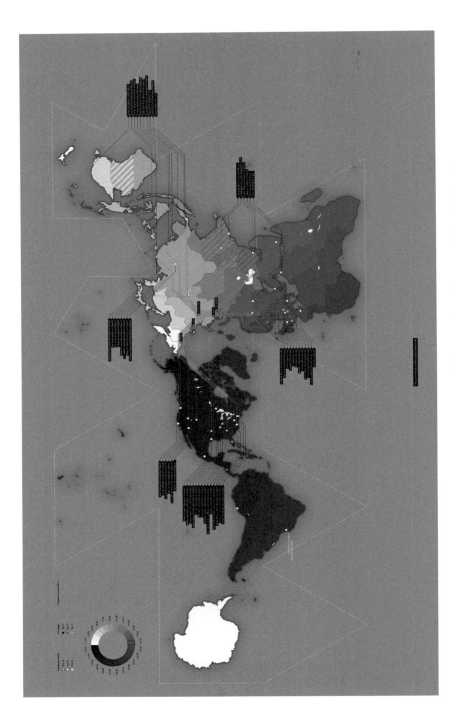

FIGURE 7.7 Arctic airfields to global flight routes. By Ron Aasholm, Xudong Yan, and Martins Smilts.

proximity enhance the potential for Arctic airport development and air traffic stopovers that efficiently tap into existing global air infrastructure. *Aerotropolis* illustrates the type-based urbanization of Soviet value-based decision-making and proposes the development of one settlement and airfield into a global airline hub.

Watershed

Watershed is a study of rare earth elements (REE) in Greenland and the landscape destruction that results from REE extraction. In addition to extraction research, including REE global uses and distribution networks, the project imagines the impact of rising sea levels and increasingly damaging extraction processes on the town of Narsaq, located a few kilometers southwest of the Kvanefield mine in Greenland. Value-based decisions relating landscape degradation to the mining towns and livelihoods that are supported by extraction relates to much larger questions of technology's impact on environment and society generally. *Watershed* questions the destruction of biologically sensitive areas for the sake of high-tech product production, REE being a crucial component to many commonly used high-tech devices. Narsaq is economically connected to the Kvanefield mine, and thus the global REE markets. In regard to value-based decisions that involve landscape and extraction, *Watershed* questions "the point of no return, in which choices that were made could no longer be reversed."

In addition to the REE research component, Watershed proposes a scenario in which the mining companies dug hundreds of meters deep into the earth's core until all resources possible were extracted and the Kvanefield mine was exhausted. The process of excavating the earth left behind a gigantic void, an erased landscape signaling the ruthless resource extraction occurring throughout the Arctic region. A few kilometers southwest from the Kvanefield mine, the city of Narsaq, originally home to only 1,500 people, experienced negative growth. *Watershed* states that in the following centuries most of the city of Narsaq was flooded and submerged as the ice sheets kept receding and the water levels continued to rise due to global warming, an environmental effect resulting from global production and overconsumption. Whenever a building was taken by the sea, its interior spaces were cast in concrete and left in place as the memory of an absence in the small northern city that once was so full of life. *Watershed* questions the paradoxical value-based relationships between urban life, landscape, and economy.

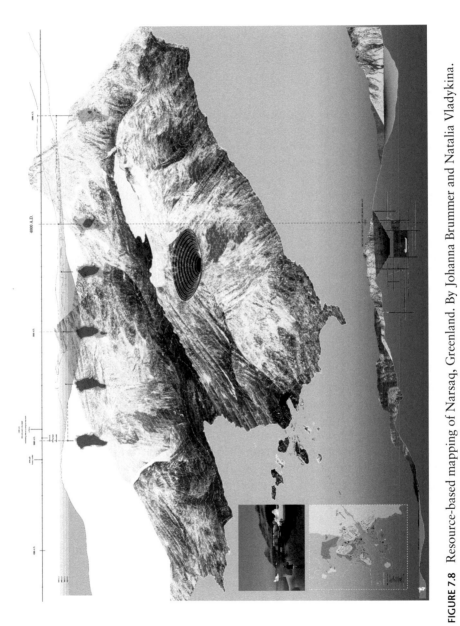

FIGURE 7.8 Resource-based mapping of Narsaq, Greenland. By Johanna Brummer and Natalia Vladykina.

Arctic Natural Resource Extraction: Oil

Geopolitical interest in the Arctic region has rapidly escalated in recent years due in part to the confirmation of vast quantities of oil and gas that resides below the Arctic seabed—a volume that comprises approximately one third of the world's resources. Stemming from the region's extreme climatic conditions, accessibility to the Arctic has historically been very limited; exploration and drilling costs, the vulnerability of extraction operations, and human health concerns are each primary risk factors that have impacted the growth of resource extraction. This study focused on the Norwegian oil and gas industry, one of the most successful energy-based industries in the world in terms of holistic economic benefit. The industry's success is visibly apparent through the exceptional quality of its host country's wealth allocation and energy distribution networks—systems supported by intelligent governance. The infrastructure that comprises Norway's oil and gas industry has quickly been expanded into the North Sea, including offshore and subsea oil platforms as well as a vast network of pipelines connecting Norway with mainland Europe. The aforementioned pipelines have spurred the development of larger port facilities and construction management industries, while also attracting the corporate headquarters of global companies—an attraction that in turn affects the living standards of towns previously based on the fishing industry.

As the project's linkage of relationships suggests, a comprehension of the historic patterns of urban development associated with the Norwegian fishing industry can be utilized as an intellectual lens through which to study the significantly more expansive oil industry. As one begins to study how fishing as an economic lifeline supported a multitude of small villages located along Norway's rugged coastline, certain "lines of engagement" emerge that paint a comprehensive picture of resource exchange as it relates to food. Storehouses and piers are built along the water. The capital flow then extends from storehouses to associative industries such as hardware, housing, and other support services. Exterior economic opportunities and pressures related to the appetite for fish drive the internal logistics of such small communities through the thresholds of value transfer. Storehouses are located near to the pier to economize offloading. Houses are located in close proximity to protect from the harsh climate while also minimizing circulatory distances relative to the harbor.

If one were to study one particularly emblematic threshold between opposing conditions of value in harbor-town environment, it would probably be that of the storehouses and boatsheds. These physical archetypes are vestiges of value. They are a resultant of a flowing stream

148 Edward Becker

of value-exchange that links even the smallest fishing towns to larger systems of commerce. Both storehouses and boatsheds exhibit a characteristic layout, and proportion is based upon an economy of means. The value-based importance of fish and boat storage impacts the logics and precision of building proportion and place. Even such base factors as available material length influence architectural proportion—and thus overall aesthetics—to a great degree, as an applied value-state beyond the application of readily available materials is simply not rational.

In a similar manner to the complexity of transmission lines in the Norwegian fishing industry previously discussed, the project *Arctic Natural Resource Extraction: Oil* comparatively analyzed a condition of value transfer between offshore oil rigs and the land-based manifestations of that value transfer. Rigs relate to pipelines which then relate to a variety of on shore physical constructs—buildings, infrastructure, etc. Urban conditions in Stavanger, for example, are directly impacted by the landscape of oil extraction facilities offshore, the linkage being an invisible, sub-surface network of resource-transference infrastructure.

Why do the patterns of urban development in Norwegian fishing towns such as Grip, Ona, and Å so closely resemble a plethora of other seaside Nordic villages such as the Finnish towns of Björkö, Nötö, and Utö? How are such consistent patterns of decision making applied in the built environment? Through a value-based reading of potential and applied value, the answer can be narrowed to the various thresholds of value exchange—social, cultural, financial—with each being intimately related to the next. To provide one additional example of lines of engagement relative to the fishing industry, one could categorize, isolate, and comparatively analyze a "line" that connects a boathouse in Nötö to a storehouse in Turku, Finland to a distribution facility on the outskirts of Helsinki to a red-brick building in Teurastamo, Helsinki where a group of women from the corner table softly slip in from the comfortable evening air to have dinner, the restaurant's interior abuzz with conversation and the smell of fresh fish, the fish's glistening scales, texture of meat, and rhythm of bone structure being reminiscent of the layerings, hierarchies, and integral relationships of the built environment within which the resource is being consumed.

The evolving web of value-based decisions that drive urbanization is constructed of threads, or "lines," of related logic. These "lines of engagement" can be utilized as an intellectual framework for architects, designers, and urbanists alike to more effectively explore and comprehend the rapidly changing urban conditions of the contemporary city. Through a value-based inquiry relative to food, money, and real estate, this chapter explicates the identification of value-add opportunities in practice as a means to more effectively comprehend the contemporary city's local and global intersections. Student projects

FIGURE 7.9 Norwegian oil infrastructure. By Stefanos Theodorou and Tommy Degerth.

illustrate the complexity of overlapping value networks and the macro-scale influences of landscape, energy, and infrastructure on the contemporary city. Unlike the prescriptive utopic visions of the past, *Lines of Engagement* questions the relevancy of such rigid urban visions as cities become increasingly

FIGURE 7.10 Traditional storehouses and boatsheds, Nötö Harbor, Finland. By Edward Becker.

fluid, borderless, and multifaceted. This intellectual framework supports the development of a more socially equitable built environment, as well as a future trajectory as to how we act upon the cities of tomorrow.

Notes

1 "Gregg Pasquarelli Interview," in *Perspecta 47: Money* (Cambridge, MA: MIT, 2014), pp. 51–56.
2 Pier Vittorio Aureli, "A Room against Ownership," in *Real Estates: Life without Debt*, ed. Jack Self and Shumi Bose (London: Bedford, 2014), pp. 42–44.
3 Sam Jacob, "Money: Time: Space," in *Real Estates: Life without Debt*, ed. Jack Self and Shumi Bose (London: Bedford, 2014), pp. 76–79.
4 George A. Akerlof and Robert J. Shiller, *Animal Spirits: How Human Psychology Drives the Economy, and Why It Matters for Global Capitalism* (Princeton, NJ: Princeton University Press, 2010).
5 "Robert Shiller Interview," in *Perspecta 47: Money* (Cambridge, MA: MIT Press, 2014), pp. 143–146.
6 Ibid.
7 "The Fiscal Topography of the Shrinking City," in *Perspecta 47: Money* (Cambridge, MA: MIT Press, 2014), pp. 198–204.
8 Neil Brenner, "Neoliberalisation," in *Real Estates: Life without Debt*, ed. Jack Self and Shumi Bose (London: Bedford, 2014), pp. 16–26.
9 Jack Self, "The Ingot," in *Real Estates: Life without Debt*, ed. Jack Self and Shumi Bose (London: Bedford, 2014), Figure E.

Chasing Lines of Engagement **151**

10 Witold Rybczynski, *A Clearing in the Distance: Frederick Law Olmsted and America in the Nineteenth Century* (New York: Scribner, 1999).

11 Urban research includes both mappings and edited text created as part of housing and urbanization studios taught at Aalto University in Espoo, Finland in Spring 2014 and Fall 2015. The studios were taught by the author and Frances Hsu, coordinator. The following students and their related projects are listed in order of inclusion in the publication: *Oil Infrastructure Mapping: Mardu, Estonia*, Disa Reuterswärd; *Resource-based Mapping of Narsaq, Greenland*, Johanna Brummer and Natalia Vladykina; *The Absolute Arctic*, Heini Emilia-Saari and Anastasia Laki; *Aerotropolis*, Ron Aasholm, Xudong Yan, and Martins Smilts; *Watershed*, Johanna Brummer and Natalia Vladykina; *Arctic Natural Resource Extraction*, Stefanos Theodorou and Tommy Degerth.

PART III
Typology

8

CHASING STRATEGIES FOR THE POST-CRISIS

Emmanuelle Chiappone-Piriou

Crisis

Today, it appears impossible to contest the analysis that our globalized world is facing a generalized state of crisis, and so are our cities. Some may still choose to respond to the many signs of the now irreversible climate change with guilty ignorance. However, faced with the multiplication of natural disasters and the scarcity of global resources, as well as with all forms of disruption in the social, political, cultural or economic spheres, the majority will tend to agree that we are indeed living in critical times.

Our perception of the crisis is still anchored to the Marxist definition as a, at times violent, sudden burst that is the condition of possible revolution, or at least of a collective reinvention. Periods of crisis lead to the shaking and annihilation of the established systems of representations; they resonate with calls for emancipation and political imagination, and see the emergence of new idioms, considered to be best suited to describe the new state of the world and to invent ways to act upon it.

Architecture is no exception. Historically, it has progressed through a series of internal crises fostered by the rejection of established models in moments of societal, political, and ecological collapse. These crises have generated calls, in the form of manifestoes or projects, for the expansion of the field and the reinvention of architecture's uses and procedures. Avant-gardists understood the social project of emancipation as having to be an aesthetical one too, and architecture has thus had to turn into a new sensitive apparatus which draws from the cross-pollination with other disciplinary spheres to produce new experiences. In particular, post-war Europe saw the emergence of an experimental architecture as a corollary to the combined societal shifts of the 1950s and 1960s and the terminal crisis of the "Modern." The post-war urbanism, as an impoverished, normative and homogenizing version of early modernism, clashed with the societal and political desire to account for singularity, exceptions, and margins. In its either joyful or more critical manifestations, this movement advocated for emancipation from hegemonic functionalism, articulated through the assignment of a new place to the individual, as a driving force within the city and society.

Our individual relationship to global phenomena has radically changed over recent years with the rise of what Benjamin Bratton calls "the stack"—the "accidental megastructure" composed of our multiple computational systems, including the Internet of Things, mobiles devices, and smart city systems.[1] With (almost) a smartphone in each hand, we have immediate access to processing power that surpasses the capabilities of almost any of the 1980s' supercomputers. Cloud and performance computing allow us to actively participate, in real time, in global financial and cultural exchanges, and to activate localized processes and practices—material and immaterial alike. Yet globalization is still perceived as an abstract and deterritorialized apparatus whose constitution and processes remain invisible. Only when it impacts our daily life negatively is it experienced in a very concrete manner. Its last and most extreme manifestation occurred as the 2008 financial crisis, a brutal and unexpected disruption of the autonomous and auto-engendering financial system. Its backlashes, however, were anything but abstract, made apparent on the labor market, the value of resources, and in real estate (particularly in the US) through the loss of home ownership for large populations, the increase in renting, and the rise of inequalities due to gentrification.[2]

Nevertheless, the past decade has given sufficient proof that the crisis has lost its regenerative power, or rather that the faith in said power has ceased to be operative. Indeed, the narrative of the crisis has been integrated as a ruling mechanism by the naturalized capitalist system and can be reproduced *ad libitum* to reaffirm and extend its domination.[3] The mechanism by which revolution and reinvention were produced has muted into a conservative one, which acts in the manner of a slow-course degenerative condition that would indefinitely postpone the conclusive event, the advent of a terminal crisis.

The correspondent uncertainty toward the future that pervades all the strata of our society is reflected in architecture. Unfortunately, architects appear to be ill equipped to face the challenges of an increasingly complex and fragmented world, and to operate in this crippling state of permanent crisis. All the well-known postures fail: theory is hesitating, manifestoes proclaiming yet another paradigm shift are piling up, and utopia has been replaced by short-term visions of a smart future. Tafuri wrote in 1976:

> Paradoxically, the new tasks given to architecture are something besides or beyond architecture. In recognizing this situation . . . . I am expressing no regret, but neither am I making an apocalyptic prophecy. No regret, because when the role of a discipline ceases to exist, to try to stop the course of things is only regressive utopia, and of the worst kind. No prophecy, because the process is actually taking place daily before our eyes.[4]

A superficial look at the state of the discipline today gives the illusionary impression that there are very few options left. Architecture appears to be navigating between the cynical celebration of the market and a withdrawal into historical models as the only ground left on which it can rouse itself from its impotency.

In this context, architects are tempted to cling onto attitudes that reposition it as an active part of the "forces trying to arrive at new social and urban structures." Fifty years ahead, the 1960s remain associated with the heroic figure of the architect, who proclaimed the expansion of his authority on the totality of the environment ("Alles ist Architekur," as Hans Hollein wrote) and took on the "revolutionary" role Bernard Tschumi describes.[5] Romantically, these moments are identified with the clear expression of political desire, and the last attempts to redefine the collective before the post-modern withdrawal into autonomy. This revolutionary attitude is an assertion of the societal, cultural, and political ambitions of architecture, all of which are currently disappearing under the conjugated actions of the mutually dependent non-architectural, and supposedly abstract forces among which are the market, the normative apparatus, or computation. Contemporary architects thus recall a historical moment in which, as Banham wrote in his 1976 recollection of the "megastuctural" moment, architecture was still relevant and "architectural design could get into the act somehow, could help resolve 'the insoluble problem of the modern city.'"[6]

Beyond the City

Our contemporary territories are forged by highly complex and volatile mechanisms: they are the result as much of local dynamics as of the set of institutions and processes that constitute the global. The ascendance of information technologies over the last decades and the mobility and liquidity of capital characteristics of the market have reached a stage at which they almost entirely organize our geographies, across multiple scales. "The big city is the place of contact of all acting elements in the world," wrote Le Corbusier in 1924.[7] The transnational infrastructures have drawn a world map whose dominant structure is constituted by global cities,[8] or such infrastructures integrate into the emergence of mega-cities.[9] As sites of high density, as well as the embodiment of our cultures, cities are the epicenter of complex phenomena shaping the world through connectivity. In this context of global integration, they are simultaneously responsible for, and suffering from, the consequences of global financial or ecological mutations. To an extent, their sustainability, rise, or decay, as well as their internal evolutions, are dependent on systems of transaction and on the competition that follows as a corollary, as not all cities benefit equally from the transnational networks.

This analysis, however, provides only a metonymic description of the urban phenomenon. Global cities do indeed stand out as single entities within a global network of interactions, both symbolically and materially, through their marketed image of supposedly unique cultural and financial hubs and their imprint, first and foremost ecological. Yet even this observation needs to be balanced. Data collection reveals inner variations within the urban fabric that blur the distinction between the city and its exterior, thus revealing a less differentiated landscape.[10] As Archizoom's *No-stop City* (1967–1971) anticipated, cities have indeed long ceased to be unified and stable realities. Instead, cities have been dissolved in an extensive urban realm that has long swallowed the rural and blurred all distinctions with the natural. Our contemporary condition is one in which the natural and the built have fully merged and innovative connections have emerged between various domains—the material and the digital, the public and the private, the human and the non-human. The *Utopia della quantità*, of which big data marks the advent, draws an informational and infrastructural map of a flat world, mainly produced by non-architectural forces.[11]

This infrastructural nature of our urban realm can nowhere be as clearly observed as in smart cities. One of the most advanced smart cities in the world, Songdo, South Korea, is branded as a city of "perfect balance" between sustainability and high-technology. Its master plan is said to be "designed around the people who live and work there."[12] However, in smart cities such as this, it is not the master plan that creates and organizes urban life. The power apparatus is not articulated through space, but through the thousands of interfaces and sensors collecting data. Not all smart cities are newly planned cities, and this apparatus appears to be merging with existing urban fabrics. No matter how traditional they may appear, our historical cities too are gradually being filled with computation, allowing for the integrated control of almost all aspects of urban life. In the face of rising inequalities and the rarefaction of resources, largely due to the urge to put a stop to the accelerating degradation of our environment, it appears difficult to contest the pragmatic or techno-utopian imperative for change. To varying degrees, according to geographical and social situations, most of us are encouraged to abide by more efficient, better-controlled urban models that regulate all aspects of daily urban life, from transmission to home automation programs.

The generic and optimized smart city could be considered the latest avatar of the top-down urban models that have been implemented since the early 20th century which, devised by the Congrès internationaux d'architecture moderne as of 1928 and theorized in the *Charte d'Athènes* (1933), continue to inform our contemporary making of the city. The "fetishization of data" that is at the heart of their functioning implies a form of reductionism:

> The smart city constructs an urban subject active only to the extent that he or she shoulders responsibilities the public sector has withdrawn from, and is otherwise fundamentally passive. The primary role imagined for such subjects is the generation of data for analysis and construction of projective models.[13]

Left to private interests, the smart city is a perfectly operating machine that, along with Facebook's optimization algorithm and other automatic systems of profiling and social modeling, is a step taken towards "algorithmic governance," articulating an "a-normative objectivity" in which the collective becomes a lure.[14]

Is architecture still fit to propose models to accommodate the complexity of the city, an entity that, embedded into multi-scalar dynamics, has ceased to be highly stable and unified? To put it as Michel Ragon did: can the architect design a "life-like" macro-structure in advance? If life is "rightly made of aleatory and unpredictability," isn't capturing its image stopping its growth and "to some extent to capture life itself"?

What role can the architect play in the emergence of urbanity when non-architectural forces are primarily responsible for shaping the city? How can architecture operate within an infrastructural world that is almost, if not completely, run by computation? Should it still strive to produce qualitative change in an era of pure quantity in which everything "from organisms to machines, from cities to ecosystems, is decomposed in discreet elements which interactions and collective behaviours are analyzed," automated, and predicted? How could it do so when, despite the extreme rationalization that characterizes our computational infrastructure, our world seems increasingly ungovernable? How can architecture implement ideas of connectivity, radical rationality, and emergence—all inherent to computation—to redefine commons and renew citizenship?

In order to address these questions, we propose to revisit two historical architectural discourses on democratization which appear to have particular resonance in today's context: Yona Friedman's *Ville Spatiale* (1959–1960) and Constant's *New Babylon* (1956–1973), both of which

160 Emmanuelle Chiappone-Piriou

contested the then-dominant power structures. This return does not suggest perfect continuity between programs and the current reflections on the how to tackle the complexity of the city. Nonetheless, along with other historical experiments such as Fumihiko Maki's research into Group Form, and Huth and Domenig's exploration of architecture as the "basic vocabulary for all societal and political debates on this evolving humanism," Friedman and Constant's visions carry lessons on how to rethink the city as system, through relationality rather form, and through active processes of choice and aggregation, in opposition to static, linear, and abstracting practices.[15]

We will thus proceed to a cross-reading of both projects, highlighting the concepts and mechanisms that bear potential for the contemporary debate. However, no matter how much resonance they appear to have with issues facing our world, both these attitudes have become fundamentally inoperative at a time when social and ecological pressures impose a redefinition of the scalar hierarchies that structure the world, as well as shift towards materiality and distributive agency.

Democratization: Against the Average Man

"Far from producing urbanity, humanists urban functionalism has dismantled the commons and undermined urban democracy."[16] Dating from 2017, this comment has a sense of *déjà vu* and highlights how the question of democratization of our cities is still addressed in terms of the emancipation from those hegemonic models. Indeed, today's situation holds a striking resemblance with the "crisis of the city" highlighted by the prospective architects of the 1950s and 1960s, the so-called "futurologists." In a time of rapid and radical socio-cultural and political evolution, the neo-avant-garde condemned the profound inadequacy of the existing urban environment to address the demographic explosion, as well as the insufficiency of the hegemonic models being implemented at the time. Inherited from the pre-war modernism, these ideals had evolved into an impoverished and homogenizing functionalism, operating in ways that conserved and reproduced established realities.

On the one hand, Friedman, who has been rediscovered by architects and artists alike at the turn of the 21st century, was one of the first to promote the notions of mobility and unpredictability against the static post-war city. Constant's *New Babylon*, on the other hand, remains the primary example of the Situationist intellectual program of a "unitary urbanism" that rejected functionalism and efficiency in favor of a spontaneous, individual definition of the urban realm. In this perspective, *New Babylon* was designed as a "qualitatively superior" social model in the form of a "built situation."

Chasing Strategies for the Post-crisis **161**

In the footsteps of the first objections raised against the modernist ambition of a "total architecture," Yona Friedman criticized, as early as 1958, the inertia of the architectural discipline and its unresponsiveness to societal and technical evolutions, while outlining the disaggregation of cities as their necessary corollary.[17] In his turn, Michel Ragon—the architectural critic and instigator of such groups as the GIAP (the International Group of Prospective Architecture, of which Yona Friedman, Guy Rottier, and Pascal Häusermann, among others, were members)—criticized architecture for being "50 years late." "How to build a city that can adapt to the unknown data of near future?"[18] The unpredictability of social phenomena was at the heart of Yona Friedman's project. As a result, he radically rejected the normativity of an urbanism that he criticized as being integrally based on statistics, and thus hermetic to adaptability. In Friedman's view, architecture had to provide models capable of accommodating both the rapid technification of society and the resultant changes in human relations. To an extent, Friedman's *Spatial City* matches the megastructural ambition to "make sense of an architecturally incomprehensible condition in the world's cities," as Reyner Banham wrote, and "to resolve the conflict between design and spontaneity, the large and the small, the permanent and the transient."[19]

Friedman shared Constant's interest in Eerhard Huyzinga's definition of the *Homo ludens* which set the foundation for the *New Babylon* project: "The liberation of the ludic potential of Man is directly linked to its liberation as a social being."[20] Man, liberated from work by automation, would be able to develop the creative modality of his being as a result of the disentanglement of labor from productive force. The corollary atomization of society and the dissolution of any institution (state and community alike) were celebrated as the condition of the liberation of the full ludic potential of the un-alienated individual. Both architects built upon notions of democratization and "human relations" to critique the modernist city; their urbanity was to be the fruit of the collective actions of numerous individuals. This framework is central to the contemporary rationale of social connectivity and access, and resonates with preoccupations about how urban analysis and planning can become relational. It connects with current investigations in how computational, interactive, hyper-local processes can reshape self-governance and democratization, along with the corresponding ideas of open source, implemented practically or referred to as a metaphor for participative architectural processes.[21]

The question of how urbanity generates subjectivities, and how these aggregate to form a common condition, is central to contemporary agendas—as it was in Friedman's *Spatial Urbanism* and Constant's "spatial sociality." In particular, contemporary urban activists recall the Situationists' *unitary urbanism*, seeking similar strategies of resistance to

162 Emmanuelle Chiappone-Piriou

the logic of efficiency and utilitarianism by re-inscribing the emancipated and desiring individuality within a larger socio-political project.[22] The contemporary promise of a full automation of the labor force also sheds new light on these hypotheses, as they hint at the possibility of a society of idleness.

In a striking parallel with our contemporary situation, Friedman analyzed the quantitative changes that architecture was faced with in a time of urban growth: architects had to work for "the many." Yet, Friedman noted, architects should resist the temptation to produce and work with a fiction: that of the "average user." Based on preconceptions, this idea implied abstraction and reduction of what the "client" or inhabitant is. Instead, Friedman claimed, "The architect loses his importance (or should lose it) to give more initiative to the inhabitants. Architects should not make houses for the average man, because such man does not exist."[23] Both historic projects tackled the difficult conceptual problem of housing the unpredictable subjectivities of the citizens while providing them with means to materialize their total freedom of movement and expression without altering it. These architectures were not only to be completed through individual action, but also fully co-designed by the empowered inhabitant. To maximize individual expression while minimizing the impact of designers, who "follow and help, as technicians, the general development," both projects offered an infrastructural response that was "non-determined and non-determinant," or as Friedman wrote, a system considered neutral because it is purely technical.[24] The urban structure was defined as a "vast network of collective services" which included water systems, power grid, sewers, and the necessary structures to allow for the individual industrialized units to be freely plugged-in and/or removed.[25]

Systems

The proto-computational nature of the *Ville Spatiale* anticipated the import of general system theory and cybernetics in social sciences in the 1950s, and the subsequent adoption of a systemic perspective in architecture.[26] This trend inspired the cybernetician Gordon Pask to declare, in the September 1969 issue of *Architectural Design*: "architects are first and foremost system designers."[27] Breaking with centuries of architectural tradition, this new understanding of the city as a general system organized through interaction and feedback, rather than a physically and aesthetically organized structure, has prevailed ever since. Not only is the analogy still easily made between cybernetic models and physical and social systems, but we now witness the implementation of cybernetics in urban governance, as discussed regarding smart cities. In the very first paragraphs of *L'architecture mobile*, Friedman briefly outlined what he would later develop in *Pour l'architecture scientifique* (1971), a protocomputational management of the urban.[28]

What he described in 1958 as the "technocracy" to come would be the guarantee of a real democratic regime—the full, impersonal, and errorless coordination of the governing mechanism by a supercomputer (*computateur*). All aspects of the collective existence were concerned: the administration first, for which the computer would elaborate and implement new legislation; secondly, the distribution of property and resources, which would be managed through a rigorous and apolitical calculation; and finally, industrial production, which would be fully automated.

That apparatus was also to act as an enabler for individual action, mobility, and expressivity, which could be manifested in unlimited fashion at the scale of the single unit. Friedman pursued and amplified this idea with the "FLATWRITER," a machine described in *Toward a Scientific Architecture* which would allow the inhabitants first to choose the configuration of their dwelling units and then to place them in the infrastructure.

The cybernetic idea of the urban system (as a set of distinct elements interacting dynamically within a coherent whole in order to produce differentiating patterns) is fully operating in Friedman's program. Against top-down centralized models, the auto-planning processes proposed in *L'architecture mobile* relied on a decentralized system that did not imply, nor produce, hierarchy. It broke with historical, vertical and unidirectional regimes of control, by associating it with communicative feedback loops. In Friedman's *Ville Spatiale*, the city was intentionally designed to be constrained to a regular, three-dimensional space-grid, only determined by a 50% occupation rate; the dwellings were to be inserted and moved at the inhabitants' will, provided the choices made respected the city's balance.

Libertarian?

It is precisely within Friedman's systemic understanding that lies the inoperability of the project for the contemporary city. The *Ville Spatiale* relies on unifying preconceptions: first and foremost that of society as a whole, of which the architect is the instigator and the guarantor. Its indefinitely extensible system would allow for, and systemize, a restrained type of individual expression strictly compatible with the system. Michel Ragon himself, in 1980, blamed the utopian urbanism of architects for its synthetic and collectivistic aspect.[29] In his *Architecture des humeurs* speculative urbanism project (2010), R&Sie(n) (François Roche) pushed Friedman's original intentions to the breaking point so as to reveal their inherent and eventual ambiguity. In the retro-futurist, nostalgic video that accompanied the project, Roche pictured an aged architect who blames the

164 Emmanuelle Chiappone-Piriou

inhabitants for the abandon, and subsequent decay, of his experimental urban iterative project.[30]

Forty years prior, Peter Hall criticized such megastructures, stating that their "auto-destruction" (by either chaotic action or abandonment) had to be addressed as a necessary consequence of the "auto-construction."[31] François Roche similarly noted that Friedman's work held on to a "schizophrenic" premise: the incompatible coexistence of a constructive, rational, and achievable infrastructure juxtaposed to the possibility of its collective "colonization." Indeed, Roche notes, this colonization stagnates as a mere "political fiction" deprived of its true vitality in order to be assimilated in an objective system, sustained by proto-computation.[32]

This system stems from the logic and objective method that Friedman later detailed in *Toward a Scientific Architecture*, in which he advocated systematic thinking, in contrast with traditional architectural empiricism and purely quantitative methods. Friedman's program can be said to share a common intellectual substratum with the epistemological Structuralist discourses. He advocated for a linguistic approach (that describes individual action as combinatorial operations taking place onto the objective infrastructure—or variation within invariance) and the use of a mathematical qualitative apparatus to mediate the individual intention without distortion.[33]

Friedman's ambition was to design a system that eliminated information short-circuits by eliminating the intermediary that is the architect. In a cybernetic vein, he described the architectural process as an "information process"—the building as "hardware" and the user as the "transmitting session." In this perspective, the architect—the expert—could be replaced by the FLATWRITER in the process of managing the information. The architect rather intervenes upstream, by designing the repertoire of configurations that is submitted to the user by means of a "universal language." The user's needs and values, termed "the message," are received and processed by the building through the graph, which is able to respond to them through "feedback."

The designed combinatorial process integrates the user's preferences and evaluates the implications for the community of each decision made by the user. When considered satisfactory, the decision, based on objective metrics and reconfigurable *ad libitum*, is implemented in the objective and stable infrastructure.[34] The modes of expression and implementation of the individual—and interaction within the community—are thus necessarily mediated by an "objective" mathematical model: a graph that allows for "the performance of calculations, the extraction of metrics, the description of rules and axioms, the examination of scenarios."

Friedman states: "Any system that does not give the right of choice to those who must bear the consequences of a bad choice is an immoral system."[35] On the contrary, here the inhabitant, having been made aware of the implications of his choices, is conceived of as being empowered and thus fully responsible. The scientific framework's formalized yet flexible logic was devised to allow for individual expression while ensuring coexistence and cooperation within the set that is the society.[36]

The graph implies a one-to-one correspondence between the mathematical apparatus and the physical spatial structure. The fact that the *Ville Spatiale* is capable of accommodating the full range of possible combinations implies that the initial system encapsulates—a priori—all the future choices that all citizens could make. The modular, open, standardized grid is thus nothing more than the physical equivalent of the graph in its form best suited to accept all possible combinatorial configurations. This reading allows one to ignore the physical characteristics of the *Ville Spatiale*'s new, spatial, urbanism (an aerial city that would overlook existing ones), and instead analyze the project as a spatial embodiment of a cybernetic system that articulates the individual to the collective within a closed whole.

Mastered by the combinatorial process implemented by the graph, change occurs by means of internal relations only. Despite the possibility of a permanent evolution through individual action, and the understanding of society as a set of relations among individuals,[37] the system is thus maintained in its unity and global equilibrium; it appears that the very possibility of entropy or dissolution is being evacuated. The *Ville Spatiale* is therefore total and autonomous, and determined only by internal changes and dynamics.

Friedman's system was still based on the premises of post-war cybernetics: described in its totality, it was designed as to be homeostatic and self-regulating. It is now largely agreed that our contemporary cities can no longer be described nor contained by such closed, stable models. Their highly hybridized and complex nature, as well as the technological evolution to planetary-scale computation and the epistemological shifts it implies, are better described and regulated through models that, drawing from the theories of chaos and complexity, embrace the non-linear character of systemic change and account for the emergent properties of large-scale environments—that is, the city.

Despite the romantic understanding of Friedman's project that now prevails—as one that reinvented the collective by unfolding the potential of individual action—the architect's system implies a direct, individual relation between the single element and the system. In the final analysis, the *Ville Spatiale* maintains the modernist assumption that only two levels exist: that of the individual, or the *micro*, and that of the collective, or the *macro*. While it does not morphologically determine the nature of the relationship between the two levels, it articulates the macro as a relatively coherent and ordered collection and organization of the micro.[38]

166 Emmanuelle Chiappone-Piriou

It can be argued, following Manuel De Landa, that the reason why the problem of the *linkages* between the micro and the macro has resisted solution is because it has been framed in reductionist terms:

> Posing the problem correctly involves, first of all, getting rid of the idea that social processes occur at only two levels, the micro- and the macro-levels, particularly when these levels are conceived in terms of reified generalities like "the individual" and "society as a whole." . . . [T]he "micro" and the "macro" should not be associated with two fixed levels of scale but used to denote the concrete parts and the resulting emergent whole at any given spatial scale.[39]

The contemporary city necessitates models that account for collective intelligence phenomena, meaning that all intelligence is considered: human and non-human alike, material and digital, and most importantly, embodied.

Breaking with the syntactic understanding of the real, which underlies Structuralism as well as first-order cybernetics, it is thus necessary to conceptualize cities in terms of emergent phenomena—as highly disaggregated, decentralized, dynamic, and multi-scalar wholes—instead of through a synthetic model such as the *Ville Spatiale*. These models need to account for change, not happening internally and smoothly in ways that keep the system on equilibrium, but rather multiple, non-linear, and at times chaotic.

Contrary to Friedman, Constant conceived a truly topological and decentralized system that could accommodate chaotic behaviors and their resulting patterns. *New Babylon* disentangled the urban condition from the traditional urban density of form and was conceived as an indefinitely extended network, limited only by the globe's dimensions.

The Injunction to Action

The planetary city of *New Babylon* was envisioned by Constant to be in a permanent state of change, triggered by the individual constant movements and desires: "Just like the painter, who with a mere handful of colors creates an infinite variety of forms, contrasts and styles, the New Babylonians can endlessly vary their environment, renew and vary it by using their technical implements."[40] These included various technical tools, including audio volume, light intensity, olfactory ambiance, temperature, etc.

New Babylon indeed broke from the traditional static and nuclear model of dwelling, which was substituted with a dynamic model of aggregation of the living units along the paths taken and drawn by the inhabitants. The units, connected to one another, formed potentially infinite chains, extensible in any direction. *New Babylon* does not stop, and all places are accessible to each and everyone.

As it has been discussed above, the functioning of the *Ville Spatiale* was underpinned by the idea that the individual definition of the environment is isolated, in that it is systematically mediated by the operator that is the computer. Yet shaping a society that is freed from any form of reductionism implies, as argued by Friedman, the refusal not only of the "average man" and of a reductionist understanding of his properties, but also the consideration of the individual's capacities and agency. Comparing his fictitious inhabitant with a painter, Constant wrote that for him, "the creative action is also a social action: direct intervention in the social, it calls for immediate answer." The creative activity is public: taking place in a shared environment, it elicits spontaneous reactions from other inhabitants. Hence, the process escapes one's control and engages in a permanent, non-linear, collective transformation of the real. The drawings of the internal ambiances of the sectors, filled with vivid colors and what appear to be light, centripetal structures, do indeed convey the impression of a chaotic and ephemeral environment.

New Babylon was designed to be a qualitatively superior social mode, a built situation in permanent mutation, generated by the daily experiences of the inhabitants:

> To us, social space really is the concrete space of encounters, of contacts amongst people. Spatiality is social. In *New Babylon,* the social space is social spatiality. Nothing allows separating space as a psychic dimension (abstract space) from the space of action (concrete space).[41]

The dissolution of the existing social relations Constant considered to be constraining (those formalized by such institutions as marriage and family) was to give rise to a fluctuant society, composed through fortuitous and ephemeral meetings and discontinuous change. The final materiality and structure of *New Babylon* was to be integrally generated by the individual actions over time—not the result of a computational, objective, mediation, as in Friedman, but that of direct negotiations among the individuals themselves.

This account for how space is conceived in *New Babylon* strongly resonates with contemporary models that account for contingency, complexity and unpredictability. Breaking from the classical definition of space as an a priori category of experience, Bruno Latour defines it as "*one* of the many connections made by objects and subjects," one that is engendered by entities.[42] Social ontology, political theory, philosophy, and science studies have operated a reshuffling of space (and time) through the relocalization of the practices and structural features that produce it, and have traded the idea of a nested scalar hierarchy (in which the world could be

168 Emmanuelle Chiappone-Piriou

grasped through a long travelling from the local to the global as in the Eames' *Powers of Ten*) for operative multi-scalar, dynamic, models best suited to describe and articulate the post-anthroposcenic world:

> The construction of a situation is the edification of a transient micro-ambience and of the play of events for a unique moment in the lives of several persons. Within unitary urbanism, it is inseparable from the construction of a general, relatively more lasting ambience.[43]

This proto-topological definition of space we find in Constant's work appears to resonate with the new perspectives taken in urban studies. In *New Babylon*, space is indeed engendered by social mobility, hence by the individuals "as they trudge along." The city's form is thus inherently dependent on their existence as much as their interactions:

> Under these conditions, social mobility suggests the image of a kaleidoscopic whole, accentuating sudden unexpected changes—an image that no longer bears any similarity to the structures of a community life ruled by the principle of utility, whose models of behaviour are always the same.

New Babylon does not exist without displacements, and all displacements generate transformations, hence specificity and heterogeneity. However, the project still deploys a

> meta-narrative of structural change for an explanation of urban life," and can be said to fall into "the trap of fetishism, in the Marxian sense of taking for real and ontologically autonomous what is rather an attribute of particular actor-networks and urban site.[44]

To address that point, we should borrow Jacques Rancière's analysis of "social critique" and Antoinette Rouvroy's account of subjectivation in algorithmic governmentality.

Following Rancière's reading, *New Babylon* appears as the ultimate emancipative apparatus, one that induces a break of the correspondence between an "occupation" and a "capacity" and the related development of new sensible and intellectual equipment. Through their individual agency, New Babylonians indeed conquer other spaces and times than those to which they were assigned by society, and thus break with established ways of feeling, acting, and enunciating. For Rancière, "solidarity of the social and the aesthetic" has historically been at the heart of working-class emancipation, of the discovery of individuality, and the parallel project of a free collectivity, and so it appears to be in *New Babylon*.

The "individually expressive humanity" proposed by Constant necessarily implies that the collective is a hybrid ensemble, aggregated through the spontaneous individual expressions as much as through the conflicts that may arise and the negotiations and compromises that may settle them. It follows that the collective is never the pure addition of individual expressions, but the emergent result of their interactions across scales and of the assemblage they produce.

In *New Babylon*, the individual expression resulted in the dynamiting of the institutions that traditionally ensured collective links. This may find some resonance in today's hyper-individualist society, in which the commons tend to narrow. While it is not our intention to sympathize with those who regret the "harmonious fabric of community" that may be lost in the process,[45] and while we believe *New Babylon* remains a fundamental project in thinking about what emancipation is, we should question the logics and narrative of hyper-individuation, and the fragmentation that comes as a corollary, in our smart environment.

Indeed, as Antoinette Rouvroy states, the new capacities of aggregation, analysis, and statistical correlation in our data-driven reality gives us the illusion that we can "grasp social reality *as such*" and emancipate ourselves from our socially imposed norms. The *a-normative* quality of algorithmic governmentality, she states, relies on "data behaviorism," the "new way of producing knowledge about future preferences attitudes, behaviours or events without considering the subject's psychological motivations, speeches or narratives, but rather relying on data."[46] This governmentality, based on purely inductive statistics coupled with profiling purposes, tends to "disregard the reflexive and discursive capabilities (as well as their 'moral capabilities') of human agents, in favour of computational, pre-emptive, context- and behaviour-sensitive management of risks and opportunities."[47]

The point here is that if smart cities (and not only the new ones) are considered as the embodiment of such a governing apparatus—that has flattened epistemology, ontology and politics—then the understanding of urbanization as a set of evolving, adaptable, localized, and complex processes needs to be scrutinized. As discussed above, second-order cybernetics and algorithmic governance have fully embraced non-linearity and self-organization as ruling mechanisms. Control is thus enacted at the infra-individual level and reproduced through those mechanisms.

The data obtained through the real-time analysis of the inhabitants' behaviors, habits, and desires is understood to produce knowledge about the reality of the city, establishing a supposed objectivity of the system. Within the narrative of crisis, the capacity to anticipate behavioral patterns and regulate them upstream is justified by the imperatives of urgent control, of detection and prevention, of immediate operationality, and of flexible adaptation to changing circumstances. In its more extreme form, urbanization conflates with risk management and optimization, it "exhibits a new strategy of uncertainty management consisting in minimizing the uncertainty associated to human agency."[48] This is relying on "data behaviorism," its predictive capacities and ubiquitous injunctions to—regulated—action.

While in *New Babylon* subjectivation was conceived as a process of individual expression of potentialities and desires contingently evolving into collective creativity, in the algorithmic governmentality subjectivation is prevented by hyper-individuation. In a sort of reversal, it is now regulation that is enforced at the very scale at which autonomization took place in *New Babylon*. While the New Babylonian was free to explore the potential dimensions of his existence, and spontaneously express full agency, the smart city inhabitant is restrained: he is required to *respond* and adapt to a series of environmental changes and stimuli that anticipate his intentions and actions. Affected in his potentiality, the subject mutates into the "user" of applications, into an agent of a computational simulation, into yet another profile in databases.

Against the supposed objectivity on which relies the smart management of the urban—of regulation of traffic, housing, use of public space, resource management, access to public services, etc.—it may be useful to turn to Jacques Rancière again and embrace his call for dissensus and a redistribution of the sensible:

> What "dissensus" means is an organization of the sensible where there is neither a reality concealed behind appearances nor a single regime of presentation and interpretation of the given imposing its obviousness on all. It means that every situation can be cracked open from the inside, reconfigured in a different regime of perception and signification. To reconfigure the landscape of what can be seen and what can be thought is to alter the field of the possible and the distribution of capacities and incapacities. . . . This is what a process of political subjectivation consist in: in the action of uncounted capacities that crack open the unity of the given and the obviousness of the visible in order to sketch a new topography of the possible.[49]

How can architecture continue to conceptualize and produce a common condition, which revives neither the traditional categories of domination nor its own binary categories: society/individual? How can it still be political today without reviving models and attitudes that are operationally inadequate to counter the hegemonic discourses and systems that, in their contemporary manifestation, pervade all levels of human life? How can architects still produce a critique and drag themselves out of the state of doubt and incapacity that the obsolescence and inoperability of traditional modes of regeneration—the crisis—has induced?

Scale Down, Perform, Aggregate (Repeat)

Through Friedman and Constant's readings, we have highlighted how our urban condition calls for models capable of accounting for its open, non-linear, and informal character. Contemporary architects, struggling with the heritage of functionalism and the inoperability of critique, have to reclaim a space for politics within which to question our traditional categorizations (nature/culture, human/non-human, living/inert), the modalities of subjectivation and of the constitution of the commons.

They may start by accounting for what does not appear to stem from any a priori political intention. The less politicized artifact—a purely functional urban planning or a building deprived of qualities—just like many mobile technological devices and the networks to which they connect us, are indeed political. They have become technical and financial human constructs and the outcomes of concrete negotiated and localized processes. To be political would thus mean to understand architecture not as a closed entity, but as a construct that, in its turn, enters into processes of assemblage, produces effects, and articulates realities across different scales and spheres. In the manner of Mel Bochner's call to render concrete the non-visual,[50] a political architecture could thus consist in revealing the mechanisms, the articulations, connections, and processes that produce our daily, and collective, environment. Against the operationality and real-time character of smart urbanism, it would consist in reintroducing delay and distance in the making of the city. It would not mean re-injecting politics into our urban, environmental, and technological environment, but rather revealing that the political has never really disappeared.

It means, as Andrés Jaque experiments with his Office for Political Innovation, disentangling the fictional discourses that pervade our society and are embodied materially and spatially, and revealing and allowing experimenting with the realities they obscure and the modalities of subjectivities they deploy. The *Cosmo* installation was designed to accommodate the 2015 summer parties at MoMA PS1. A pop infrastructure, *Cosmo* was integrally constituted with some of the technical apparatuses necessary for the water treatment process; by making them visible, it unveiled the complex mechanisms of water de-pollution that are essential to New York City's sustainability, but that, as they are delocalized our of the State of New York, remain perfectly invisible to the inhabitants. Tubes, pools, and algae culture systems gave a material (and party-like) reality to these vital and unknown processes.

172 Emmanuelle Chiappone-Piriou

To some extent, the project follows up on Yona Friedman's intuition that society not only contains people, but objects too, and that there exists a system of influences among them.[51] Moving further, *Cosmo* accounts for the vitality of matter and of objects, and more broadly, it enmeshes human relations, technology, and the built environment to a much higher degree than Friedman did. In an Actor-Network perspective, it unfolds the water treatment system in opposite directions, treating it as an assemblage constituted by many interactions, between human and non-human agents alike, as well as an actual entity that enters other discontinuous processes of a higher order. In *Cosmo*, the architectural gesture lay in the operation of rematerializing these invisible processes, which it did by scaling them down. *Cosmo* thus acted as an indicator, in the heart of New York, of the territorial inequalities that these water de-pollution processes enact and sustain, hence participating in the emergence of a new (aesthetic) sensibility.

This same process of revelation of the infrastructural nature of our world underpins *Domesticated Mountain* (2012) by artist Andreas Angelidakis. The project reflects on the absolute condition of suburbia that is the Internet, and on the changing nature of dwelling within it. The fundamental expression of individuality that is the home is redefined in terms of accumulation, as the materialization of the purchasing activities we have online. The views of the house show mountains of boxes that have been moved to the site by a delivery van; over time, the house continues to develop by means of the compulsive acquisition of more goods via the Internet and the accumulation of the correspondent delivery boxes. As such, the home becomes the material manifestation of our direct participation in the supposedly abstract and deterritorialized processes of the global market.[52]

Being political, however, does not simply consist in opposing an illusionary transparency to the computational flattening of our world. It is rather a question of operating redistribution of the sensible, but also of knowledge, and of opening up the black boxes of the mechanisms that organize and unify the political, the social, and the financial regimes.[53]

The *Block'Hood* game designed by architect Jose Sanchez (Plethora project) does exactly that. "Is a neighborhood alive? Pulsating with life? Can it learn? Or adapt? Can a city be an ecosystem?" enquires the game teaser. The player is invited to build a neighborhood where "communities and species coexist," and to ensure its sustainability and the conditions of coexistence within it. *Block'Hood* reveals the systemic and infrastructural nature of the models according to which our environments are produced, organized, and managed: the player builds a neighborhood block by block, through aggregation (a block can be a housing unit, a store, a tree, a wind turbine, etc.), each of which has inputs and outputs and enters into an interdependent relation with the others in order to constitute a productive network. The player thus has to define and connect blocks in such a way as to avoid the entropy and decay that would be generated by abandonment or a lack of interrelation of the blocks, thus ensuring sustainability and generating growth. The game has an educational purpose, and allows players to learn not only about the ecological challenges that face our cities, but also the interrelational mechanisms that sustain them. Here, the gamer—the citizen—is addressed through reflexive abilities, desires and capacities for decision, and not merely as a "user" or a "profile." The notion of community is present both within the game and in the processes through which it is constituted, as the players are able to alter and repurpose the game.

The game consists in the "third term" invoked by Rancière, capable of establishing a common object of discovery and appropriation for the architect and the inhabitant alike, faced with which no specific form of expertise or knowledge would prevail over another. It breaks with the "a priori distribution of the positions and capacities or incapacities attached to these positions."[54] Specifically, the discrete combinatorial ontology of computer games allows the gamer to develop a contingent assemblage, unexpected to the developer. The establishment of such a term—in the form of a parliament, an (archi)scene or a platform, digital and/or physical—could lift architecture from the impasse it has talked itself into, one stuck between the inability to act in which the necessary failures of universalist programs has led it and the promotion of the utopias of the "rear-guard,"[55] whose innovative attires operate as an anesthetic that suppresses any possible consequence of the said system. This third manner "proposes to conceive (architecture) as a new scene of equality where heterogeneous performances are translated into one another."[56] This term could allow for unpredictability and contingency to hatch, and be the core around which the agency of the inhabitant as much as that of the architect could reform.

Conclusion

This chapter has stated the urgency of revising the models through which our contemporary urban condition is being analyzed, and acted upon, in what is believed to be a time of permanent crisis. It has insisted on rejecting, once and for all, the purely top-down models that have shaped cities through simpler times and still persist today.

We have unfolded two historical projects that were designed as alternatives to the crisis of the modernist city, and which still carry lessons for the current post-crisis situation. Friedman's *Ville Spatiale* and Constant's *New Babylon* both embodied the political, social, and theoretical claim for a re-evaluation of what the collective is, in opposition to the organic classical structuring of reality as well as of the city. They advocated mobility against the static city, individual emancipation against an extensive and homogenizing definition of society, and democratization against control.

Yet, as we have seen, it is necessary to distinguish between the manners in which each project manifested and actualized its original ambition. Through the study of the scientific axiom on which it is based, the *Ville Spatiale*, on the one hand, appears to have relied on the understanding of society as a homeostatic whole, sustained in equilibrium by a technocratic proto-computational system. *New Babylon*, on the other hand, presented us with a truly non-linear and spontaneous form of urbanization occurring through individual action. Yet we have argued that the computational turn has reversed the mechanisms of control that now operate at the very scale of the individual.

While each critique may seem to unfold in opposite directions, celebrating complexity on the one side and warning against fragmentation on the other, we would like to stress the necessity of maintaining this complex position if we want to address our current post-crisis situation: sustaining locally emerging, non-linear, self-organizing processes as modes of resistance against top-down systems, while at the same time scrutinizing those very processes as having been absorbed by the ruling apparatuses of the smart city. We need to oppose the extensive, top-down, anthropocentric organizing of the real that has led to the present ecological crisis as much as we need to resist the narrative of the crisis and the imperatives of urgency, efficiency, permanent evolution, and adaptation that come as a corollary within the new environmental regime of *smart* control.[57]

In the manner of Tristan Garcia in his twofold analysis of the disintegration of the "we,"[58] we maintain that the nostalgia for a stable and apprehensible urbanity and the urge for one that can accommodate our contemporary complexity may not be reconciled easily, or at least not immediately: none appears sufficient, yet none marks the end of the city. As Garcia states, what remains lively, and operational, is the narrative: the narrative of how our cities come to be and operate, the revealing of their infrastructural nature and transversal dynamics, as well as of the many agents and assemblages that constitute it, hyper-locally, and the tentative description of how the commons can be reinvented. To paraphrase Garcia: "Our aim is to watch, everywhere around us, for the image of the city that will form in the years to come."

Notes

1 Benjamin H. Bratton, *The Stack: On Software and Sovereignty* (Cambridge, MA: MIT Press, 2016).

2 Mark Uh, "From Home to Rent: Who Lost the American Dream?" *Trulia*, February 11, 2016, https://www.trulia.com/blog/trends/own-to-rent/ (accessed June 29, 2018).

Chasing Strategies for the Post-crisis **175**

3 Comité invisible, *A nos amis* (Paris: La fabrique éditions, 2014); see also Naomi Klein, *The Shock Doctrine: The Rise of Disaster Capitalism* (New York: Metropolitan Books, 2008). As underlined by Klein, Milton Friedman's capitalist doctrine is funded on the narrative of crisis, real or perceived:

> Only a crisis—actual or perceived—produces real change. When that crisis occurs, the actions that are taken depend on the ideas that are lying around. That, I believe, is our basic function: to develop alternatives to existing policies, to keep them alive and available until the politically impossible becomes the politically inevitable.

https://bfi.uchicago.edu/news/post/milton-friedman-his-own-words (accessed June 29, 2018).
4 Manfredo Tafuri, "Preface," in *Architecture and Utopia: Design and Capitalist Development* (Cambridge, MA: MIT Press, 1976), pp. ix–x.
5 Either we could become conservative, that is, we would "conserve" our historical role as translators of, and form-givers to, the political and economic priorities of existing society. Or we could function as critics and commentators, acting as intellectuals who reveal the contradictions of society through writings or other forms of practice . . . . Finally, we could act as revolutionaries by using our . . . understanding of cities and the mechanisms of architecture . . . in order to be part of professional forces trying to arrive at new social and urban structures.

Bernard Tschumi, *Architecture and Disjunction* (Cambridge, MA: MIT Press, 1996), p. 9.
6 Reyner Banham, *Megastructures: Urban Futures of the Recent Past* (London: Thames and Hudson, 1976). p. 32. The revolutionary attitude is also, finally, the affirmation that, to regain its agency in a contemporary world characterized by a growing complexity and fragmentation, when urbanity emerges at the conjunction of the material and the digital, architecture needs to redefine its own limits, once again opening up to other disciplines, and incorporating other forms of knowledge and skills.
7 Le Corbusier, *Urbanisme*, cited in Jacques Lucan, *Le Corbusier, une encyclopédie* (Paris: Editions du Centre Pompidou, 1987), p. 169 (my translation).
8 Saskia Sassen, *The Global City: New York, London, Tokyo* (Oxford: Princeton University Press, 2001).
9 Parag Khanna, *Connectography: Mapping the Future of Global Civilization* (New York: Random House, 2016).
10 Matthew Gandy, "Where Does the City End?" *Architectural Design* 82(1) (2012): 128–133.
11 Andrea Branzi and Archizoom Associati, "City, Assembly Line of Social Issues/ Ideology and Theory of the Metropolis," in *No-stop City, Archizoom Associati*, Casabella nos. 350–351, July–August 1970 (Orléans, France: Editions HYX, 2006).
12 Songdo International Business District, "Masterplan," http://songdoibd.com/about/ (accessed June 29, 2018).
13 Adam Greenfield, "Practices of the Minimum Viable Utopia," in *4D Hyperlocal: A Cultural Tool Kit for the Open Source City*, ed. Lucy Bullivant (London: Wiley, 2017), pp. 16–25.
14 Antoinette Rouvroy and Thomas Bern, "Gouvernementalité algorithmique et perspectives d'émancipation: le disparate comme condition d'individuation par la relation?" *Réseaux* 2013/1(177) (2013): 163–96.

176 Emmanuelle Chiappone-Piriou

15 We choose to specifically analyze the similarities between the programs, leaving the many fundamental differences aside for the clarity of the argument developed in the text.
16 Alejandro Zaera-Polo, "The Posthuman City: Imminent Urban Commons," in *4D Hyperlocal: A Cultural Tool Kit for the Open Source City*, ed. Lucy Bullivant (London: Wiley, 2017), pp. 26–35.
17 Yona Friedman, *L'architecture mobile* (1962). The first version was typed and distributed by Friedman in 1958.
18 Ibid.
19 Banham, *Megastructures*.
20 Constant Nieuwenhuys, *New Babylon: art et utopie*, ed. Jean-Clarence Lambert (Paris: Cercle d'art, 1997), p. 51.
21 Lucy Bullivant, ed., *4D Hyperlocal: A Cultural Tool Kit for the Open Source City* (London: Wiley, 2017).
22 Lara Schrijver, "Utopia and/or Spectacle? Rethinking Urban Interventions through the Legacy of Modernism and the Situationist City," *Architectural Theory Review* 16(3) (2011): 245–258.
23 Friedman, *L'architecture mobile*; my translation.
24 Ibid.
25 Nieuwenhuys, *New Babylon*.
26 For the relevance of Friedman's work for today's do-it-yourself and user-centric culture, computation and online connectivity, see Theodora Vardouli, *Design-for-Empowerment-for-Design: Computational Structures for Design Democratization* (Cambridge, MA: MIT Press, 2012).
27 Gordon Pask, "The Architectural Relevance of Cybernetics," *Architectural Design* (September 1969): 494–496.
28 Yona Friedman, *Toward a Scientific Architecture* (Cambridge, MA: MIT Press, 1975).
29 Michel Ragon, "Urbanisme prospectif et/ou urbanisme utopique," *Espaces et sociétés: revue critique internationale de l'aménagement, de l'architecture et de l'urbanisation urbanisme et utopie* 32–33 (1980): 15–42.
30 The *Architecture des humeurs* consists in a bio-political, non-reductionist process of urban aggregation in which the urban structure and organization is subject to the individual conscious and unconscious desires and intentions. A series of computational, mathematical and machinist procedures are designed to articulate the link between the collective and the individual by means of "improbable and uncertain successive indeterminations, aggregations and layouts." These protocols are developed on the basis of the collection of both physiological data (based on neurological secretions) and desires expressed by the inhabitant. The project reverses Friedman's principle of a pre-determined global structure housing the living units, to propose that the "layout of the residential units and the structural trajectories are conceived and developed here as posterior to the morphologies that support social life and not as an a priori." The algorithmic treatment and the incremental and recursive structural optimization protocols developed thus allow for the architectural form to emerge and adapt. The scenario included a robot capable of 3D-printing the structure through time, according to the data gathered.
31 Peter Hall, "Monumental Folly," *New Society*, October 24, 1968, cited in Banham, *Megastructures*.
32 François Roche and Camille Lacadée, "Yona Friedman®," *new-territories*, February 25, 2014, www.new-territories.com/blog/?p=1347 (accessed June 29, 2018).
33 Vardouli, *Design-for-Empowerment-for-Design*. Friedman himself never directly referred to Structuralism.

34 See Friedman, *Toward a Scientific Architecture*.

35 Ibid., p. 13.

36 "I call society a set of individuals in which there exists some sort of 'relation' between any two individuals belonging to the set." Friedman, "Appendix (1972): Society = Environment," in *Toward a Scientific Architecture*, p. 143. In his drawings, not only did Friedman schematize the relationships between the individuals (represented as points connected by lines), but also the influences amongst them. Friedman's view of the city was one in which everyone person was linked to any other by intermediaries.

37 Both propositions were to replace the existing urban fabric, not by contaminating it but, more radically, by ending it useless and archaic. The *Ville Spatiale* was to rise on piles above the existing city, agricultural and natural zones alike; little is said about the existing city, apart from the fact that it would be intensified by the new urbanism. Constant imagined the progressive replacement of the existing agglomerations, slowly disaggregated by the evolution of the lifestyle and rendered obsolete by the attractiveness of the newly built, better adapted, sectors of *New Babylon*, up to the point that the full network is connected.

38 R&Sie(n)'s partly unconscious *Architecture des humeurs* replaced a synthetic top-down system with an equally synthetic purely emergent one. That explains, we believe, that it presented the same (fictional) risks of failure.

39 Manuel DeLanda, *A New Philosophy of Society: Assemblage Theory and Social Complexity* (London: Continuum, 2006), p. 32.

40 Constant Nieuwenhuys, "New Babylon: Outline of a Culture" (original in Dutch, "New Babylon, een schets voor een kultuur"), rewrite of a chapter from an unpublished manuscript written in German between 1960 and 1965, published in *New Babylon*, trans. by Paul Hammond (The Hague: Haags Gemeentemuseum, 1974), pp. 49–62. Reproduced in Mark Wigley, *Constant's New Babylon: The Hyper-architecture of Desire* (Rotterdam: Witte de With Center for Contemporary Art/010 Publishers, 1998), p. 162.

41 Nieuwenhuys, *New Babylon*, p. 51.

42 Bruno Latour, "Spheres and Networks: Two Ways to Reinterpret Globalization," *Harvard Design Magazine* 30 (2009): 142.

43 Constant Nieuwenhuys and Guy. Debord, *Amsterdam Declaration*, trans. by Paul Hammond (original in French, *La déclaration d'Amsterdam*, written in Amsterdam, November 10, 1958), *Internationale Situationniste* 2 (1958): 31–32. Reproduced in Mark Wigley, *Constant's New Babylon: The Hyper-Architecture of Desire* (Rotterdam: Witte de With Center for Contemporary Art/010 Publishers, 1998), p. 87.

44 Ignacio Farìas, in *Urban Assemblages: How Actor-Network Theory Changes Urban Studies*, ed. Ignacio Farìas and Thomas Bender (New York: Routledge, 2010).

45 In *The Emancipated Spectator*, Jacques Rancière describes the nostalgia for a "harmoniously weaved community," one in which everyone was assigned to its rank and function, as the pivotal node of the "post-critique, embodied both by a "right-wing frenzy" and a "left-wing melancholy." "Right-wing frenzy," he writes, matches the denunciation of the market, medias and spectacle with the denunciation of the democratic individual, considered to be only preoccupied by the satisfaction of his desires. In doing so, the right-wing frenzy correlates the dissolution of the traditional institutions that defined the human society with the triumph of the market. On the other hand, the "left-wing melancholy," in its post-Situationist form in which "the truth is but a moment of the false," hankers for the "lost social link," broken by modernity. The melancholy stems from the belief that, in the inverted logic of the spectacle, every dissenting

178 Emmanuelle Chiappone-Piriou

attempt is only nurturing the system it opposes and every expression of collective intelligence is being swallowed.

46 Antoinette Rouvroy, "The End(s) of Critique: Data-behaviourism vs. Due-process," in *Privacy, Due Process and the Computational Turn: Philosophers of Law Meet Philosophers of Technology*, ed. Mireille Hildebrandt and Ekatarina De Vries (London: Routledge, 2012).
47 Ibid.
48 Ibid.
49 Jacques Rancière, *The Emancipated Spectator*, trans. by Gregory Elliot (London: Verso, 2009), pp. 48–49.
50 See Mel Bochner, "Primary Structures," *Arts Magazine* (June 1966): 32–35.
51 See Friedman, "Appendix (1972): Society = Environment," p. 151.
52 This project resonates with Georges Perec's *Les Choses*, in which the happiness of the young couple is fully dependant on the things they buy and thus ineluctably delayed, as much as it does with Waled Beashty's *FedEx* sculpture series, in which the sculptures physically bare the consequences of their shipping modes, through FedEx boxes.
53 Philippe Morel, "A Few Remarks on the Politics of 'Radical Computation,'" in *Paradigms in Computing, Making, Machines, and Models for Design Agency in Architecture*, ed. David Jason Gerber and Mariana Ibanez (Los Angeles, CA: eVolo Press, 2014), pp. 123–40.
54 Rancière, The *Emancipated Spectator*, p. 12.
55 Tafuri, "Preface."
56 Rancière, The *Emancipated Spectator*, p. 22.
57 Maroš Krivý, "Towards a Critique of Cybernetic Urbanism: The Smart City and the Society of Control," *Planning Theory* 17(1) (2016): 1–23.
58 Tristan Garcia, *Nous* (Paris: Editions Grasset & Fasquelles, 2017).

9

CHASING AMBIGUOUS CONDITIONS OF COEXISTENCE

Peter Winston Ferretto

Introduction

Only after a second glance do you realize that things aren't quite what you expected them to be. Lift interiors in Hong Kong, specifically domestic lifts, appear to be the same as most other lift interiors around the world. Possibly the decor is richer in ornament than an equivalent European lift, but the 1.5 meter-square ubiquitous cabin is a standardized component that simply gets installed and allowed to operate following programmed algorithms. In fact, your cognitive faculties cease to function in these commonly recognized "background" spaces. It is as if your brain goes into default mode, basing conclusions on preconceived assumptions about what is staring straight at you. On closer inspection, you realize that what you thought to be "standard" has been subtly manipulated: the lift buttons marking the floors of the apartment have been tampered as to omit any presence of the number 4 (4, 14, 24, 34. . .) due to its negative local "bad omen" connotations. Pronounced in Cantonese the word "four" phonetically sounds the same as "death," resulting in a paradoxical Spike Jonze situation where a building has no 4th, 14th, 24th floor, etc.[1]

Such a small, in most people's eyes inconspicuous, alteration embodies the notion of "Hong Kong Conditions." The conditional city is, in many ways, a reaction to the anaesthetized and anonymous city architects and urban planners so often pay attention to. Conditions in this context belong to the background city we inhabit, but are unable to acknowledge. The city we live in, yet fail to observe, collectively dismissed and marginalized by experts who, in their unyielding attempt to improve our habitat, seem to have lost the ability to appreciate the banal and quotidian urban presence. You will never find an architect who claims authorship of the background city; shame and indignation prevail. By definition, the urban "background" is an orphan and circumstantial soul that at best can be described as an illegitimate urban byproduct only acknowledged via its antonym, the foreground city.

Contrary to the foreground city (the city of icons and architectural statements we are so often told constitutes its identity, from the Eiffel Tower in Paris to the Guggenheim in Bilbao), the background city is preoccupied with coexisting, adapting, and avoiding all manifestations of its ego. In short, the background city insists on being invisible. For better or worse, the present reality of cities, the "here and now" of our urban existence, is actually shaped by that 99% we refuse to discuss. Rather than dismiss such pervasive urban agglomerations, this chapter seeks to observe and interrogate the mechanisms and tropes of this non-city.

Just as one can never recall the sound of background noise, the background city cannot be reproduced, only recognized. Yet within this infinite sea of homogeneous scenarios, behind the scenes, back-stage, lie countless moments of inhabitation, existences that can only be brought into focus manually, by sheer determination. In a manner similar to tuning a radio, one has to tune in to the right city wavelength to be able to absorb and appreciate its intimate world of micro inhabitation, the invisible latent energy that makes every background scene distinct. We are no longer following a flat and generic urban landscape, but have entered a parallel actual world that anthropologists define as the cultural identity of a place (Mathews 2013).

Inhabited Urban Conditions from an Architectural Perspective

At the core of what defines an urban condition is the notion of how we inhabit space. These two words "inhabit" and "space" require constant adapting and re-adapting to become an urban condition, for example the physical mutation of spaces to accommodate human existence, participation, and engagement. Conditions do not follow predetermined or preconceived ideals of spatial inhabitation, rather they reflect a constantly adapting space, a space that is arranged in association with time and behavior.

Conditions are grounded in "the local mind," an argument advocated by the Italian anthropologist Franco La Cecla in his book *Mente locale* (1993), where he argues that the relationship between the inhabitant and the environment are not regulated by "spatial experts" such as architects, politicians, and administrators, but by local people.[2] Conditions, according to La Cecla, represent the anti-ubiquitous places of the city, the city formed by the people who manipulate their surroundings via established "spatial structures," to borrow the term coined by Claude Lévi-Strauss.[3] In this context, the urban conditions refer to shared spatial practices that embody the memory of a culture and define the social traditions of the place, including how it adapts to new necessities, by digesting or cannibalizing urban codes and regulations.

To frame the discussion surrounding the interpretation of conditions within an architectural discipline, it is important to situate the idea in relation to the concept of contingency.

Architecture is seldom associated with the notion of contingency. Ever since Vitruvius' triad *utilitas, firmitas, venustas* (commodity, firmness, delight) set out in "De architectura" (Pollio and Morgan 1960), the discipline has become dominated by "agents of coherence" (Till 2013, p. 28) that impose visual order, and by association political influence, on the everyday environment in which we live.[4] To a certain extent, one could argue, the same mantra still prevails today. The concept of order is embedded deep into the modernist architectural project: "To create architecture is to put into order" (Le Corbusier 1991, p. 32).

Modernity, or more specifically the modern project, the ruthless practice of purification, separated nature and culture, categorizing previously overlapping disciplines into distinct entities. In his book *Architecture Depends* (Till 2013), the architect and academic Jeremy Till further elaborates the above point by making reference to the Polish sociologist Zygmunt Bauman. According to Bauman, the modern project has at its core the suppression of all vulnerable and contingent elements of human existence, within which architects "operate in a state of permanent denial of the residual power of any other order" (Till 2013, p. 34).

Modernity's effect on the manner in which contingent conditions are valued was developed by the French sociologist and philosopher Bruno Latour, who in *We Have Never Been Modern* (1993) argues that in the pursuit of perfection, modernization has "compartmentalized previously interwoven forces into mutually exclusive entities." Complex hybrid networks that existed for centuries in our pre-modern society have been rationalized, via strictly objective standards. Within this framework, architecture is evaluated as either functional or aesthetic, but never collectively as a hybrid contingent body. In the opinion of Latour, it is important to re-establish networks that "allow us to pass with continuity from local to global, from human to non-human" (Till 2013, p. 57), highlighting the importance and relevance of overlapping spheres of science, culture, and architecture.

The notion of "inhabited urban condition" is by no means a new field of research. The topic has in recent years become the source of extensive literature from a wide range of disciplines and experts. By contextualizing

182 Peter Winston Ferretto

the present arguments and positions, this chapter situates the Hong Kong condition within the present academic and professional discussion, and ultimately founds its relative theoretical position.

Conditions of Place

Beyond modernity, the relationship between place and space is a critical component in understanding how urban conditions are inhabited. According to the German philosopher Martin Heidegger, space is something that has been vacated, freed within a defined limit (Heidegger 1971). The concept of limit here relates the description of where something starts, as opposed to where something ends. Heidegger traces the etymology of the word to the Greek word *orismos*, concluding that spaces receive their essence from place, and not from space.

This position *vis-à-vis* the place where the condition occurs is essential in deciphering the existence of a condition.[5] For example, in one of the conditions analyzed in Shau Kei Wang later in this chapter, the inhabited relates directly to the traces and memories of a long-gone seashore line the community still respect and react to in their everyday life. The memory of the place remains embedded in both the local customs and physical vestiges of a prior life in the form of temples to the local divinity Tin Hau, who used to protect sailors embarking on perilous sea journeys and today continues to protect locals from contemporary evils.[6]

The meaning of everyday urban conditions we encounter is informed to a considerable degree by the fact that they inhabit shared worlds. The way they exist in the world is essentially structured by others. "The world of Dasein is a with-world," Heidegger claims (Wrathall 2005, p. 52). As a result, our interpretation of conditions is dictated by the way others understand and interpret conditions, or in the case of Hong Kong, how others have interpreted and responded to these conditions beforehand.

Conditions without Architects

Rather than center the thesis of this chapter on Hong Kong's macro intense urbanism, which has been the focus of numerous books, most recently *The Making of Hong Kong: From Vertical to Volumetric* (Shelton, Karakiewicz, and Kvan 2011), the attention here shifts toward small-scale micro situations typically dismissed as marginal or outright forgotten.

The idea originates from Bernard Rudofsky's book *Architecture without Architects*. In his introduction, the author states: "*Architecture without Architects* attempts to breakdown our narrow concepts of the art of building by introducing the unfamiliar world of non-pedigreed architecture" (Rudofsky 1964, p. 6), developing in the course of the book a taxonomy of anonymous, vernacular, and spontaneous architectural examples. Here, however, the focus is the architectural conditions that respond to Hong Kong's challenging spatial limits—where their existence varies in degrees of precariousness that are directly associated to their temporal status.

Urban conditions inherently work against the rigidity of the city, the city set out by planners, developers, and architects who seem to incessantly wax lyrical about public space. In fact, both words "public" and "space" have today become benign branding tools synonymous with the prevalent desired lifestyle. Collectively, architects and planners, via their speculative modus operandi of renderings and artificial visions, have contributed to a homogenous city that is alien to its very inhabitants.[7] Here, every new neighborhood is an upgraded replica of the previous. Present-day Hong Kong is overflowing with examples, such as areas in east Kowloon, Tiu Keng Leng, and Tseung Kwan O. Endless repetition of high-density housing typologies is interspersed with ubiquitous retail malls. Upon introduction, one feels immersed (as a result of certain demographic regulations, one mall per 100,000 inhabitants) in a state of constant *déjà vu*.[8] Paradoxically, it is in these areas that inhabited urban conditions re-create a level of abnormality, a break from the prevailing state of anonymity.

Conditions as Material Transformations

Transformations, *vis-à-vis* the physical change from one state to another, allow us to address the idea of urban conditions from another standpoint, such as conditions of materiality. Material and spatial conditions are characterized by the Danish architect Ander Abraham in his book *A New Nature: 9 Architectural Conditions between Liquid and Solid* (2015) as composite concepts capable of coexisting in the same space, creating a series of interconnected events. According to Abraham (2015, p. 31), architecture constitutes a very small part of "composite urban condition" within the modern city made up of constant transformation.

Conditions as a state of material transformation, although deviating slightly from the trajectory of the research in question, open a new way of thinking about architecture in the city. Conditions cease to be read as autonomous objects, more or less receptive to the local context, but become inseparable from context: there cannot be an inhabited condition without a material context.[9] Abraham's text further differentiates conditions from objects, where conditions are not defined by boundaries or form, but by multiple connections that he relates back to the French philosopher Jean-François Lyotard's idea of a "multiplicity of little narratives."[10]

Typically, to understand architecture one has to take a step back, to be able to visualize the object from a distance in terms of façade and form. On the contrary, to be able to fully comprehend a condition, one has to remain inside the phenomena and absorb the composite nature of the forces at play from physical, audial, visual, and mental. According to Abraham (2015, p. 43), if architecture can be defined as a condition (of everything made by man), the "composite" dimension is its only manifestation. Large areas of the contemporary urban metropolis are governed by indeterminate forces bonded, in the words of Abraham, by a unique "character." The material presence of the city, the composition of apparently random associations—that is, concrete and plastic, wood and stone—consolidate into spatial conditions that make the city legible, and hence inhabitable.

The relationship between form and non-form of a condition is critical to Abraham's thesis, as the condition in his view stands in a state of constant genesis. He cites an indirect example to elucidate the point: a pool of water is a condition that has no form, but is a result of a specific action of spilling a liquid. To this extent, many of the urban conditions of Hong Kong result in indirect associated actions brought to life when juxtaposed with multiple other composite narratives.

Conditions within the Grid

According to Albert Pope (1996, p. 2), "the contemporary city, the city that is, at this moment, under construction, is invisible." Much of the contemporary urban residuum found in our cities, rather than being ignored or forgotten, suffers from being unknown and inaccessible. With reference to the American city, Pope argues that suburbia's characteristics completely alienate conventional urban readings, and have become an unprecedented form of urban development.

Without an adequate conceptual framework in place, the amorphous, unquantifiable spaces of the contemporary city will remain inaccessible not only to those who live in them, but also to those who design them. In response to this, Pope articulates a meticulously crafted argument around how the open city of the "grid" establishes an autonomous logic that allows the city to transform—the grid being identified as the key component allowing endless urban permutations to evolve.

Contrary to many other modern cities, Hong Kong, given its historical and geographical setting, did not develop from a predetermined *forma urbis*, but established itself in reaction to its extreme topography.[11] Understanding this difference allows us to identify how Hong Kong has come to exemplify many of the conditions Pope highlights, although his thesis does not directly name Hong Kong. It could be argued that Hong Kong's constraints have given way to a reactive city of continuous adaptation to specific conditions, a careful urban calibration.

Conditions of the In-between

Rethinking the notion of contemporary urban spaces produced several recent publications which focus on the topic of "urban interstices" as representative territories where new social situations arise.[12] Interstitial conditions are by nature small spaces, and by default surrounded by other events and buildings. The morphology of the space and its inhabitation are always correlated, and the gap between (to quote the architecture landscape theorist Luc Levesque) generates, "something that is attractive and stimulating, an intensity that escapes the intentionality of planning: something paradoxical, from which inspiration can be drawn" (Levesque 2013, p. 21).

This intrigue with the urban gap has also been applied to Hong Kong in *Hong Kong In-between* (Borio and Wüthrich 2015). Following a research methodology developed by Atelier Bow-Wow in Tokyo,[13] Borio and Wüthrich explore the urban "back of house" condition where the "real city" occurs, arguing that these gaps act as lubricant to the engine of the city. Interestingly, the book concludes with a series of participatory projects exploring how these, so called "negative spaces" can become a positive identity of the city via minimal interventions that change people's attitudes and allow such spaces to be reappropriated.

Reading Hong Kong's Urban Dialects

Hong Kong is in a constant state of transformation, where every square meter of its urban territory is transformed into an artificial, highly technical landscape. The interrelation between city and landscape, from infrastructural facilities to reclaimed land, is the product of a highly engineered pragmatic thinking (policy) of control. Yet, with an urban density of more than 30,000 inhabitants per square kilometer and an average residential area of about 11 square meters per person (Jenni 2015), together with a multi-assemblage of layers, another side of this unique city is often taken for granted.

Hong Kong's Density

Of primary relevance to understanding Hong Kong's conditions are its demographic density and its extreme topographical setting (an island surrounded by mountains and sea). A population of more than 7 million inhabiting an urban land area of just 120 square kilometers yields a concentration of people approaching 600 per hectare (Shelton, Karakiewicz, and Kvan 2011, p. 19). Hong Kong is a city where local practices still survive the relentless

186 Peter Winston Ferretto

march toward homogeneous modernization. Paradoxically, though, in this process of survival, such daily practices have become invisible to the casual passerby, merging into the background as anonymous contingent moments. These urban micro conditions, literal manifestations of the "everyday urbanism," to quote Margaret Crawford (Chase, Crawford, and Kaliski 2008), represent the indissoluble connection between habitat and instances of social life, putting into question our traditionally modern interpretations of urbanism focusing on static and permanent conditions.

The urban conditions confronted in Hong Kong are based on the unique ground reality of the city—a landscape that constantly transforms, relying on its temporary existence. This kinetic urban reality, common to many Asian cities, generates a temporal background of overlaying circumstances each associated with a unique byproduct: planning codes, building regulations, and government covenants. [14] To this effect, urban conditions are relative entities, dependent upon specific spatial relationships. At first sight, this might not be evident, but only appears the more you digest their condition via observation, mapping, and drawing. These urban relationships contribute to a general condition of intensity reliant on multiple networks of activity.

The Hong Kong Discourse

> Hong Kong edifices are not built to be beautiful, they are built in a pragmatic way: rational and efficient. Hong Kong architecture is nothing more than an immediate expression of the specific condition. [MAP Office]
>
> *(Peckham 2011)*

Many architects and critics have acknowledged and investigated these situations before. The most recent in-depth investigation of the topic has been produced by MAP Office, a multidisciplinary Hong Kong-based architectural practice led by Laurent Gutierrez and Valerie Portefaix, who, as their website claims, document how human beings subvert and appropriate space.[15] Another important study, *Hong Kong Typologies*, written by the Swiss architects and ETH professors, Christ & Gantenbein, traces a taxonomy of Hong Kong's modern architectural heritage. Their position is that since all conditions in Hong Kong are radical (political, topographical, demographical, financial, and climatic), the associated architecture of the city is radical—or, one could argue, practical to the extent that functionality and efficiency become radical. A list of thirty-six examples of 20th-century buildings, each belonging to a specific type—pencil tower, gallery building, vertical factory, and shop house—is identified. These examples collectively reinforce strict regulations, imposed by the local planning authorities and applied to the extreme conditions, and ultimately combined to produce a quasi-fictional reality.

The book also includes a series of contributions by local academics; of specific interest is "The Origin of Hong Kong Building Types" (Tieben 2010), which outlines the history of the urban built fabric of Hong Kong. In a quest for efficiency to establish the "Made in Hong Kong" brand, Hong Kong's population increased by 1 million every decade to reach the 7 million of today (Tieben 2010, p. 39). According to Tieben, Hong Kong's rapid urbanization is strictly correlated to historical events, most importantly the creation of the People's Republic of China (1949), which started the wave of mass immigration. In the 1950s, Hong Kong consolidated its position as a free port, with the geopolitical situation (Korean War, 1950–1953) forcing the city into manufacturing. Many industrial estates were built next to mass housing complexes using similar designs and construction methods. With the value of domestic export continuing to rise, in the 1960s Hong Kong started to specialize in new industries, such as electronics, watches, toys and clothing—all labor-intensive.

In this regard, much of Hong Kong's architecture can be explained by this search for efficiency and the maximum exploitation of site borne in mind. Hong Kong building types, according to Tieben, are fully imbedded into the vibrant life of the metropolis, where everyday life is strongly related to the condition of hyper-density.

Urban Dialect

Inhabited urban conditions are a form of urban dialect indigenous to the area. These conditions reflect quotidian occurrences and at the same time present fragile temporality. They represent episodes disappearing at any one moment. The next moment allowing the residents to dwell, as they want; playing mah-jong with friends, gambling while smoking, and impromptu picnics.[16] According to La Cecla (1993, p. 38), these events, allow people to "acclimatize" themselves with their immediate environment. Representing instances that develop over time, local customs evolved over generations and through form of mentality rely on local practices and adaptations to circumstance.

Dialect, the language of the people, is implanted with infinite nuances and subtleties that go back centuries in the history of a culture. In the same manner, urban dialects relate to how people dwell within their respective environments, differentiating themselves from the standard language (the formal city). By not being composed of static structures, but reliant on mental patterns, or as La Cecla (1993, p. 70) states, "mental maps," inhabitants have built-in strata of information: a collection of memories, events, and rituals. These maps constitute a common reference point of spatial occurrences, and relate to the idea of urban condition. Conditions in this sense are relationships in the guise of meeting places, shortcuts, festivities, superimpositions, card games, and the secret alleyways of local inhabitants. This alter-identity, rather than the city being composed of architectural artifacts, means that they develop together with their inhabitants through complex networks that are typically disregarded by local planning authorities (in the name of modernization) as elements that should be at best avoided, and at worst eradicated. The identity of a city, according to their mindset, should be established by a set of regulations that install order (planning) and coherence into neighborhoods, with the unfortunate side effect of eliminating local urban dialects.

If the local urban dialect is embodied in the everyday condition, the common mother tongue language of Hong Kong, is defined by rules, the plethora of codes that regulate the city. Hong Kong is a city of regulations—one could describe it as the contemporary version of the Forbidden City (the palace in Beijing where no one could enter or leave without the emperor's permission). In Hong Kong, the "forbidden" relates to the denial of any common practices being performed in public spaces such as smoking, gambling, cycling, picnics, drinking, hanging out washing, drying food, fires, walking dogs, and cooking. Everything has to be sanitized and regulated, in the process pushing people to the edges, to undefined zones, residual spaces, no-man's lands where life can happen, where people can behave normally.

Hong Kong Conditions

> Our gaze travels through space and gives us the illusion of relief and distance. That is how we construct space, with an up and a down, a left and a right, an in front and behind, a near and a far. When nothing arrests our gaze, it carries a very long way. But if it meets with nothing, it sees only what it meets. Space is what arrests our gaze, what our sight stumbles over: the obstacles, bricks, an angle, a vanishing point.
>
> *(Perec and Sturrock 1997, p. 81)*

Over the course of the last two years, at the Chinese University of Hong Kong, this urban research project aims to decipher exactly those conditions "our sight stumbled across," as Perec describes above. The condition here becomes a tool to interrogate the collective DNA of how people inhabit such an extreme city, at the same time allowing the formulation of a position from which we can actually learn. Too often, in our quest to explain given urban situations, architects rush to assess. By association, they pass judgment, rather than assessing and postulating solutions. This study seeks to accept and uncover the process behind how the city operates: from the invisible interconnected networks to the adjustable and adaptive systems that Hong Kong constantly generates to survive.

The five conditions chosen, each representing a specific category of urban coexistence, were selected to portray a multifaceted cross-section of Hong Kong's urban inhabitation. In this chapter, all the examples exclusively focus on Hong Kong Island, excluding important areas of Hong Kong such as Kowloon and the New Territories that would require a more extensive study. The research involved extensive fieldwork mapping, initially undertaken with graduate students at CUHK School of Architecture as part of an elective topical class in 2016, and later developed with Sungyeol Choi, a Research Assistant investigating the residual urban spaces within Hong Kong.[17]

The *modus operandi* revolved around two key components: photography and three-dimensional drawing. The photograph allows the inhabitation to be recorded, in a similar manner to August Sander, who concentrated on always taking portraits of his models in their natural working environment.[18] Each photograph sanctions a specific form of urban dwelling, while the 3D drawing reveals the morphology of the space, acting as a form of translation of the photograph, exposing the structure of the space in question. Borrowing from Christopher Alexander's "pattern language," a form of philosophy cultivates the exploration. This dual method of recording and digesting is critical in describing the condition at stake:

> At the core . . . is the idea that people should design for themselves their own houses, streets and communities. This idea . . . comes simply from the observation that most of the wonderful places of the world were not made by architects but by the people.
> *(Alexander, Ishikawa, and Silverstein 1977)*

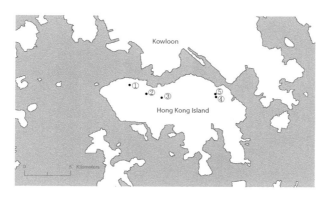

FIGURE 9.1 Location of the five urban conditions. Image by Peter Ferretto and Sungyeol Choi.

In a comparable manner, this research follows Alexander's format of treating urban conditions as entities that identify how local architecture spontaneously responds to given problems or situations. To this extent, the research presented here is empirical and relies on observing the social subculture of the city at work.

1: Occupy

Tucked away in a non-descript alley, Li Sing Street, off Queens Road West on Hong Kong Island, between the traditional neighborhoods of Sheung Wan and Sai Ying Pun, is a small fruit and vegetable store. This parasitic store embeds itself into a 30 centimeter leftover alcove. In this urban empty shelf, thinner than your conventional domestic bookshelf, lies a one-man business where the dimensions of the shop dictate every aspect of this ingenious business operation. Food displayed, security shutters, delivery, amount of food stored, and opening hours all depend on the extreme shop dimension.

The condition, a result of the vertiginous commercial rents achievable in Hong Kong and a series of urban/architectural contingent circumstances, is a common example of how a marginal and, to most people, insignificant space is occupied and transformed into a fully functioning commercial venture. When you look closer, it isn't simply the physical dimensions of the store that are taken to the extreme. The legality and the logistics of the situation are also shrewdly exploited. Technically, no commercial business

FIGURE 9.2 Shelf store: fruit and vegetable shop in Sheung Wan. Image by Peter Ferretto and Sungyeol Choi.

can invade the public road with permanent structures. Hence, the store works around temporary transformations, enabling the shop to all but disappear when not in use. The logistics likewise take advantage of the urban setting, with the adjacent alley being pedestrian-only. This forces the store to rely exclusively on motorbike delivery, with no associated storage space.

At a time when large parts of Hong Kong are rapidly being gentrified, Sai Ying Pun being a prime example, and entire neighborhoods are being artificially inseminated with massive hermetic developments, this condition represents an urban fragment of "reciprocity" (La Cecla 2014, p. 102).[19] It is an example of a micro transitional space, without which the city loses its "fraternal" dimension, as with the non-confrontational engagement with the real life of its citizens.

2: Byproduct

Hong Kong is a city that came into existence by accident.[20] The engineering acrobatics required simply to allow the city to function are almost preposterous. This site, located between a complex road network and the steep topography of the terrain on Government Hill, exemplifies this infrastructural "byproduct" condition. Historically the site, located in the vicinity of the Eliot Canal, built at the turn of the 20th century to provide water for the nearby Ice-house, has been the home to several important institutions, such as hospitals, the Catholic Cathedral, and many school buildings.

FIGURE 9.3 Infrastructural spaces—Mid-Levels. Image by Peter Ferretto and Sungyeol Choi.

Today the site is completely bypassed, sitting below a 40 meter-high viaduct that connects the prosperous Mid-Levels area to Central (the financial heart of Hong Kong). The resulting "terrain vague," to use the term coined by the Catalan urbanist Solà-Morales (1995), is an abandoned and unproductive space representing the anonymous reality of the city, an "urban pause" that allows the city to breathe.[21] These conditions are as much part of Hong Kong's urban ecology as the famous landmark sites we are all aware of.

The inefficient character of the "byproduct" condition represents an important urban phenomenon. This uncontaminated void becomes unaffected by Hong Kong's quest for efficiency and real estate development. Formative spaces act as interior urban realms from one end of the spectrum to the homogenized interiors of the Hong Kong Mall at the other. Their indeterminacy allows them to go unnoticed and at the same time offers opportunities for how the present status quo can be subverted.

3: Mitigating

The geological history of Hong Kong is vital in understanding the city's built environment. The majority of the island consists of granitic rock, an extremely hard land-bed that precludes most subterranean developments. Compared to most other Asian metropolises, it is common to come across multi-story car parks entirely above ground, even given the high land values—a direct manifestation of the island's geological landscape.

FIGURE 9.4 Superimposed rationalism, Braemer Hill. Image by Peter Ferretto and Sungyeol Choi.

Broadview Terrace (the name gives away the housing's primary asset) is a high-end residential compound built in 1974 on Cloud View Road in Braemer Hill, offering spectacular views over Hong Kong's harbor. Built right on the edge of the granite cliff, to maximize both views and plot coverage, the development has a bionic structure erected along the precipice to comply with two building codes: to accommodate private vehicle access and provide emergency fire access to all elevations. The result is the superimposition of a Terragni-esque structural white grid over the raw, exposed granite mountain, which, taken in isolation, produces an abstract reinforced concrete grid as a testament to the city's constant struggle to inhabit nature.[22]

This common mitigating condition, a form of topographical domestication, generates an artificial datum, a flat level from which a building line can be erected. Although the notion of artificial land is typically associated with reclaimed sea land in Hong Kong, such engineering techniques of adapting the existing topography equally create a manufactured condition of land colonization. Pure pragmatic functionalism assumes its own structural design identity, becoming an unforeseen city aesthetic.

4: Ritual

Shau Kei Wan, located in the northeastern part of Hong Kong Island, is a relatively suburban district (an oxymoronic statement given its population in excess of 70,000, who live in a density of approximately 30,000

FIGURE 9.5   Hung Shing Temple, Shau Kei Wan. Image by Peter Ferretto and Sungyeol Choi.

people per square kilometer). This region evolved from an 18th-century fishing village into a socially engineered hyper-dense landscape. However, the striking feature, given this radical transformation, is how the local community retain and live their everyday lives incorporating the vestiges of their traditional rituals.

Up to the late 1970s, Shau Kei Wan harbor used to be setting for a large, informal floating settlement, housing more than 20,000 inhabitants in floating structures that have all but disappeared.[23] Today, even though the fishing culture has vanished, the local community maintain a strong connection to the fishermen's spiritual beliefs, with temples dedicated to goddesses such as Tin Hau, who is venerated in the many scattered temples that remain embedded into the fabric of the neighborhood.[24]

This small, subsidiary temple to the adjacent main Hung Shing Temple, sits at the foot of a hill that used to house a large informal settlement.[25] The building, no bigger than a typical garden shed (3 × 3 meters), houses a statue of the scholar Hung Shing Ye, usually surrounded by fruit offerings. The open entrance is flanked by spiral incense burners. A local banyan tree, requiring steel bracing, perilously hangs above the roof of the temple, inducing a three-way state of symbiosis between building, nature, and spirit. The clear relationship here between people and place, via the participation of quotidian rituals, engenders an urban condition that goes far beyond contemporary "real estate" thinking and helps form a society rooted in invisible networks.

5: Residual

FIGURE 9.6 Mobile station master's office, Shau Kei Wan Bus Terminus. Image by Peter Ferretto and Sungyeol Choi.

The final condition, also located in Shau Kei Wan district, 200 meters south of the temple mentioned above, is a residual condition produced as a derivative of three intersecting transportation infrastructures. The Island Eastern Corridor Expressway is a subsidiary bypass and an elevated pedestrian walkway. Ensconced below this transportation knot is Shau Kei Wan's main Bus Terminus, a perfectly efficient exercise in converting a potential urban wasteland into a thriving and propagating public amenity.

The more you look, the more you discover in Shau Kei Wan. Every aspect of this three-dimensional urban jigsaw has been cleverly adapted to incorporate public amenities. From functional public staircases becoming impromptu terraces for people to rest and watch the evolving daily narratives to the flyover acting as an integrated bus shelter, life seems to permeate this contingent site. Yet it is only through a slow process of mapping the territory that one is fully able to comprehend the complexity of the dynamics at work.

Stuck to a huge concrete pier supporting the flyover above is a temporary mobile facility equipped with a fiberglass cabin (the station master's office), a disused oil tank (an impromptu garden with local ferns and a rose tree), a mini-shrine to the Han Dynasty warlord Kuan Yu (a three-tier red timber bookshelf structure), and a six-compartment locker unit (red metal, with associated changing room). To many, this humble and anonymous condition, apparently disconnected from any urban discourse, has little relevance in explaining and justifying how the present Hong Kong works. However, this residual condition demonstrates how commonly discarded urban spaces rely on a network of adjacencies, contextual and cultural, in order to connect seemingly disconnected and abandoned spaces.

Toward a Culture of Condition

> Increasingly we live in a "'cultural supermarket'" in which the world's cultural forms, in areas from food to religion to music to architecture, are to some extent available for appropriation by everyone.
>
> *(Mathews 2013, p. 55)*

The cultural identity of a place from an anthropological perspective, as argued by the Hong Kong-based anthropologist Gordon Matthews, has historically been associated with the "way of life of the people." In this context, Hong Kong's cultural identity is, and one can argue has always been, in a state of flux, neither culturally "pure" nor culturally "free." Hong Kong is a city that lies between extreme polarities of the political, national, economical, and architectural. In architectural terms, there is the extremely formal (designed and branded architecture) contrasted with the informal, unplanned, organic city (adaptive, temporary, and

CONDITION

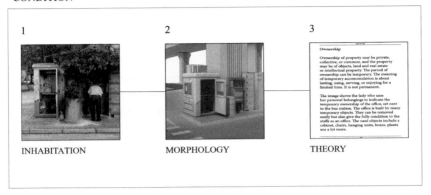

FIGURE 9.7 Diagram of the research methodology. Image by Peter Ferretto and Sungyeol Choi.

spontaneous architecture). Precisely between these two positions lies the architectural identity of Hong Kong.

"Condition" is a word with multiple readings: as a noun it relates the state of something, its appearance, quality, and circumstances, while as a verb it implies influence, constraint, and control. These two understandings are critical to the thesis of this chapter. On the one hand, the urban condition narrates the physical characteristics of our city, as described in the first section of the chapter. In particular, the situations that belong to the "background city" and how everyday practices of inhabitation—the hyper-local—help establish an "urban dialect" which mostly remains extraneous to the authorities that plan our cities. The second position, the notion that reflects the meaning associated with influence and control, relies on observation and interpretation through drawing.

Working in a similar manner to an ethnographer, the research outlined in this chapter presents readings taken from direct observations, a collection of moments and situations (condensed into five conditions) representing an empirical record of the present, the "here and now" of a city in constant flux. The interpretation of conditions, which I classify as a form of urban hermeneutics, is an important methodology to decipher the nuances of the city. This methodology employs a three-part process—Photograph/Inhabitation, Drawings/Morphology, Text/Theory—in order to distinguish and decode often-discarded urban situations.

Most of the conditions highlighted in this chapter would not typically be associated with the recognized identity of Hong Kong. They represent a taxonomy of the "other" Hong Kong, to borrow the concept coined by Foucault (1984). These in-between worlds, neither here nor there, belong somewhere between utopia and dystopia, or the heterotopia of Foucault, acting as vessels connecting the city to its roots, to the memories of a world not so far away, that has evolved into the present condition. Foucault remarks that the perfect example of heterotopia is a boat, a floating piece of space that belongs to no fixed place except the infinity of the sea.

Architecture has the power to affect people's lives, beyond the functional and the practical. To this effect, this chapter explores how the customs and rituals of the "urban dialect" provide a background to our lives and contribute to a shared reality. To conclude: "The relationship between space and activity is evidently neither a compelling certainty nor open and random, but complex and variable" (Jones 2016), where Hong Kong's background is complicit in this complexity, molding our habits, beliefs, and expectations, and most importantly, providing a framework of relationships. The framework of the background city enables architecture to be understood as a coexistent platform, beyond Vitruvius' paradigm of *utilitas, firmitas, venustas*, as mentioned in the introduction to the chapter, but rather related to space, time, and memory. Memory has the ability to both preserve the past and also adapt and manipulate the present, and in this respect alludes to the driving word of this chapter: "condition."

Acknowledgments

The initial part of this study was carried out with students from the School of Architecture, Chinese University of Hong Kong, enrolled in the elective class "ARCH5131: Hong Kong Condition."

The main research is part of a larger project titled *Urban Pauses: Reclaiming Hong Kong's Residual Urban Spaces* (2016), supported by the General Research Fund (GRF), a competitive grant awarded by the Research Grants Council of Hong Kong.

Finally I would like to thank Mr. Sungyeol Choi, the Research Assistant who helped me assemble the material for this chapter.

Notes

1 This is a reference to the director Spike Jonze's magic realism film *Being John Malkovich* (1999), where the protagonist works in a strange low-ceilinged office located on the 7½th floor of the Mertin-Flemmer Building in Manhattan.
2 La Cecla uses the Italian word *ambiente*, which, although it translates into English as "environment," embodies a wider notion, suggesting elements of atmosphere and ambience associated to places and spaces.
3 A reference to Lévi-Strauss' structuralist epic *Tristes tropiques* (2012).
4 This point is argued by Jeremy Till is his book *Architecture Depends* (2013), where he establishes a counter-notion of architecture as a contingent discipline inherently dependent on external and unpredictable agents to become reality.

5 Heidegger uses the word *Dasein* to describe our way of being—that is, existing in a place with particular things and established ways of doing things.
6 Tin Hau, a Chinese sea goddess venerated throughout Southern Asia, is the patron protector of sailors and fishermen.
7 I refer here to Hong Kong, but this argument could easily apply to so many other contemporary cities.
8 This is a hypothetical number; for a detailed retailed planning policy. See Planning Department, Government of Hong Kong Special Administrative Region, *Hong Kong Planning Standards and Guidelines: Summary* (March 2017), https://www.pland.gov.hk/pland_en/tech_doc/hkpsg/sum/pdf/sum_en.pdf (accessed June 29, 2018).
9 To understand the urban materiality of Hong Kong, it is important to differentiate between formal and informal materials. The formal—that is, the materials that belong to the domain of capital-"A" architecture (buildings designed by architects) has a relentless repetitive quality such as the ubiquitous marble ceramic tile that clads endless public and private surfaces. In contrast, the informal materials, the everyday materials that belong to lower-case-"a" architecture (informal, temporary street buildings), constantly adapt and possess a tactile and visceral quality.
10 For further reading, see *The Postmodern Condition: A Report on Knowledge*, (Lyotard, Bennington, and Massumi 1984), where the idea of grand, universal narratives is contrasted with metanarratives—that is, small and local narratives.
11 Following the First Opium War, Hong Kong was ceded by China to Britain under the Treaty of Nanking, signed on August 29, 1842, becoming a Crown Colony of the British Empire.
12 See Brighenti (2013).
13 Atelier Bow-Wow is an architectural office in Tokyo formed by Yoshiharu Tsukamoto and Momoyo Kaijima, who have published several books about the city most notably *Made in Tokyo* (2001).
14 The concept of the "kinetic city" has been elaborated by the Indian architect and MIT professor Rahul Mehrotra, who advocates the potential of designing for informality in the city. According to Mehrotra, the kinetic city is about activity, not architecture.
15 www.map-office.com (accessed June 29, 2018).
16 Mah-jong is a famous Cantonese board game played with 144 domino-like tiles on a square table.
17 General Research Fund, Research Grants Council of Hong Kong, *Urban Pauses: Reclaiming Hong Kong's Residual Urban Spaces* (2016).
18 August Sander (1876–1964), a German Portrait photographer, famous for his *Faces of Our Times* documentary.
19 In Hong Kong, gentrification is today generally associated with the arrival of the Mass Transit Railway (MTR) subway system in a neighborhood, with the MTR coincidentally opening a new station in Sai Ying Pun in 2015.
20 Contrary to other major Chinese cities such as Guangzhou, Beijing, or Shanghai, which developed historically following an urban structure, Hong Kong was developed by the British as a reactive engineered city, with trade as the main driver. Large parts of Hong Kong's territory come from reclaimed land, and infrastructure constantly mitigates the island's harsh topography.
21 A term I am currently researching in connection to the notion of "residual spaces" in Hong Kong. See note 17.
22 This refers to Giuseppe Terragni's rationalist magnum opus, the Casa del Fascio building in Como, Italy (1932–1936).

23 The last remaining examples of a floating village can be found in Lantau Island, in the fishing town of Tai O.

24 See note 6.

25 The temple of Hung Shing is dedicated to the scholar Hung Hei, a righteous government official who won the approval of the local people during his tenure in office through his scholarly study of astronomy, geography, and mathematics, eventually establishing an observatory in the area to predict meteorological changes. Ever since, prayers to him are thought to contribute to the wellbeing of fishermen and sea traders.

Bibliography

Abbas, A. *Hong Kong: Culture and Politics of Disappearance* (Hong Kong: Hong Kong University Press, 1997).

Abbas, A. "Building Hong Kong: From Migrancy to Disappearance," in *Drifting: Architecture and Migrancy*, ed. S. Cairns (London: Routledge, 2004), pp. 129–141.

Abraham, A. *A New Nature: 9 Architectural Conditions between Liquid and Solid* (Zurich: Lars Muller Publications, 2015).

Alexander, C., Ishikawa, S., and Silverstein, M. *A Pattern Language: Towns, Buildings, Construction* (Oxford: Oxford University Press, 1977).

Borio, G., and Wüthrich, C. *Hong Kong In-between* (Zurich: Park Books, 2015).

Brighenti, A.M., ed. *Urban Interstices: The Aesthetics and the Politics of the In-between* (London: Routledge, 2013).

Certeau, M.D. *The Practice of Everyday Life* (Berkeley, CA: University of California Press, 2006).

Chase, J., Crawford, M., and Kaliski, J. *Everyday Urbanism* (New York: Monacelli Press, 2008).

Christ, E., and Gantenbein, C. *Hong Kong Typologies* (Zurich: ETH-DARCH, 2010).

Emerson, T. "From Lieux to Life," *AA Files* 45/46 (2001): 92–97.

Foucault, M. "Of Other Spaces: Utopias and Heterotopias," *Architecture/Mouvement/Continuité* 5 (1984): 46–49.

Heidegger, M. "Building Dwelling Thinking," in *Poetry, Language, Thought* (New York, 1971), pp. 141–160.

Herzog, J., and de Meuron, P. "How Do Cities Differ?" in *The Inevitable Specificity of Cities*, ed. J. Herzog, R. Diener, M. Meili, P. de Meuron, M. Herz, C. Schmid, and M. Topalovic (Zurich: Lars Müller Publishers, 2015), pp. 15–19.

Herzog, J., Diener, R., Meili, M., de Meuron, P., Herz, M., Schmid, C., and Topalovic, M., eds. *The Inevitable Specificity of Cities* (Zurich: Lars Müller Publishers, 2015).

Jenni, R. "Engineering Territory," in *The Inevitable Specificity of Cities*, ed. J. Herzog, R. Diener, M. Meili, P. de Meuron, M. Herz, C. Schmid, and M. Topalovic (Zurich: Lars Müller Publishers, 2015), pp. 160–196.

Jones, P.B. *Architecture and Ritual* (London: Bloomsbury Academic, 2016).

Kaijima, M., Kuroda, J., and Tsukamoto, Y. *Made in Tokyo* (Tokyo: Kajima Institute Publishing, 2006).

La Cecla, F. *Contro l'urbanistica* (Milan: Giulio Einaudi, 2014).

La Cecla, F. *Mente locale* (Milan: Eleuthera, 1993).

Latour, B. *We Have Never Been Modern* (New York: Harvester Wheatsheaf, 1993).

Le Corbusier. *Precisions on the Present State of Architecture and City Planning*, trans. by E.S. Aujame (Cambridge, MA: MIT Press, 1991).

Levesque, L. "Trajectories of Interstitial Landscapeness: A Conceptual Framework for Territorial Imagination and Action," in *Urban Interstices: The Aesthetics and the Politics of the In-between*, ed. A.M. Brighenti (London: Routledge, 2013), pp. 23–53.

Lévi-Strauss, C. *Tristes tropiques* (London: Penguin Classics, 2012).

Lyotard, J.-F., Bennington, G., and Massumi, B. *The Postmodern Condition: A Report on Knowledge* (Minneapolis, MN: University of Minnesota Press, 1984).

Mariani, M., and Barron, P. *Terrain Vague: Interstices at the Edge of the Pale* (New York: Routledge, 2014).

Mathews, G. "Cultural Identity in the Age of Globalization: Implications on Architecture," in *The Domestic and the Foreign in Architecture*, ed. S. Lee and R. Baumeister (Rotterdam: 010 Publishing, 2013), pp. 47–54.

Mehrotra, R. "Negotiating the Static and Kinetic Cities: The Emergent Urbanism of Mumbai," in *Other Cities, Other Worlds*, ed. A. Huyssen (Durham, NC: Duke University Press, 2008), pp. 205–218.

Peckham, R. *MAP Office* (Hong Kong: RAM Publications, 2011).

Perec, G., and Sturrock, J. *Species of Spaces and Other Pieces* (London: Penguin Books, 1997).

Pollio, V., and Morgan, M. H. *Vitruvius: The Ten Books on Architecture* (New York: Dover Publications, 1960).

Pope, A. *Ladders* (New York: Princeton Architectural Press, 1996).

Rudofsky, B. *Architecture without Architects: A Short Introduction to Non-pedigreed Architecture* (New York: Doubleday, 1964).

Scott, J.C. *Decoding Subaltern Politics: Ideology, Disguise, and Resistance in Agrarian Politics* (London: Routledge, 2013).

Shelton, B., Karakiewicz, J., and Kvan, T. *The Making of Hong Kong: From Vertical to Volumetric* (London: Routledge, 2011).

Solà-Morales, I. "Terrain Vague," in *AnyPlace*, ed. C.C. Davidson (Cambridge, MA: MIT Press, 1995), pp. 118–123.

Tieben, H. "The Origin of Hong Kong Building Types," in C. Gantenbein, *Hong Kong Typologies* (Zurich: ETH-DARCH, 2010), pp. 33–55.

Till, J. *Architecture Depends* (Cambridge, MA: MIT Press, 2013).

Tsukamoto, Y., and Kaijima, M. *Made in Tokyo* (Tokyo: Kajima Institute, 2001)

Tsukamoto, Y., and Kaijima, M. *Bow-Wow from Post Bubble City* (Tokyo: INAX Publishing, 2006).

Wrathall, M. *How to Read: Heidegger* (New York: W.W. Norton, 2005).

10

CHASING A GENEALOGY OF X

Choon Choi

Introduction

Whereas an X in mathematics stands for the unknown, an X in architectural drawings stands for emptiness—a void. By connecting four corners of an area with two lines, an X indicates an empty space open to below within architectural drawings. If the shape of a void is rectangular, the X appears more balanced and symmetrical, but it becomes more eccentric with more complex shapes. It is not imperative to indicate a void with an X, and many architects find it to be graphically too obtrusive, instead opting for a written description of "open" or "void" within the open area, or filling it with a hatch pattern. But Korean architects are rather faithful about the use of the X, embellishing their plans with the X with curious enthusiasm. It is a feature they seem eager to show off prominently in the foreground. The voids created by an X can be found in unexpected places all over Korean cities, and these nameless spaces may be described, but not defined; sensed, but not seen; blocked, but not filled. It is "a sign, alas, that would last an instant only to vanish for good."[1]

In most cases, architects themselves are unable to elaborate on the precise form or shape of their voids, as voids in Korean architecture are not spatial or morphological, but mostly territorial. Early use of voids in contemporary Korean architecture first appeared in accidental outdoor spaces such as peripheral gaps created through setback requirements, or "dry areas," which are underground air shafts exempt from floor area ratio calculations. These open areas were not intentionally shaped or sculpted, but simply leftover spaces, to be covered up later through illegal roof extensions to increase floor areas. Primarily motivated by greed, these discreet voids lack the poetic, contemplative atmospheres typically associated with void spaces. Conversely, a grand double-height space symbolizes wealth and status. Having enough space to leave empty signifies excess wealth, and tall void spaces have become objects of desire among the expanding middle class.

Soon, the void was no longer an issue of merely claiming extra breathing room for the wealthy, as the urban scene of Seoul became more chaotic and more fragmented. A need for a more organized network of void spaces became progressively more urgent during Korea's economic rush toward an imminent collapse in the mid-1990s. Korean architects aggressively voiced their opposition to this "fragmented reality stained with greedy commercial savagery," calling the urban street scene of Seoul "a ridiculous mask hiding the perverted desires of the *petite bourgeoisie*."[2] The group of architects supported Seung's call for architecture of poverty focused on the spaces between buildings—the void, interstitial territories that were no more than competitive battle grounds for territorial disputes between property owners. They sought to portray calm, well-designed empty voids as the most important design features in their architectural projects. They upheld traditional open spaces such as *madang* and *maru* as the basic planning tools for Korean architecture, and tried to reinterpret their spatial logic within an expanded urban realm. A typical Korean home features some form of central open space, simulating a courtyard, or *madang*, in a traditional *hanok*. Unlike the Japanese spatial concept of *ma*, or in-between space, the idea behind the *madang* of Korean architecture is more utilitarian and practical. More *carnivalesque* than contemplative, Korean courtyards are meant for an indeterminate combination of active and festive functions. As the bland apartment blocks lost status as the *de facto* housing type in Korea, the courtyards and other forms of central voids gained greater popularity within residential architecture during

FIGURE 10.1   Courtyards in *hanoks*. Image provided by SPACE Group.

the past decade. Apart from *madang*, voids in Korean architecture fall into two other categories—the "ultimate space," which, as defined by Kim Swoo-guen, is vertically carved into section or elevation, and the invisible void, referring to mostly sentimental residual spaces, marked by erasure, removal, and absence. To understand Korean cities, we need to ignore what is visible and tangible, but instead follow the traces of these different types of voids hidden within the depth of rooms and corridors. If we gain access into these intimate zones of imagination, we can peek into the discreet inner desires and resilient memories that have shaped Korean cities in ways seemingly indecipherable to outsiders.

Waiting for X

> To reach the goal of creating the totality of life by means of art. . . .the first step was, then, to create the imaginary space wherein this totality might exist as an independent and self-sufficient reality--a reality that would not attempt to represent the objective world nor be an allegory of that world, but would have its own life and objectivity, though in a different sense.[3]

The most common type of voids found in Korean architecture may be called the flat void, a hole in the floor plate that seldom continues beyond the single level immediately below the hole. A flat void is more conceptual than spatial, in that the X denotes a territorial gap rather than a spatial volume. The X for a flat void prominently shows up in floor plans, but quickly disappears in sections, as its flat sectional interruption can only be faintly indicated by lighter line weight. Sometimes the X disappears altogether, including in floor plans, if the void is open completely to the sky. Its outline demarcates a zone of shared common usage that cannot be monopolized by a single user. It is also a realm of indeterminacy, as no specific use is prescribed to it. This lack of definition is the very essence of Korean courtyards, and many cultural scholars have identified it as a source of Korean identity. As Yoo Heung-joon, a popular cultural historian, claimed: "it's a kind of space that can't even be named because it serves no particularly useful purpose, but such spaces extend the vitality of buildings and diversify our lifestyles."[4] The void space in the middle of Yoo's own house, in fact, was one of the most widely published and disseminated images of Korean architecture.

Perhaps no other contemporary architect has done more to popularize flat voids in Korean architecture than Seung H-sang (born 1952), who designed the famous house for Yoo named Sujoldang. When the house was built in 1993, it was hailed as the most sophisticated reinterpretation of Korea's cultural heritage into contemporary architecture, and

204 Choon Choi

marked the beginning of Seung's prolific career as an architect of the "urban void":

> What Seung has discovered was to absorb with enthusiasm the values of non-functionality, indeterminacy, and useless void. In his Sujoldang project, he divided the tiny courtyard into three segments or four if you include the parking area. These four voids of various sizes and functions ultimately created a sense of spatial vastness that defies its 200 square-meter parcel. Each of those subtracted spaces was absolutely not wasted but a void with a cause.[5]

By organizing the house as a series of voids, Seung was able to appeal to the Confucian bias that is deeply ingrained within the psyche of Korea's cultural elite, and he further embellished it with a sense of intellectual sophistication through appropriation of images from Beckett and Giacometti's *Waiting for Godot* as his primary source of inspiration. In fact, Seung published a photo of the stage scene below the photographs of Sujoldang, taken directly from the book *Dialogue in the Void* by Matti Megged. The texts from this book and the images of Giacometti's work provided a pivotal turning point in Seung's career, and those of many of his contemporaries during the following decade. The persimmon tree in the courtyard of Sujoldang indeed directly referenced Giacometti's melancholy tree on the stage in *Waiting for Godot*. But, standing next to a traditional stone fence topped with *kiwa*, or black ceramic tiles, the reference became more nuanced and complex. The placing of a lacquered chair behind the tree, and the wooden floor pattern, commonly used for semi-indoor platforms, also contributed to the perceptual complexity of the courtyard. By infusing a small house with an intense mixture of phenomenal subtlety and Confucian philosophy, Seung deftly defied blatant historicism and naïve allegories that had plagued many of his predecessors. With Sujoldang, Seung firmly established the discourse of voids as the main organizing element for contemporary Korean architecture, and his concept of indeterminate voids has consistently dominated the discourse on Korean identity.

Seung often credits Dokrakdang as the main source of inspiration for his design philosophy. Indeed, the persimmon tree of Sujoldang offers a more direct resemblance to the tree in the courtyard of Dokrakdang than to the tree in *Waiting for Godot*. Built as a reclusive country estate for a renowned neo-Confucian scholar Hoejae in the early 16th century, Dokrakdang sits low on the ground surrounded by eight rocks and four mountains. The house is organized as a group of courtyards, each defined by stone walls with buildings situated along the periphery of each courtyard. The main pavilion is entirely tucked behind the fence, and it disappears within the vista beyond. In his own drawing of the house, Seung illustrates how the essence of the house is in the abstract organization of voids. He explains how attention to details or formal elaboration of built mass were dismissed as irrelevant, and Hoejae exclusively focused on relationship between void spaces. Both indoor spaces and outdoor courtyards were treated with equal weight and habitable spaces were drawn merely as thickened walls surrounding the courtyards: "The most important task is to create a void. That void is in itself the essence of their existence."[6]

Building upon the accolades for Sujoldang, Seung published his first design manifesto, *The Beauty of Poverty*, in 1996, in which he turned the question of aesthetic composition into a moral agenda. "The Beauty of poverty," Seung exclaims, "upholds utility over possession, sharing over accumulation, voids over solids," and equates spatial voids with frugality and generosity.[7] Seung's call for restraint, reserve, and thrift resonated deeply within the Korean society as it faced the first major global financial crisis that began in 1998. The basis of his arguments almost directly quoted Lao-tzu's teachings in *Tao-te-ching*, and the popularity of the *Tao-te-ching* as the *raison d'être* of voids in Korean architecture may be attributed to Amos Ih Tiao Chang's book *The Tao of Architecture* (1956), which was translated into Korean in 1984 by Professor Yoon Jang-seob of the Seoul National University. Seung's definition of his courtyards as a "space of no particular use but a reservoir for the diversity of lives" closely echoes Chang's description of a void as "that which is intangible . . . beyond the power of man, existing as a permanent reservoir from which the potential of life may be drawn as the need arises."[8] Seung and other Korean architects' habitual recitation of the following maxim attest to the dominant influence of Lao-tzu on Korean architecture:

> Molding clay into a vessel, we find the utility
> In its hollowness;
> Cutting doors and windows for a house, we find utility
> In its empty space.
> Therefore the being of things is profitable, the non-being
> Of things is serviceable.

The Swinging Lorenzo

To escape the myopic utopian vision of the flat void as an intellectual hideout, we need to travel further back in time to the 1970s, when one of the first modern architects of Korea, Kim Swoo-guen (1931–1986), introduced his theory of "ultimate space." Kim divided space into three categories—basic, functional, and ultimate. The ultimate space for him harbored the invisible force that allowed human beings to fulfill their

FIGURE 10.2 Hilltop bar. Image provided by E.S. Lim and the Kim Swoo Geun Foundation.

existential desires. Whereas a flat void quickly vanishes in section, or only a faint suggestion of its apparition remains in thin lines, the *vertical void* forms Kim's ultimate space, appearing mostly in elevation and section. Kim's vertical void is more three-dimensional and spatial than a flat void, and when it is situated adjacent to a public street, it can extend the street life into the inner territory of a building. Extending both horizontally and vertically, the ultimate space is also an illusory technique to expand a tiny space beyond its physical boundaries into an imaginary void through a labyrinthine juxtaposition of rooms.

Architect Kim Swoo-guen entered the fragile scene of post-war Korean architecture with a messianic charisma, winning the national design competition of the Korean National Assembly in 1959, when he was still a graduate student at Tokyo National University of Fine Arts and Music. Upon returning to Korea, Kim became the favorite architect of the military regime of Park Chung-hee, who hired him for a succession of government-initiated mega-projects, starting with the Hill Top Bar at Walker Hill (1961), the Freedom Center (1963), and the Sewoon Arcade (1963).

His influence was far-reaching, both as a generous patron of all artistic genres and a promoter of the avant-garde through his own journal, *SPACE*. As the mentor and teacher of a large group of leading architects that still dominate the profession in Korea, including Seung H-sang, Kim defined what it meant to live as an architect in Korea.

Kim's legendary personality, characterized by his charisma and braggadocio, gained a mythical status through many tales recounted by his apprentices and acquaintances. In one of the earlier stories, Kim reportedly stepped inside the cross-shaped girders underneath his inverted pyramid structure of the Hill Top Bar when construction workers refused to take off the concrete formwork for fear of collapse, and stayed there for the whole day until the entire formwork was dismantled. In 1977, a *Korea Herald* article called him "the most admired—and the swingingest architect in South Korea," in a special report on the opening gala

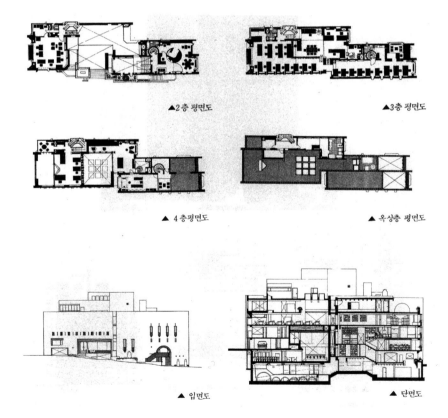

FIGURE 10.3 Plans and sections of the SPACE Group. Image provided by SPACE Group and the Kim Swoo Geun Foundation.

for the new Space Theater. It was the "hottest invitation in town," with 100 members of the exclusive Tokyo-Seoul network of cultural elites, but Kim's new building for his company, the SPACE Group, was the brightest star of the evening.

The original SPACE Group Building, built in two separate phases in 1971 and 1977, is arguably still the most famous work of modern architecture in Korea, with its influence over the collective imagination of Korean architects far exceeding its modest size. It was the first demonstration of his theory of "ultimate space" for a non-religious building type. It stood tall over traditional *hanoks*, with empty courtyards that surrounded it on three sides. Beginning with a central outdoor open space on the ground floor that divides the two wings, three large X signs appear on the third floor, another on the fourth floor, overlooking the drafting room below, and the last two on the fifth floor with roof gardens below. These seven voids are clearly visible in the main section as tall double-height spaces, extending through the skylights adorning the roof slab above. A large X over a generous void space is clearly visible in each floor plan, and unlike most void spaces in other Korean buildings, these vertical void spaces

FIGURE 10.4 Saemteo Building. Image provided by Choon Choi.

remain visible in sections as well. A café, a theater, a gallery, and three floors of offices and his private residence occupy a tightly knit maze of rooms that add up to just over 1,000 square meters. Divided into twenty different interior levels, the building displays an impressive array of vertical voids, stretching the limit of geometry in all directions.

The vertical X of the SPACE Group became more open and civic in Kim's public buildings built in the late 1970s. They began to engage streets and public plazas more actively, and the few civic-minded clients who understood Kim's intention to give up private space for public use willingly sacrificed rentable floor area to be used as "urban voids." Paying homage to the prevailing urban theories developed by José Luís Sert during the same period, Kim's inner network of courtyards and public passageways carved out more and more of the ground floor areas in Kim's public buildings. Kim's other projects completed in the same period, such as the Saemtoe Building (1979), the Arko Museum (1979), or the Arts Complex at Seoul National University (1973), generously incorporated stepped plazas, courtyards, and passageways that opened up the buildings to the surrounding context. Through his masterly deployment of the ultimate space and the urban void, Kim pioneered an alternate path for managing the public open spaces of Seoul. Such mastery provided a critical link to Seung's idea of the urban void—a term borrowed from Eduard Bru's urban theory: "It is not free space in the strict sense of the term, but rather space amongst things. It is the result of the existence of unresolved tensions that have made its occupation impossible."[9]

The open space under Kim's Saemteo Building is still one of the best examples of this type of urban void. A brick building with four waffle slabs stacked at 2.7 meter floor-to-floor height appears surprisingly tall and vertical in elevation thanks to a clever compositional manipulation of narrow windows and, more importantly, the double-height open space on the ground floor. Behind the tall columns, a stone-paved public passageway carves out a large volume of space on the ground floor. Beautifully paved in granite stone blocks, the intimate courtyard tucked behind tall columns is accessed from three sides, with the entrance to a glass-walled café occurring at the intersection of the three axes. Leaving almost half of the ground level entirely as void, and accessible to public, was an unprecedented gesture of civic generosity. The intimate scale and atmosphere of the recessed plaza is still one of the best examples of privately owned public space in Seoul. It is perhaps not a coincidence that Seung H-sang began his own practice inside the Saemteo Building, until he built the Iroje Building nearby. Seung also designed the rooftop addition and the renovation of the Samtoe Building in the year 2000, meticulously preserving the ground-level plaza even while inserting a new elevator shaft.

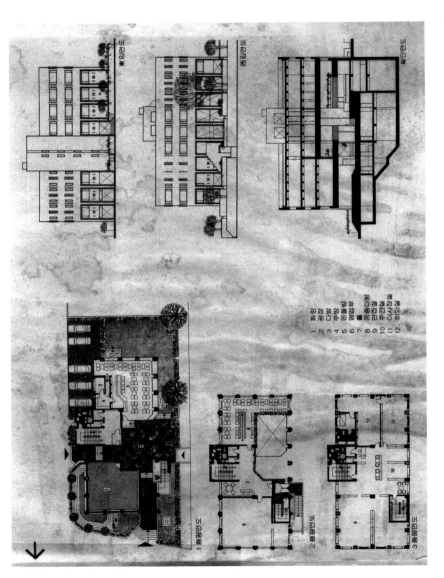

FIGURE 10.5 Plans and sections of the Saemteo Building. Image provided by SPACE Group and the Kim Swoo Geun Foundation.

Memories of X

> An increasingly rapid slippage of the present into a historical past that is gone for good, a general perception that anything and everything may disappear—these indicate a rupture of equilibrium.[10]

French historian Pierre Nora's observation that "we speak so much of memory because there is so little of it left" aptly describes the current urban context of Seoul, where any trace of the past that conjures memories inspires a fervent following among lovers of history. Whereas the first two generations of architects, such as Kim Swoo-geun and Seung H-sang, were entirely consumed by the problem of how to manage the chaos during Korea's breathless economic development, the current generation of architects no longer has much chance to make new buildings. The large-scale urban developments that so irritated Seung no longer make any financial sense in the new era of economic stasis. Further, the few areas that survived Korea's initial phase of urbanization and the subsequent flood of high-rise developments remain stuck in a state of fossilized decay. Their residents are still hopeful that the influx of capital for major redevelopment is inevitable and immanent, prompting the neglect or abandonment of their supposed temporary environments. In other words, these neighborhoods in waiting have now become urban ruins. The spray-painted X that once marked a building for demolition has become a permanent mural. Only traces of inherently weak mnemonic armatures remain inside these urban wastelands. Meanwhile, fragile but more enduring tales embedded within these ruins can survive long past the end of the physical lifespan of the buildings themselves. Some architects eagerly debate the historical values, or lack thereof, of such buildings, still convinced that there is scope for another heroic star-architect to emerge from the crowd. They are too proud, or simply blind, to see that architects are no longer asked for a utopian vision. They refuse to admit that the void marked by an X is no longer architectural, but historical. Today, architects in Seoul are not dreamers of the future, but guardians and archivists of the stories from the past. The main task for architects of the current generation is how to fill the gaps in history—the voids in our collective memory—and to reconnect the present to the past. Like explorers who search for the spot marked by an X on a treasure map, the current generation of architects in Korea eagerly collect, archive, and forage through historical texts and images in search of the past their elders had dismissed. Without any aesthetic or political agenda, they work with matters of memory to reconfigure a new historical context in which to situate each new project. Any wall that seems saturated with memories, regardless of its architectural pedigree, is now considered a precious artifact that can shed new light into historical voids.

The most direct means of re-materializing voids of memory through architecture is the restoration and reuse of old structures. In working on anonymous old buildings, it is important to adapt a more flexible attitude toward history which recognizes that every building contains, beneath its surfaces, murmurs of conversations waiting to be resumed. A successful restoration of a building can merge the memories of the past and the imagination of the present into the same fold of time. An exceptional example of such a project is the Nook in Huamdong, Seoul (2015) by KYWC. Barely over 30 square meters in size, the original house was built by a Japanese family in 1920, but most of its original timber structure was still intact. Because most of the buildings from the colonial era were demolished after liberation, including the General Government Building, which was demolished in 1995 after a long debate, few colonial-era buildings have survived. To preserve this rare historical relic, KYWC, led by architect Kim Seung-hoy, carefully peeled off multiple layers of residues and restored the interior of the house to its original state. When the Japanese brothers who used to live in the house visited it, they saw the floral relief on the concrete retaining wall still intact and recounted their forgotten memories of youth springing from the flowers. The Nook House has been restored as a site of memory, or *lieu de mémoire*, defined by Nora as a place that is "simple and ambiguous,

FIGURE 10.6   Nook in Huamdong. Image provided by Kim Jae Kyoung and KYWC.

natural and artificial, at once immediately available in concrete sensual experience and susceptible to the most abstract elaboration."

Asian cities are saturated with invisible, mythical memory that shapes and dominates the collective imagination even today. Through a breathless process of urban transformation within a relatively short period of time, many Asian cities suffer from a dismal discrepancy between the present reality and the past narratives. The enduring vividness of collective memory passed down over thousands of years aggravates the discomfort. Without an intimate understanding of these mythical memories, an architect cannot make buildings that resonate with the fragile context. Whereas restoration of old buildings like the Nook in Huamdong can appear overly nostalgic, the other means of materializing the void of memory is more regenerative and rational. Recognizing that forgetting is as important as remembering for a society to maintain its vitality, we at times need to admit that removal of a physical structure sometimes leads to an unshackling of a buried narrative from its lifeless container.

Cities like Seoul, where vivid memories from the past continue to dominate our collective imagination, desperately need to fill the void of memory and restore a sense of historical continuity. A civic conversation that intimately engages with the past must be resumed with every new construction. Historical knowledge leads to a strong sense of identity, which in turn allows the new generation of architects to speak on equal footing with the voices from the past. History is too often used as a shortcut for jump-starting an architectural project through imitation of precedents, or as an embellishment for adding a false patina of sophistication. Instead, it should serve as a solid foundation for strengthening our cultural identity, and as a platform for participating in a conversation that will fill the various historical voids.

Acknowledgment

"The Genealogy of X" was presented as a lecture performance at the Museum of Modern and Contemporary Art, Seoul, as part of the exhibition entitled *Void*, from October 2016 to March 2017.

Notes

1   An intuition, a vacillating frisson of illumination as if caught in a flash of lightning or in a mist abruptly rising to unshroud an obvious sign—but a sign, alas, that would last an instant only to vanish for good.

    Georges Perec, *A Void (La disparition)*, trans. by Gilbert Adair (New York: HarperCollins, 1994), p. 116.

2 H-Sang Seung, *The Beauty of Poverty* (Seoul: Mikunsa, 1996).

3 Matti Megged, *Dialogue In the Void: Beckett & Giacometti* (New York: Lumen Books, 1985).

214 Choon Choi

4 Heung-joon Yoo, "My Definition of Sujoldang Based on Empiricism," in *Urban Void* (Seoul: National Museum of Modern and Contemporary Art, 2002).
5 Ibid.
6 Seung, The Beauty of Poverty.
7 Ibid. (my translation).
8 Amos Ih Tiao Chang, *The Tao of Architecture* (Princeton, NJ: Princeton University Press, 1956).
9 Eduard Bru, "The Urban Void," *Quaderns d'arquitectura I urbanisme* 183 (1989): 50–57.
10 Pierre Nora, "Between Memory and History: *Les Lieux de Mémoire*," *Representations* 26 (1989): 7–24.

AFTERWORD

Chasing Composition

David Salomon

Where do *things* come from? How are they formed? How does what exists now come into being? How can we understand objects and processes that we do not have access to via our senses? Such questions are routinely asked by scientists and historians. They are also the ones being asked by the contributors to *Chasing the City*.

What these urban stalkers share with previous students of the city is a focus on the underlying logics of the ubiquitous events, processes, and entities that are hiding in plain sight. The "things" they are interested in are not limited to buildings, streets, and parks. They include an expanded field of infrastructural elements, ones that manage and accelerate the flow of water, goods, information, energy, people, and capital. The spotlighting of spatial voids, the calling out of awkward and invisible structures—both physical and informational—reveals a desire and a belief that the first step to changing reality is representing it. Hence the emphasis on the various documentary strategies of mapping, diagramming, photographing, etc.

Unlike other urban investigations, there is no attempt to generalize and propose an objective once-and-for-all solution based on these idiosyncratic findings. Nor is any attempt made to combine these ad hoc discoveries into a priori spatial types found in so many master plans. Thus, the questions at hand are: What whole can we make out of these disparate parts? What can be done with the data that has been discovered by these miners of the city? Can these same analytical processes that enable one to study the city be used to literally re-form it? In other words, how can this research be turned into compositions?

Composition and research—the former seems so outdated, formalist, and subjective, the latter so contemporary, scientific, and objective. What

216 David Salomon

makes them compatible and complementary is their shared commitment to experimentation and invention. Not unlike aspects of architectural education, these are methods that search for questions that do not have specific answers and seek out problems that do not yet exist.[1]

In architecture, composition is conventionally understood as an internal disciplinary operation (traditionally associated with axial and symmetrical arrangements) that addresses the manipulation of surfaces, shapes, and spaces. In contrast, research solicits the objective external material—or noise—that this potentially closed system needs to make it a relevant social institution. While clearly distinct, they are never separate from one another, as each has to adjust and adapt its modes and methods to account for the other's operations and effects.

As recognized and redefined by a number of thinkers, composition and research have affinities with the strategies and findings found in *Chasing the City*, namely, their emphasis on using eclectic, if not subjective, methods for generating new knowledge out of what already exists. In comparing the differences between research and science, Bruno Latour helps to establish the affinity between research, composition and aesthetics:

> Science is certainty; research is uncertainty. Science is supposed to be cold, straight, and detached; research is warm, involving, and risky. Science puts an end to the vagaries of human disputes; research creates controversies. Science produces objectivity by escaping as much as possible from the shackles of ideology, passions, and emotions; research feeds on all of those to render objects of inquiry familiar.[2]

While this definition is distinct from the conventional understanding of research, it should be noted that none of the qualities attributed to it by Latour contradict the normative requirements for "good" research to be rigorous, its methods explicit, and its findings original and significant.[3] Where it does differ is in its recognition of the subjective forces present in any research enterprise—even the most empirical ones.

Such a definition of research has many affinities with art, specifically avant-garde art—that is, art that questions the very status of what art "is." Both are experimental—both procedurally and conceptually—in that they use new tools, tropes, techniques, and sensibilities for constructing new realities. As Alan Colquhoun notes, the romantic/modern understanding of composition represented a radical shift from the classical tradition. In the modern concept of composition, objects and images were not representations of ideas; rather, composing became an independent way of knowing the world. In this newly conceived position:

> *Composition* came to mean a creative procedure in which the artist created "out of nothing" and arranged his material according to laws generated within the work itself . . . . Form was no longer thought of as a means of expressing a certain idea, but as indissoluble from, and coextensive with, the idea. Composition therefore was able to stand for an aesthetic of immanence in which art became an independent kind of knowledge of the world.[4]

Despite its denials, modernists were reliant on "compositional procedures precisely to the extent that the architecture avoided repetition of previous formal solutions and the meanings—embedded in them."[5] In other words, the composition would be generated out of the specifics of any given situation, not from a set of already established organizational tropes, images, or forms. In other words, any knowledge it contained was embodied within the work itself, and could thus be produced in a myriad of ways and forms. This is also the strategy of those hunting the city today. The city, as well as its infrastructures and the surrounding landscapes, are understood as a metaphorical mine/archive, serving as a highly specific source for finding multiple forms, generating new information, and creating new sensibilities.

The philosophers Gilles Deleuze and Felix Guattari state: "composition is aesthetic, and what is not composed is not a work of art."[6] Further, all aesthetic practices have a very specific task: to produce sensations. Sensations are not to be confused with individual perceptions or feelings, but are a compound of percepts and affects which are independent of those who encounter them. In other words, sensation is embedded in the work itself. Sensations do not allude to or depend on something else—for example, ideas, meanings, or subjective perception—for their being or efficacy. Works of art are not signs, they are things[7]—things that are composed.

Such things and sensations, they argue, are essential for producing alternative visions of the world (what Jacques Rancière calls "distributions of the sensible") and for supplying additional sensibilities for generating and occupying them.[8] Composition, art, and sensation are not pleasurable distractions, nor do they reveal existential truths. Rather, they produce the unimagined future out of the all too real present. Underlying this concept—that aesthetic production provides a method for linking the specificity of the present with an infinite set of possible futures—is that the relationship between the known and the unknown, the self and the stranger, the generic and specific, etc., cannot be established through linear and rational means alone. Rather, they can only be examined and communicated through sensorial experience and aesthetic skill.[9] This is consistent with how the scholars of the design process Wang and Ilhan define the creative act:

218 David Salomon

> A creative act is characterized by the imaginative and original generation—with aesthetic value as a high priority—of utilitarian objects .... The provenance of a creative act is essentially unpredictable in nature, if by prediction is meant the ability to reproduce the moment of creation, or the empirical attributes of what is created, by pre-determined formulations or frameworks.[10]

In a recent essay, Latour also takes up the concept of composition. He too defines it as a means of joining the particular with the general:

> From universalism [composition] takes up the task of building a common world; from relativism, the certainty that this common world has to be built from utterly heterogeneous parts that will never make a whole, but at best a fragile, revisable and diverse composite material.[11]

Latour recognizes the affinity of this heuristic mode of production with aesthetic practices—both being constructive rather than critical: "For compositionism, there is no world of beyond. It is all about *immanence.*"[12] For Deleuze and Guattari (as for Colquhoun), immanence is an essential, internal quality of artistic objects. For Latour, it is central to generating different types of aesthetic aggregations—social, technological, political, etc.

Aggregating is a very different forming technique from subdividing. The latter is often found in the uniform geometric urban schemes produced by classicists and modernists alike. In contrast, aggregation uses a variety of means to combine unlike things into difficult wholes. Aggregation is not limited to the random piling-up of stuff. It can also mean creating complex patterns by linking elements according to a sophisticated structure or logic—elements and structures that are already present in the city.

City compositions can be as unique as the context that generates them. There are many things and many ways to research and compose the city, including: Rowe and Koetter's collaging of urban and architectural tropes; the Office for Metropolitan Architecture's stacking and packing of diverse programs to make mosaic-like buildings and landscapes; Philip Rahm's accumulation of temperature, humidity, and light waves to create unnerving atmospheres inside and outside of buildings; MVRDV's transformation of statistics and graphs into compelling candy-colored objects and spaces; and Urban Lab's intertwining of water features and functions with urban street systems.

As with the authors in *Chasing the City*, these practices recognize that the elements and structures one finds in the city are not understood as inert entities and cannot be conceived of as pre-made materials. Instead, they must be thought of as "matter."[13] In other words, they must be understood as having their own internal and immanent logics. These logics must be understood before they are made. This research is itself aesthetic and immanent, as it manipulates and produces surprisingly plausible scenarios and sensations "out of the nothing" that is right in front of us. Rather than having to imagine and represent things that were never there, it uses what is present to envision what might yet be possible.

In all of these practices one finds not only composition, but design as well. That is, these tactics integrate the competing requirements posed by actual urban problems. However, addressing those problems is not how the work is produced, nor can it account for the unique and significant "blocs of sensations" they produce. These new sensations are made possible by the sustained research done on form, programs, statistics, garbage, poverty, culture, information technology, climate, thermodynamics, etc.— and by their skill in translating these things into alluring and engaging shapes, spaces, and surfaces.

Chasing and making the city compositionally—with its emphasis on constructing and making connections, sensations, and affects directly through the manipulation of urban matter(s) at hand, and without relying on any transcendent idea, belief, geometry, or subject—is a surprisingly efficient method for assembling disparate elements into an infinite variety of "diverse composite materials": a set of composites that includes people, political parties, buildings, and businesses. Perhaps most significantly, this aesthetic approach—which by definition is both rational and irrational; objective and subjective—untethers infrastructure from its utilitarian roots and frees it from the expectation that it must be monofunctional and optimized. The focus on the creation of sensations and sensibilities is not superfluous; rather, it enacts a different kind of productivity.

The efficiency of aesthetic infrastructure rests on its ability to integrate different functions with one another rather than optimizing any one of them—aggregating the competing functions and identities into a complex but still legible composition.[14]

To conclude, Chasing the City compositionally does not mean beautifying utilitarian objects. It is not something done after all the data is in and the infrastructure in place. The facts and the functions must themselves be composed. As long as architectural compositions are fed with "risky" and "uncertain" research from a variety of sources and urban situations, they can be simultaneously original and grounded, significant and speculative, thorough and experimental. The research has started. Let the compositions begin.

Notes

1 See Donald A. Schön, "Toward a Marriage of Artistry and Applied Science in the Architectural Design Studio," *Journal of Architectural Education* 41(4) (1988): 4–10.

2 Bruno Latour, "From the World of Science to the World of Research," *Science* 280(5361) (1998): 208–209.
3 Jeremy Till, "Architectural Research: Three Myths and One Model," first published as "Three Myths and One Model," *Building Material* 17 (2008): 4–10, https://jeremytill.s3.amazonaws.com/uploads/post/attachment/34/2007_Three_Myths_and_One_Model.pdf (accessed June 29, 2018).
4 Alan Colquhoun, "Composition Versus the Project," in *Modernity and the Classical Tradition* (Cambridge, MA: MIT Press, 1989), pp. 33–34.
5 Ibid., p. 34.
6 Ibid., p. 191.
7 Gilles Deleuze and Felix Guattari, "Precept, Affect and Concept," in *What Is Philosophy?* (New York: Columbia University Press, 1994).
8 Jacques Rancière, "The Aesthetic Dimension: Aesthetics, Politics, Knowledge," *Critical Inquiry* 36(1) (2009): 1; Felix Guattari, "The Object of Ecosophy," in *Chaosmosis* (Bloomington, IN: University of Indiana Press, 1995).
9 See Gregory Bateson, "Style, Grace, and Information in Primitive Art," in *Steps Toward an Ecology of Mind* (New York: Ballantine, 1972), pp. 128–152, for the relationship between skill and the function of art as a "corrective" to cognitive purposefulness.
10 David Wang and Ali O. Ilhan, "Holding Creativity Together: A Sociological Theory of the Design Professions," *Design Issues* 25(1) (2009): 5–21.
11 Bruno Latour, "An Attempt at a 'Compositionist Manifesto," *New Literary History* 41 (2010): 474; emphasis in the original.
12 Ibid.
13 See Jesse Reiser and Nanako Umemoto, "Matter," in *Atlas of Novel Tectonics* (New York: Princeton Architectural Press, 2006).
14 David Salomon, "Toward a New Architecture: Aesthetic Thinking, Synthetic Sensibilities," *Journal of Landscape Architecture* 11(1) (2016): 52–63.

INDEX

abandoned xiv, 52–54, 85, 108, 192–195
Abraham, Ander 183–184, 199
abstraction xiv, 14, 75, 87, 91, 94, 162
adaptation 26, 37, 93, 103, 170, 174, 184, 187
administration xiii, 105, 111, 116, 163
Agamben, Giorgio xiii–xvii
agency xii, 14, 35, 67, 69, 114, 129, 130–37, 139, 160, 167–73, 175–78
aggregation 160–61, 166, 179, 172, 176, 218
agriculture xv, 40–43, 51, 70, 89–97, 105, 117, 177
AI/Artificial Intelligence 72
Alberti 115
aleatoric 20–23, 28, 36
Alexander, Christopher 189–90, 199
algorithm/algorithmic xviii, 16–18, 35, 68, 74–75, 80, 122, 159, 168–70, 175, 176, 179
Alphabet and the Algorithm, The 18, 35
Amazon xviii, 66–68, 72–74, 81, 220
Amos Ih Tiao Chang 205, 214
analyze/analysis 26, 40–42, 132, 148, 159, 162, 165, 173, 176, 182
Angelidakis, Andreas 172
anomalic 20–23, 28
anomaly/anomalies 21
antidrone 6, 37–38, 48

anti-utopian 3–4, 39
apparatus xii–xviii, 155–58, 163–69, 171–74
a priori 67, 165–67, 171–183, 176, 216
Architectural Association 137
Architecture Depends 181, 197, 200
Archizoom 158, 175
arctic xv, 140–45, 147–51
A Room Against Ownership 133, 150
Atelier Bow-Wow 185, 198
Artifact 75, 85–89, 107–8, 117, 138, 171, 188, 211
atmosphere/atmospheric 71, 197, 202, 209, 218
Aureli, Pier Vittorio 133, 150,
awkward 6, 11–15, 16–18, 22–28, 30–35, 215

balloon 40, 47–53, 57, 58, 60
Baltimore, Maryland xiv
Banham, Reyner 4, 8, 19–20, 33, 35–36, 157, 161, 175, 176
bathymetry 117
Bauman, Zygmunt 181
Beaumont, Texas 113
behavioral patterns 133–35, 166, 169
behavior of cities 2–7, 22
Beijing, China 188, 198
Belanger, Pierre 120, 126
Benjamin, Walter xv–xviii, 156, 174

Index

Bentham, Jeremy xiii–xv
Berens, Carol 107, 125
Berger, Alan xv, xvii, 79
bigness 37–39, 57, 66
Bilbao, Spain 107–8, 180
biodiversity 41, 99
bio-fuel 44–46
Birth of a Territory, The xv–xvii, xvii–xviii
Block'Hood game, The 172
Borio and Wüthrich 185, 199
Bratton, Benjamin 156, 174
Brenner, Neil xvi, xvii, 80, 150
Brooklyn, New York 110–11

Cacapava do Sul 94–95, 105
Canguilhem, Georges xiii–xviii
capitalism xv–xviii, 35, 63, 66, 76, 81, 122, 126, 136, 150, 175
Carpo, Mario 18, 35
catalyst/catalyze 22, 40, 46, 59, 63, 69, 86, 120, 133–34, 139
character 14–16, 22, 35, 68, 72, 165, 171, 184, 192
Charte d'Athènes 159
chase/chasing 4–7, 30, 35, 86
Chicago, Illinois xvi, 64, 67, 79, 175
Christ & Gantenbein 186, 199
Ciudad Ojeda 85
climate change/global warming xv, 37, 46, 57, 91, 103–5, 117, 140–45, 156
cloud xv, xvi, 63, 79, 156, 193
Colquhoun, Alan 216–18, 220
Columbia River 63
commodity/commodities/commodification xv–xvi, 4, 40, 76, 87, 181
complexity: ecological 34, 91; informational 40; relational xv, 15–20, 24–28, 34, 156–60, 197; systematic/network xvi, 13, 68, 134, 148–49, 169, 181, 188; territorial 126, 195–97; theoretical 17–20, 165–74, 177–97; urban 1–3, 5, 11–14, 16–20, 109, 127, 138–39, 156, 160, 174–75
components 1–3, 6, 15, 20–29, 30–34, 88–89, 123, 189
composition 29, 66, 105, 184, 205, 209, 215–19, 220
computation xiii, 156–74, 176–78
computer xv, 22, 156, 163–73

communication xiii–xv, xvi, 3, 23, 26, 62–66, 73, 75–77, 79, 87, 122
community xvi, 5–6, 46–47, 54, 58, 73, 77, 110–11, 126, 140, 161, 164–73, 177, 182, 194
Condition of Postmodernity, The: An Enquiry into the Origins of Cultural Change
consumption xv–xvi, 3, 6, 64–67, 76, 86–88, 122, 129–30, 145
container 62, 65–66, 86, 213
contingent/contingency 16, 85, 104, 167, 170, 173, 181, 186, 190, 195, 197
Co-op Zimmer 133
Corner, James xv, xvii, 14, 35, 55, 148
Correa, Felipe 58, 85, 104
Cowen, Deborah 62, 79
Crawford, Margaret 186, 199
cybernetics 162–66, 169, 176–78

da Cunha, Dilip 38, 57
Dallas, Texas 17, 29, 32
dam 41–46, 49–51, 57, 59–60, 63
data 3, 29–30, 47, 63–68, 80, 158–61, 169–70, 176–78, 215, 219
data behaviorism 169–70
Davidson, Cynthia 12, 35, 200
Debord, Guy 23–24, 36, 70–71, 177
dead zone(s) 43–46
decentralize 2, 163–66
Deleuze, Gilles xiii, xvii, 14, 35, 114, 123, 126, 217–18, 220
democratization 159–61, 174, 176
dependent/dependence 2, 4, 20, 94, 122, 135, 140, 157–58, 168, 186, 197
dérive 23, 36
desire 11, 13, 16, 33, 67–76, 80, 109, 135, 156–57, 166, 169–73, 176–77, 183, 202–6, 215
de-urbanized 44, 49
deviance/deviant/deviation xv, 21
dialogue 3, 38, 58, 204, 213
Discipline and Punish xii, xiii
discourse xii, 4, 6, 104, 129, 159, 164, 170–71, 186, 195, 204
displacement xvi, 19, 168
display xv–xvi, 20, 50 142, 190, 209
dispotifs/dispositives xiii–xvii
Dissociated Technology 87–89 103
DNA 18, 21, 188

Index **223**

document xv, xviii, 40, 46–57, 59–60, 62, 66–69, 75, 166, 186, 198, 215
Dokrakdang 204
Domenig, Günther 160
Domesticated Mountain 172
Dubai 62
Dutch Dialogues 38, 58
dynamics 26, 71, 87, 130–39, 157–59, 163–66, 174, 195

Eames, Ray and Charles 28, 36, 168
Easterling, Keller xv, xvii, 79
ecologic/eco-logic 17–18, 20, 101–4
ecology/ecological 3, 6, 16–19, 29, 32, 34, 42, 45, 51, 86, 94, 99–100, 107, 117–24, 155, 158–60, 173–74
Ecologies of Power 120, 126
economy 46, 62, 66, 79–80, 91, 94, 107, 121, 137, 145, 148, 150
ecosystem 16, 33, 63, 86, 99, 103, 105, 134, 139–40, 159, 172
ecotone 99
edge 12, 26, 51–55, 91–101, 105, 107–111, 137, 188, 193, 200
efficiency 2, 63, 67, 69, 77, 81, 160, 162, 174, 186–87, 192, 219
efficient xi, 5, 52, 87, 114, 117, 138, 145, 158, 186, 195, 219
Eiffel Tower 21, 180
elastic/elasticity 3, 123
Eldon, Stewart xv, xvii,
emergent: complexity xvi, 3–4; processes/technologies xii, xvi, 39, 120, 135–36, 147; systems 62–63, 86; urban emergence 3–4, 21, 23, 35, 62–63, 130, 155–59, 165–69, 172, 175–77, 200
engage 24–25, 34, 46–49, 94, 112, 139, 167, 209, 213
engagement 6, 37–40, 44, 49, 54–57, 102–3, 127–32, 138–40, 147–49, 180, 191
Espoo, Finland 138, 151
equilibrium 12, 35, 165–66, 174, 211
evolution/evolutionary 4–8, 12, 15–16, 22, 26–28, 33, 106, 117–24, 129, 135, 158–65, 174, 177
exchange 3, 6, 18, 26, 63, 97, 127–29, 133–36, 140, 147–48, 156
existential 16, 206, 217
exploit/exploitation xii, xvii, 89, 133, 137, 140, 187, 190

extraction xii, xv, 3–4, 6, 85–88, 91–98, 111–14, 122, 139–40, 145–48, 151, 164

Facebook 68, 73, 80, 159
Far from Equilibrium 12, 35
FedEx 63–66, 73, 178
field 1, 40, 47–48, 65, 71, 75, 116–20, 129, 155, 170, 181, 189
flexibility 5, 8, 122, 132
flood 41–46, 49–57, 91–92, 146, 211
fold/folding/unfold/unfolding 3–5, 14, 19, 26, 35, 130, 165, 172–74, 212
Forbidden City 188
forces: economic/logistic 85, 107, 127; military 112; natural 57, 102–4, 117; of fragmentation xiv; social 156–62, 175; subjective 216; urban 2, 4–5, 19, 26–34, 123, 181, 184–86, 191–93, 205
Fordist xv, 67, 129–32, 139
fossil fuels 86, 89–93, 103
Foucault, Michel xii–xviii, 196–97, 199
fragmentation, urban xiii–xv, 3–5, 67–69, 107, 124–25, 169, 191
fragmentation and complexity/chaos 156, 174, 175, 202
fragmentation of habitats 99–101, 105
framework(s): infrastructural 85–86,; process frameworks 5; theoretical/ conceptual 39–40, 69, 114, 117–18, 148–50, 161, 165, 184, 200, 218; urban structure as 7, 58, 86, 100, 135, 181, 197
free trade zone 87
Friedman, Yona xvi, 4, 8, 159–74, 175–78
futurologists 160

Garcia, Tristan 174, 178
Garden City of To-Morrow 11
Geist, J.L. xv, xviii
geography xii–xvii, 73, 89, 116, 122, 126, 199
GIAP/International Group of Prospective 161
global communications xii–xvii, 3–6, 62, 65–67
globalization :economics and resources 24, 37, 63–64, 79–80, 85–88, 91–94, 103, 108–114, 126, 140–50, 172, 205; global city(ies) 2, 6–7,

224 Index

11–16, 79–80, 129–39, 155–58,
  175–77, 200
global village 73
Google xvi, xviii, 62–63
Gran Chaco 89–91, 97–99, 105
Greece xvi
Group Form 160
Guarani Aquifer 91–98, 105
Guattari, Felix 14, 35, 126, 217–18, 220
Guggenheim 130, 180
Gulf of Mexico 43–46, 51, 56
Gulf Restoration Network 56–57,
  58–60

hand held devices xii–xvii, 67–69,
  156, 171
Hanok 202, 208
Harvey, David xiv, xviii, 121–22, 126
Häusermann, Pascal 161
Haverfield, Francis 7
Heidegger, Martin 182, 198–200
Helsinki, Finland 127–30, 148
heterogeneous/heterogeneity xii–xiii, 7,
  168, 173, 218
heterotopia/heterotopic xiii–xviii,
  197, 199
Hippodamus 1–3, 7
historicism 4, 7, 12, 107–8, 127–29,
  163, 197, 204, 211–13
Hoejae 204–5
Homo ludens 161
Hong Kong 179–97, 198–200
Houston, Texas 108
Howard, Ebenezer 11
humanism/humanist 160
Huth, Eilfried 160
Huyzinga, Eerhard 161
hybrid/hybridize 48, 64, 100, 137,
  165, 169, 181
hydrology/ hydroscapes 46, 60,
  89–99, 104

ideal/ idyllic xiii, 1–5, 11–14, 16–17,
  35, 37, 39, 115, 130, 137, 160, 180
identity 4–7, 11, 14–17, 20–26, 30–35,
  94, 134, 140, 180, 185, 188, 193,
  195–96, 200, 203–4, 213
imageability/image 16–21, 35–36, 124,
  158–59, 174, 211
impact behavior 108–9
implantation 3–4, 24, 187
independent/independence ix, 203,
  216–17

index/indexing xii, xv, 115–17
industrial xiii–xv, 6, 42–44, 46–55, 64,
  64, 67, 72–75, 79–81, 89, 107–09,
  121, 124, 125, 162–63, 187
information systems xii–xviii, 62–67,
  79–81, 122, 157–58, 164, 215–220
infrastructure xvii, 6, 16, 19, 37, 40–48,
  51, 57–59, 64–67, 74, 79, 85–99,
  103–4, 111, 116, 124–25, 127–28,
  135, 138–149, 151, 157–164,
  171–74, 185, 191, 195, 198, 215–19
inherent/inherency 1–6, 13–14, 29,
  107, 114, 132–33, 159, 163, 168,
  183, 197, 211
instrument xiii, 72, 75, 116, 129
integral 2, 5–6, 12, 35, 148, 161, 171
integration/integrate 1–6, 12, 16–28,
  34–35, 37–40, 45, 57, 107–8, 125,
  136, 156–58, 164, 195, 219
interdependent/interdependence 30,
  35, 88, 172
internet xii, xv–xvii, 156, 172
interrogation 7, 15, 180, 188
Iran xvi
irregularity 2–5, 21–22, 115

Jaque, Andrés 171
Jonze, Spike 179, 197
Jorn, Asger 23, 70

Kempf, Petra 25
Keynes, John 135
Kim Swoo-guen 203–11
Koetter, Fred 218
Koolhaas, Rem 37–38, 57, 81
Kowloon Walled City 20
Kunshan, China 117
Kwinter, Sanford 12, 35

La Cecla, Franco 180, 187, 191,
  197–200
laminate/delaminate 2
landscape(s) xvii, 6, 12–13, 57, 65–71,
  74, 79, 91, 99–103, 110–14, 117,
  119–25, 126, 127, 139–40, 142,
  145–49, 158, 170, 185–86, 192–94,
  200, 217–18
Landscape Architecture 38, 58, 80, 91,
  126, 127, 220
Landscape Urbanism xviii, 6, 106–9,
  110–14, 119–25, 126, 180, 217–18
Latour, Bruno 167, 177, 181, 200,
  216–18, 220

layer/layering 2, 5, 11–16, 18–25, 118, 127, 139, 148, 185, 212
Learning from Logistics: How Networks Change Our Cities 63–66, 79
Leatherbarrow, David 115, 126
LeCavalier, Jesse xvi, xviii
Le Corbusier 157, 175, 181, 200
Lerup, Lars 108, 125
level 33, 70, 107, 114–18, 126, 193, 203, 209
Leveling the Ground 115, 126, 145
logistical urbanism 63
logistics/logistical xii–xvi, xviii, 6, 8, 48, 62–69, 72–77, 79–80, 85–88, 89, 94, 97, 103, 105, 114, 120–21, 125, 147, 190–91
logistic landscapes 63, 79
Los Angeles, California xiv, 4, 8, 33, 35–36, 67, 116, 126
Los Angeles: The Architecture of Four Ecologies 4, 8, 33, 35–36
Louisville, Kentucky 63, 68, 79
Lynch, Kevin 16, 21, 35–36
Lyotard, Jean-Francois 183, 198–200
Lyster, Clare xvi, xviii, 6, 79

madang and maru 202–3
Maki, Fumihiko 18, 35, 160
manifesto 5, 37–39, 155–56, 205, 220
manufactured landscapes 106–8, 110–14, 119–25
manufacturing xv–xvi, 6, 37, 62–63, 86, 106, 111–20, 187, 193
map/mapping xii, xv, 5–6, 12–15, 18–19, 23–35, 38, 40–42, 48, 58–60, 70, 76, 79, 103, 105, 106, 113, 117, 119–21, 128, 131, 140–46, 151, 157–58, 175, 186–89, 195, 211, 215
MAP Office 186, 198, 200
Martin, Reinhold xvi, xviii
Marxist/Marxism 76, 126, 133, 155, 168
Marx, Karl 76, 126, 133, 155, 168
mass production xv, 64, 67, 71–76, 81, 133, 145, 163
masterplan/master-plan xii, 2–4, 57, 60, 94, 102, 123, 158, 165, 175, 215
Mathur, Anuradha 38, 57–58
matrix 4, 105, 123
Matthews, Gordon 195
Mayne, Thom 18, 35

McDonaldization 16, 35
McPhee, John 68, 80
megalopolis xv
megastructure xvi, 8, 70–73, 156, 161, 164, 175–76
Megged, Matti 204, 213
Memphis, Tennessee 63–64
Mente Locale 180, 200
meronym/metronymic 20–23, 28, 36
metacity xv–xvii
metropolis xii–xv, 76, 86, 107, 175, 184, 187, 192
Meyer, Hans 58, 133
Mid-Levels 191–93
migratiry ecology(ies) 99–104
military 6, 79, 106–8, 110–14, 119–21, 125, 126, 142, 206
Mississippi River 39–57, 58–60
Missouri River 42–46
mobile technology , 67–76, 80, 156, 171
mobility/mobilize xv, 3, 40, 49, 59, 71–76, 120, 141–42, 156–63, 168, 171–73, 176, 194–95
Modern/Modernism xii–xv, xviii, 4, 7, 12, 37, 156–62, 165, 173, 176–77, 180–88, 198, 200, 205–8, 213, 214, 216–18, 220
morphology xvi, 66, 118, 185, 189, 196
Mulholland, William 116, 126
Mumbai 57, 63, 200
municipalities 2–6, 67, 93, 107–8, 116
MVRDV 218

Naked City 24, 70
narratives 6, 15, 39–41, 67, 121, 156, 168–69, 174, 175, 183–84, 195–96, 198, 213
neoliberal/neo-liberal xv–xvi, 67, 137, 150
Neo-Utopian Paradox xv–xvi, 1–7, 11–13, 17, 37–39, 54, 156–58, 173, 175–76, 197, 199, 205, 211
network: actor-networks 46–48, 51, 56–57, 58–60, 168, 172, 177; ecological networks 43, 100, 145–49; logistical networks 63–68, 75–76, 79, 141, 145–49, 162, 166, 171–73, 191, 194–95, 202, 208–09; network systems xiii, 6, 16, 46–48, 86–89, 122, 129, 141, 158, 162, 166–68, 177, 181, 186–89 ; network theory 39–40, 66–68, 122, 158, 186
Newark, New Jersey 63

226 Index

New Babylon 65, 69–77, 80, 159–74, 176–77
New Geography xii–xvii
New Orleans, Louisiana 38–57, 58
New Urbanism 4, 177
New York, New York 31, 64, 76, 138, 171–72
Nieuwenhuys, Constant xvi, 65, 69–77, 79–80, 159–74, 176–77
Nolli, Giambatista 12
Nolli Map 12
No-Stop City 158, 175
Nueva Loja 85

Oakland, California 63
Ogallala Aquifer 91
Ohio River 42–43
oil 46, 85–90, 99, 104–5, 128, 140, 147–50, 151, 195
Olmstead, Frederick Law 138, 151
OMA 57
open-source/open source xii, 40, 48, 161, 175–76

Panopticon xiii–xv
paradigm xv, 4, 19, 79, 156, 178, 197
Paris, France xv–xvi, xvii, 8, 21–24, 63, 70, 180
Parisian Surrealists xv
Pask, Gordon 162, 176
Pasquinelli, Matteo xiii–xvii, xviii
Pearl River Delta 63
Pedra do Segredo 94
phantasmagoria xv
Philadelphia, Pennsylvania 110–11, 126
pipeline 6, 85–104, 105, 147–48
plandemonium 39
planners 4, 11–12, 24–26, 72, 108, 125, 132, 138, 179, 183
Plethora Project 172
plummet line 116–117
Pope, Albert 184, 200
porosity 108–09, 119
Post-Crisis 7, 173–74
post-Fordist xv, 67, 129–132, 139
post-industrial 66, 107–9, 121, 124
Postmodern/Post-Modern xiii–xiv, xviii, 2, 107, 157, 198–200
Postmodern Geographies: The Reassertion of Space in Critical Social Theory xiii–xiv, xviii
production xv, 5–6, 62–64, 67, 72–76, 81, 85–89, 92, 103–4, 107–8,
110–14, 119–25, 133, 145, 163, 217–18
psychogeography/psychogeographic 23–24, 35–36, 70, 76
Public Lab/ *Public Lab River Rat Pack* 38, 46–57, 58–60

QR codes 75

Ragon, Michel 159–61, 163, 176
Rancière, Jacques 168–73, 177–78, 217, 220
reciprocity 2, 16, 24, 32, 33–34, 108, 133–36, 191
redevelopment 34, 54, 91, 107–11, 125, 211
resource extraction xii, xv, 6, 37–40, 42–46, 59, 85–88, 91–94, 111, 114, 140, 145–49, 151, 170
resources, ecological/natural xii, xv, 37–40, 42–46, 59, 85–88, 91–94, 100, 103–4, 105, 117, 122, 126, 155–63
resource transference 127–31, 139–40, 145–49, 151
resources, urban xii, xv, 3–6, 14, 155–63, 170
revolution 64, 155–57
revolutionary xvi, 33, 157, 175
rewire/rewiring 6, 89–99, 99–104
RFID tags 75
rhizomatic/rhizome 121–23
riverfront 52–55, 60
Roche, François 163–64, 176
Rome, Italy 12, 79, 115
Rottier, Guy 161
Rouvroy, Antoinette 168–69, 175, 178
Rowe, Collin 218

Saarinen, Eliel 130
Sanchez, Jose 172
San Francisco, California 68, 110–11, 118
Sassen, Saskia 63, 79, 175
Seattle, Washington 28, 114
second production 85, 103
Seoul, South Korea 7, 202–10, 211–13, 214
Serres, Michel xvii, xviii,
Seung H-sang 202–9, 211–12, 213, 214
Shane, David Grahame xiii, xv, xviii, 18, 35
Shanghai, China 22, 198

Index **227**

Shau Kei Wang 182, 193–95
Shiller, Robert 135, 150
ship/shipyard xv, 6, 51, 54, 65–66, 106–110, 111–121, 123–25, 126, 140–42
Shoffer, Nicholas 70
Silicon Valley 63, 79
Singapore 22
singular/singularities 2–3, 6, 11, 17–22, 34, 38–39, 62, 73, 107–8, 114–15, 122–23, 135, 156
Sitte, Camillo 4, 7
Situationst International 4, 6, 23–24, 36, 68–73, 76, 81, 160–61, 173, 176–77
social critique 24, 168–74, 175–78
Soja, Edward xiii–xiv, xviii
Somani xv, xiii
South America 85–103
Space Group Building 202, 207–10
spatial fix xiv 121–23, 126
spatio-temporal networks 66–69
Special Economic Zones xv, 62
speculate/speculative 1, 5–7, 35, 38–40, 42–46, 49–51, 57, 59, 76, 121, 124–25, 139, 163, 183, 219
sprawl xvi, 16–17, 66, 108, 120
Spread Networks 64
standardize/standardization 2, 7, 31, 142, 165, 179
St. Louis, Missouri 46–57, 58–60
Structuralism/Structuralist 164–66, 176, 197
subjectivity/subjectivation xv, 69, 161–62, 168–71, 215–19
sublime xv
Sujoldang 203–5, 214
superimposition 4, 11–12, 17, 22–24, 34, 70, 188, 192–93
Sydney, Australia 107–8
synthetic 6, 19, 34, 108, 116, 163–66, 177, 220

Taipei, Taiwan xvi
Tao of Architecture 205, 214
technology/technological xviii, 2, 6, 24, 35, 37, 47, 67–69, 72–77, 79–81, 85–86, 87–88, 103–04, 106, 116, 122, 130–39, 145, 157–58, 165, 171–72, 178, 218–19
technopoles 63
Tel Aviv 63
Terasawa, Kazumi 20

Territory/territorial: as geopolitical 64, 66, 110–14, 120–22, 126, 129, 139–40, 201–6; as region 6, 14, 38–42, 71, 85–89, 91–96, 99, 103, 105, 107–8, 110–14, 120–22, 139–40, 156–57, 172, 176, 201–6; as urban space xii–xvii, xvii–xviii, 1–2, 79, 110–14, 120–22, 185, 189, 195, 198–200
Till, Jeremy 181, 197, 200, 220
topology/topological 4, 80, 166–68
topography/topographical 3, 19, 117, 120, 126, 136, 150, 170, 184–86, 191–93, 198
transplantation 7, 13, 20
transport/transportation 6, 44–51, 65, 80, 85, 87–91, 97, 105, 113, 122, 141, 195
typology/typological xii, xvi, 5–7, 16, 20, 22–24, 74, 129, 142, 183, 186, 199–200

Uber 66
United States Navy xv, 106, 109–12, 118–25
unpredictable/unpredictability 2–4, 14, 21, 30, 108, 119–123, 159–62, 167, 173, 197–98, 218
UPS 63, 68, 79
urban fabric 26, 33, 108, 122–25, 158, 177
Urban Lab 218
Uruguayana 89, 97–98
Uruguayana-Porto Alegre 89
U.S. Army Corps of Engineers 45, 51–52, 59–60
utopia xiii–xvi, 2–7, 11–13, 17, 37, 39, 54, 80, 130, 137, 149, 156–58, 163, 173, 175–76, 197, 199, 205, 211

Vaux, Calvert 138
Ville Cybernetique 70
Ville Spatiale 159, 163–67, 173–74, 177
Vital Awkwardness 15–23, 33
Vitruvius 181, 197, 200
void 6–7, 12, 107–9, 145, 192, 201–09, 211–13, 214, 215
von Hertzen, Heikki 130
VÖR 130

Waggonner & Ball 38, 58
Waldheim, Charles xii, xviii, 79, 121, 126
Walmart xvi, xviii

228 Index

Washington, D.C. 58, 109, 125
water level 41–46, 53–57, 58,
　145–46
watershed 38–48, 57, 58–59, 91, 105,
　112, 140, 145–47, 151
waywiser 115–16
We Have Never Been Modern 181, 200
Wigley, Mark 71, 80, 177

X, traits of 201–5, 208–10, 211–13

Yangtze Delta 117, 126
Yoo Heung-joon 203–5, 214
You Are the City 25

Zipcar 66
zones of elasticity 121–23